Upgrading to Compete

Global Value Chains, Clusters, and SMEs in Latin America

Carlo Pietrobelli
Roberta Rabellotti
Editors

Inter-American Development Bank

David Rockefeller Center for Latin American Studies
Harvard University

©2006 Inter-American Development Bank
1300 New York Avenue, N.W.
Washington, D.C. 20577

Produced by the IDB Office of External Relations

To order this book, contact:
IDB Bookstore
Tel: (202) 623-1753
Fax: (202) 623-1709
E-mail: idb-books@iadb.org
www.iadb.org/pub

The views and opinions expressed in this publication are those of the authors and do not necessarily reflect the official position of the Inter-American Development Bank.

Cataloging-in-Publication data provided by the Inter-American Development Bank Felipe Herrera Library

Upgrading to compete : global value chains, clusters and SMEs in Latin America / Carlo Pietrobelli, Roberta Rabellotti, editors.

p. cm.
Includes bibliographical references.
ISBN: 1597820326

1. Small business—Latin America. 2. Small business—Growth—Case studies. 3. Industrial clusters—Latin America. 4. Competition—Latin America—Case studies. I. Pietrobelli, Carlo, 1959- II. Rabellotti, Roberta. III. Inter-American Development Bank.

HD2341 U87 2006
338.642 U87--dc22

LCCN: 2006932328

Acknowledgments

This book draws on the empirical findings of the project "Clusters, Value Chains and Competitiveness," carried out for AGORA'2000, Italy, on behalf of the Micro and SME Division, Department of Sustainable Development (SDS/MSM) of the Inter-American Development Bank (IDB), and directed by Carlo Pietrobelli and Roberta Rabellotti. The editors wish to thank Manuel Albaladejo, Pablo Angelelli, the late Alessandro Bolondi, Claudio Cortellese, Juan José Llisterri, Carlos Guaipatín, Chris Freeman, the late Sanjaya Lall, Carlo Manfredi, Jörg Meyer-Stamer, Rajah Rasiah, Frédéric Richard, Andrés Rodríguez-Clare, Giovanni Stumpo, and Morris Teubal, who provided comments and support at various stages of the study.

Moreover we greatly benefited from participation and discussions in the many seminars where preliminary drafts were presented. These include the IDB in Washington, D.C., and Buenos Aires, UNCTAD in Geneva, the IberPYME Conference in Guadalajara, the ECLAC-UAM workshop in Mexico City, the Universities of Modena, Novara, and Bocconi in Italy, the Science Policy Research Unit (SPRU) at the University of Sussex, U.K., the Universidad Nacional de General Sarmiento in Buenos Aires, the Universidade Federal do Espírito Santo in Victoria, Brazil, the Department of Trade and Industry in Pretoria, South Africa, the Asia-Europe Institute at the University of Malaya in Kuala Lumpur, Malaysia, and Peking University. We thank all the colleagues that on these occasions discussed our work and helped refine it by putting it under a true global scrutiny. Finally, we are especially grateful to Álvaro Ramírez, Juan José Llisterri, Pablo Angelelli, and Claudio Cortellese at the IDB, as well as to the IDB's Office of External Relations for review, editing, and production of the volume.

Carlo Pietrobelli and *Roberta Rabellotti*
Rome and Milan
September 2006

Contents

Index of Topics by Chapter

Figures

Tables

Preface

Most enterprises in Latin America and the Caribbean are micro, small, and medium sized. Over 95 percent of the approximately 17 million estimated businesses in the region are micro-, small, and medium-sized enterprises (MSMEs). These businesses employ a significant portion of the population—over 50 percent of total employment in many countries in the region. Yet the contribution of MSMEs to gross domestic product does not match the weight of these enterprises in the business structure and in employment, because there is a large gap between MSMEs and large enterprises in productivity and competitiveness.

Low productivity in MSMEs is not due solely to the small scale on which they operate. Other causes tend to be more important, such as inefficient management, use of inadequate technologies, a high level of informal business that limits access to markets, a low level of cooperation with other enterprises, weak institutions of support, and a regulatory environment that is biased against smaller-sized businesses. Against a backdrop of growing openness and globalization, as is now being experienced by Latin America and the Caribbean, an MSME sector with such weaknesses may find it difficult to face international competition, which in turn may have negative social consequences.

This book arose out of a study commissioned by the Micro, Small and Medium Enterprise Division of the Inter-American Development Bank aimed at researching cases based on Latin American experiences with competitive cooperation among enterprises, whether brought about as a result of specific policies or spontaneously. The aim was to thereby draw lessons from models generated in the region itself as a result of the economic conditions and business culture of Latin America and the Caribbean. The intention here is to make a contribution to conceptualizing the processes of improved competitiveness based on cooperation among enterprises and also to contribute to improving and renewing government policies and programs and private initiatives aimed at increasing MSME productivity in the region.

Starting with a conceptual framework that incorporates recent advances found in the literature on clusters, value chains, innovation, and sector learning patterns, the authors present a collection of case studies illustrating the conditions that best serve to improve productivity in MSMEs.

The selection of case studies reflects the distribution of MSMEs in Latin America and the Caribbean by economic sectors. Most of the case studies therefore involve clusters and value chains based on natural resources and traditional manufacturing. But the book also analyzes cases in the new economy, such as software development in several regions of Mexico. Comparison of this collection of new studies and other cases that the authors draw from the literature provides a detailed picture of the institutional, governance, and technology/sector conditions that can facilitate innovation and competitiveness by MSMEs that are part of clusters or value chains. On the basis of this work, the authors also suggest a series of actions for the public and private sector, aimed at achieving three complementary objectives: facilitating the development of open economies, promoting links among enterprises, and strengthening the position of MSMEs in value chains.

Another aspect highlighted by the authors is that public policies and programs and private initiatives to increase the competitiveness of MSMEs participating in clusters and value chains must have characteristics specific to economic sectors, where it is market dynamics that set the priorities for action. This recommendation is consistent with experiences in the projects that the Inter-American Development Bank is supporting in the region, which show that the greatest incentive for enterprises to participate in cluster development programs lies in generating business and benefits that the participants can take advantage of immediately, in addition to being able to benefit from the generation of externalities. Collective efficiency is therefore directly linked to the idea of the business as a center and pivotal point for fostering and developing clusters and value chains.

IDB Group institutions have for some time recognized the importance of MSMEs in Latin America and the Caribbean, as well as the challenges they face. These institutions are accordingly working together with the countries of the region and with the private sector to provide the financial and technical resources needed to spur MSMEs' development. One of the areas singled out for promoting the competitiveness of MSMEs is that aimed at promoting cooperative arrangements among enterprises, and between enterprises and public and private institutions. IDB interest in these arrangements has been increasing in recent years. The operational instruments used chiefly by the Bank for financing these activities encompass financing national or local programs that include companies of all sizes, from large multinational corporations to small groups of local microentrepreneurs.

These IDB efforts have not been isolated. In the past decade, most aid agencies and almost all the governments in the region have launched initiatives to encourage business cooperation and the setting up of public-private institutions to design competitiveness policies.

This book is the product of the joint effort of an international team of researchers from Italy and Latin America and the Caribbean working together with IDB professionals. The research work received funding from the Consulting Trust Fund of Italy. To all we express gratitude for their valuable contributions.

We are confident that the findings presented in this book will enrich the academic debate and will inspire public and private actors in the region to develop new policies and innovative projects to enhance the competitiveness of MSMEs in the region.

Antonio Vives
Acting Manager
Sustainable Development Department

Chapter 1

Clusters and Value Chains in Latin America: In Search of an Integrated Approach

Carlo Pietrobelli and Roberta Rabellotti

Does enterprise participation in global markets ensure sustainable income growth? Policies have often been designed in the belief that this is true, but competitiveness and participation in international markets may take very different forms, and developing countries do not always benefit. This book presents a series of rich and original field studies from Latin America, conducted by the authors with the same consistent methodological approach, and represents a theory-generating exercise within clusters and economic development literature.

The main question addressed is how Latin American small and medium-sized enterprises (SMEs) may participate in global markets in ways that provide for sustainable income growth, the "high road" to competitiveness. In contrast, the "low road" is often typically followed by small firms from developing countries, which often compete by squeezing wages and revenues rather than by increasing productivity, salaries, and profits.

The split between the high and low roads to competitiveness is often explained by the different capabilities of firms to *upgrade* (Humphrey and Schmitz, 2002a; Kaplinsky and Readman, 2001; Porter, 1990). Upgrading is usually defined as the ability to make better products, to make products more efficiently, or to move into more skilled activities. In this book, we explicitly link the ability to upgrade to innovation, and define upgrading as *innovating to increase value added.*

Although SMEs often lack the internal capabilities to participate effectively and fruitfully in global markets (Peres and Stumpo, 2000, 2002), they may still carry out successful upgrading processes. Many of the case studies in this volume suggest that policies may sustain these upgrading efforts targeting the high road to competitiveness.

Capitalizing on one of the most productive areas of the recent literature on SMEs, we focus our research on small enterprises located in *clusters*. Rich empirical evidence (Humphrey, 1995; Nadvi and Schmitz, 1999; Rabellotti, 1997) shows that when small firms are located in clusters, in both developed and developing countries, they are often able to overcome some of the major constraints they usually face, including a lack of specialized skills and difficulty of access to technology, inputs, market information, credit, and external services. However, the literature on clusters focuses mainly on *local* sources of competitiveness from intracluster vertical and horizontal relationships that generate *collective efficiency* (Schmitz, 1995) and often neglects the increasing importance of external linkages. Because of the spread of information technologies and recent changes in production systems, distribution channels, and financial markets, enterprises and clusters are increasingly integrated into value chains that often operate across many different countries. The literature on global value chains (GVCs) (Gereffi, 1999; Gereffi and Kaplinsky, 2001) calls attention to the opportunities for local producers to learn from the global leaders of the chains, which may be buyers or producers. The internal governance of the value chain importantly affects local firms' potential for upgrading (Humphrey and Schmitz, 2000).

Evidence on Latin America presented in this book reveals that firms often participate in clusters as well as in value chains, and therefore that both the local and the global dimensions operate simultaneously. Both forms of organization offer opportunities to foster competitiveness via learning and upgrading. But firms also face constraints, such as limitations on upgrading in some forms of value chains, and inadequate competitiveness of clusters with less developed external economies and joint actions. Analyses of both clusters and value chains were conceived and developed to overcome the sectoral dimension (i.e., differences across sectors) in the study of industrial organization and dynamism. Research on clusters, by focusing on agglomerations of firms specializing in different stages of the *filière*, moved beyond the traditional units of analysis of industrial economics, the firm and the sector. In the value chain literature, the main distinction is between buyer-driven and producer-driven chains (Gereffi, 1994), and sectors usually fall into one of these two categories. Nevertheless, we find that even with our focus on SMEs that are both located in clusters and involved in value chains, the characteristics of the particular industrial sector play an important role affecting the upgrading prospects of SMEs.

The strength and original contribution of this book lies in the tremendously rich field studies of clusters, which represent a solid knowledge base and inspiration for further theory generation. The volume as a whole is itself an effort of "appreciative theorizing" (Nelson, 1995), a theory-generating exercise with strong and detailed case studies, all adopting the same theoretical and methodological approach, itself a rare feature in similar exercises. The field studies provide useful hints and inspire more rigorous theory building and consistent quantitative testing.

The original approach consists of taking into account the cluster, value chain, and sectoral dimensions at once. The causal logic of the book leads us to explore the hypothesis that enterprise upgrading is simultaneously affected by firm-specific efforts and actions and by the environment in which firms operate (Figure 1.1) The firm's environment is crucially shaped by three characteristics: (1) the collective efficiency of the cluster in which SMEs operate, (2) the pattern of governance of the value chain in which SMEs participate, and (3) the peculiar features that characterize learning and upgrading patterns in specific sectors.

In this introductory chapter we discuss the state of the literatures on clusters and global value chains, focusing on their areas of overlap and complementarity. Then we introduce the notion of upgrading and explain why sectoral differences crucially affect the upgrading prospects of firms and clusters. In order to take into account sectoral characteristics and their

Figure 1.1. The Causal Logic of the Book

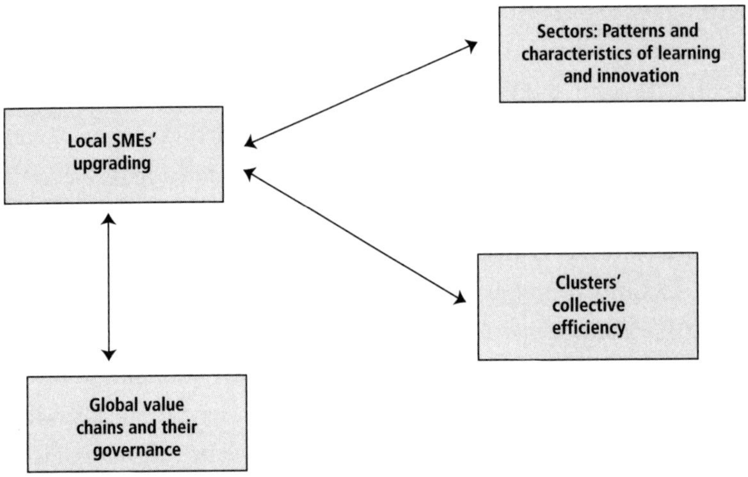

effects on a firm's pattern of innovation and learning, we introduce a new taxonomy of sectors, based on the concepts underlying the Pavitt taxonomy and applied to the industrial reality of Latin America. The chapter ends with a presentation of the methodology of the study and with a final section that outlines the content of the book.

Clusters and Value Chains

This research builds on two major branches in economic analysis: institutional economics, which acknowledges the central role that institutions play in determining economic agents' behavior and performance (for example, Nelson and Sampat, 2001; Putnam, 1993; Williamson, 2000), and evolutionary economics, which focuses on the evolutionary nature of technological change (for example, Nelson and Winter, 1982; Dosi et al., 1988). For our purposes, it is useful to explore briefly different conceptions of organizations and institutions. *Organizations* are consciously created formal structures with an explicit purpose. The organizations with which firms interact may be other firms, including suppliers, customers, and competitors, or nonfirm organizations, such as universities, research institutes, standard-setting agencies, financial institutions, technical schools, government agencies, and business organizations (Edquist, 2002). Firms that are pursuing technological innovation, learning and upgrading, crucially interact—more or less closely—with other firms and nonfirm organizations. Of particular importance for innovation and upgrading are interactions that go beyond arm's-length market transactions and that involve more than information about prices and quantities. Laws, regulations, social rules and norms, technical standards, and cultural habits constitute the *institutional* context within which firms and organizations interact. Such institutions may importantly foster or hinder the interactive learning processes that are essential conditions for upgrading. Importantly, all these relationships have a fundamental dynamic nature, as firms, market structures, and institutions *co-evolve* over time (Nelson, 1998).

Within this general theoretical background, this book focuses on how enterprise upgrading is affected simultaneously by clusters' collective efficiency, value chains' pattern of governance, and the sectoral features that affect learning and innovation. In the rest of this section we explore, in turn, clusters and collective efficiency, and value chains and their governance structures. In the following section, we turn to types of upgrading and present our new taxonomy of sectors, linking upgrading with sectoral characteristics.

Clusters

During the 1990s, a new approach to small-scale industry in developing countries was stimulated by the successful performance of the industrial districts in the developed world, particularly in Italy. The ability of clustered firms to be economically viable and to contribute strongly to the growth process in industrial districts has attracted a great deal of interest in development studies (see, for example, Schmitz, 1995; Rabellotti, 1997, 1999; Humphrey, 1995; Nadvi and Schmitz, 1999).

The literature on industrial districts is broad, and the numerous scholars across disciplines and regions of the world who have contributed to this debate have used a variety of definitions (see Paniccia, 2002, for a recent review). In this study, we refer to industrial districts of the Marshallian type, as first defined by Becattini (1987).

Among the characteristics of industrial districts, sectoral specialization and geographical concentration of SMEs is common in developing countries, with a wide range of cases now well documented in the literature (for reviews on Africa see McCormick, 1999, and on Latin America see Albaladejo, 2001; Pietrobelli, Rabellotti, and Giuliani, Chapter 9 in this volume). However, the existence of a critical mass of specialized and agglomerated activities, even with strong historical roots, does not necessarily imply that these clusters also share all of the other characteristics that identify the Marshallian type of district. Nevertheless, clustering can be considered a major facilitating factor for a number of subsequent developments (which may or may not occur), including division of labor and specialization, the emergence of a wide network of suppliers, the appearance of agents who sell to distant national and international markets, the emergence of specialized producer services, the emergence of a pool of specialized and skilled workers, and the formation of business associations. To capture the positive impacts of these characteristics on the competitiveness of firms located in clusters, Schmitz (1995) introduced the concept of *collective efficiency* (CE), defined as the competitive advantage derived from local external economies and joint actions. Clustering offers opportunities for powerful externalities that may be appropriated by the SMEs in the cluster and may facilitate the development of joint actions among local actors.

The concept of *external economies* (EEs) was first introduced by Alfred Marshall in his *Principles of Economics* (1920), in which he wrote about economies external to the firm but internal to the district. External economies are (positive or negative) unpaid, out-of-the-market-rules side effects of the activity of one economic agent on other agents. In industrial districts the most common external economies are the creation of a market for specialized skilled labor; the creation of a market for inputs, machinery, and specialized inputs (increased availability; competition on price, quality and service), allowing a fine division of labor; improved market access; and easy access to specialized knowledge about technologies and markets and rapid dissemination of information.

According to Schmitz (1999a), incidental external economies are important in explaining the competitiveness of industrial clusters, but a deliberate force is also at work, namely, *consciously pursued joint action* (JA). Such joint action can be of three different types (Nadvi, 1999). Joint action within vertical linkages includes backward ties with suppliers and subcontractors and forward ties with traders and buyers. Joint action within bilateral horizontal linkages between two or more local producers can include joint marketing of products, joint purchase of inputs, order sharing, common use of specialized equipment, joint product development, and exchange of expertise and market information. Joint action within multilateral horizontal linkages among a large number of local producers, particularly through cluster-wide institutions, includes cooperation in business associations and business development service centers.

The combination of incidental external economies and the effects of active cooperation determines the degree of collective efficiency of a cluster and, dynamically, its potential for fostering SMEs' upgrading. Both are crucial: incidental, passive external economies may not suffice without joint actions, and joint actions hardly ever develop in the absence of external economies. Therefore, our focus is necessarily on the role of intracluster vertical and horizontal relationships that generate collective efficiency or, in other words, the increasing returns from incidental external economies and from joint actions.

However, recent changes in production systems, distribution channels, and financial markets, accelerated by the globalization of product markets and the spread of information technologies, suggest that more attention must be paid to external linkages.[1] To this end, the *global value*

[1] Markusen (1996), broadening the definition of industrial district, discusses four types of districts. Especially in the "satellite platform" type, consisting of a congregation of branch facilities of externally

chain approach (Gereffi, 1999) takes into account activities occurring outside the cluster and, in particular, helps to explain the strategic role of relationships with key external actors.

Value Chains

The idea of a value chain is based on the series of activities needed to turn raw materials into finished products and sell them and on the value added at each link (Gereffi, 1999; Kaplinsky and Readman, 2001; UNIDO, 2002). Rarely do individual companies alone undertake the full range of activities required to bring a product from conception to market. The design, production, and marketing of products involve a chain of activities divided among different enterprises that are often located in different places, sometimes even in different countries. Increasingly, firms from several countries are involved in value chains that have a global reach and thus can be called global value chains.

From an analytical perspective, the value chain approach is useful because the focus shifts from manufacturing alone to include the other activities involved in the supply of goods and services, including "intangibles" phases such as distribution and marketing (Kaplinsky, 2000; Wood, 2001). The flows of information, as well as goods, in the chain are captured by this concept, making it clear that linkages between firms are often non-arm's-length and involve skills and knowledge that are scarce and can command large financial rewards. All activities contribute to total value, but it is crucial to identify those activities providing higher returns along the value chain in order to understand the global distribution of value added.

The focus of value chain research is on the ongoing relationships among the various actors involved in the chain and on their implications for development (Humphrey and Schmitz, 2002b). The concept

---

based multiplant firms, she acknowledges the importance of external linkages. Guerrieri, Iammarino, and Pietrobelli (2001) further develop this approach and apply it to clusters in Italy and Taiwan.

of *governance* is central to the analysis of the relationships among actors in the chain. At any point in the chain, some degree of governance, or coordination, is required to decide what is to be produced (design of the product), how it is to be produced (the production process, technology, quality standards), and how much is to be produced. We deem it necessary to write of governance, rather than only coordination, as the proactive involvement and participation of all the actors within the value chain is crucial. This governance may occur through arm's-length market relations or through nonmarket relationships. In nonmarket relationships, following Humphrey and Schmitz (2000), we distinguish among three possible types of governance: (1) *network*, implying cooperation among firms of more or less equal power that share their competencies within the chain; (2) *quasi hierarchy*, involving relationships between legally independent firms in which one is subordinated to the other, with a leader in the chain defining rules with which the rest of the actors must comply; and (3) *hierarchy*, in which a firm is owned by an external firm.

The global value chain literature also stresses the role played by the GVC leaders, particularly the buyers, in transferring knowledge along the chains. For small firms in less developed countries, participation in value chains is a means of obtaining information on the needs of global markets and of gaining access to those markets. Although this information has high value for local SMEs, it is less clear what role the leaders of the GVCs play in fostering and supporting the SMEs' upgrading process. Gereffi (1999), focusing primarily on East Asia, asserts the rather optimistic view that GVC leaders almost automatically promote process, product, and functional upgrading among small local producers (see below for a discussion of the different forms of upgrading). A more differentiated picture of the role of GVC leaders in SME upgrading in Latin America emerges from the studies in this book.

Consonant with the present approach, Humphrey and Schmitz (2000) discuss the prospects of upgrading with respect to the pattern of value chain governance. They conclude that insertion in a quasi-hierarchical chain offers very favorable conditions for process and product upgrading but hinders functional upgrading; networks offer ideal conditions for all forms of upgrading, but they are the least likely to occur among producers in developing countries. In addition, Humphrey and Schmitz's more dynamic approach suggests that chain governance is not static and may change because (1) power relationships may evolve when existing producers (or their spin-offs) acquire new capabilities; (2) establishing and maintaining quasi-hierarchical governance is costly for the lead firm and leads to inflexibility because of transaction-specific investments; or (3) firms and clusters often do not operate only in one chain, but rather simultaneously in several chains, and therefore may apply competencies acquired in one chain to supply other chains (Humphrey and Schmitz, 2002b).

In sum, both modes of organization of production, that is, both the cluster and the value chain, offer interesting opportunities for the upgrading and modernization of local firms, and they are not mutually exclusive. However, in order to assess the potential contributions of clusters and value chains to innovation and upgrading of local SMEs, we need to understand the organization of interfirm linkages and the internal governance structure of value chains. In addition, as we explain in the following section, the characteristics of the industrial sector of a SME's dominant specialization also play a role and affect the SME's prospects for upgrading.

The Sectoral Dimension of SMEs' Upgrading

The concept of upgrading—making better products, making them more efficiently, or moving into more skilled activities—has often been used in studies on competitiveness (Kaplinsky, 2000; Porter, 1990) and is related to innovation. Here we define upgrading as innovating to increase value added.[2] Enterprises may upgrade in various ways, such as by entering

[2] In this context, innovation is clearly not defined only as a breakthrough into a product or a process that is new to the world. It is rather a story of marginal, evolutionary improvements of products and processes that are new to the firm and that allow the firm to keep up with an international (moving) standard. This involves shifting to activities, products, and sectors that sustain higher value added and enforce higher entry barriers. See, among others, Katz (1987), Lall (1992), and Pietrobelli (1998).

higher-unit-value market niches or new sectors or by undertaking new productive (or service) functions. Four types of upgrading have been distinguished for enterprises within a value chain (Humphrey and Schmitz, 2000).

Process upgrading is transforming inputs into outputs more efficiently by reorganizing the production system or introducing superior technology (e.g., footwear producers in the Sinos Valley: Schmitz, 1999b). *Product upgrading* is moving into more sophisticated product lines in terms of increased unit values (e.g., the apparel commodity chain in Asia upgrading from discount chains to department stores: Gereffi, 1999). *Functional upgrading* is acquiring new, superior functions in the chain, such as design or marketing, or abandoning existing lower-value-added functions, to focus on higher-value-added activities (e.g., Torreón's blue jeans industry upgrading from *maquila* to "full-package" manufacturing: Bair and Gereffi, 2001). *Intersectoral upgrading* is applying the competence acquired in a particular function to move into a new sector (e.g., the use of competence in producing televisions in Taiwan to make monitors and then to upgrade into the computer sector: Guerrieri and Pietrobelli, 2004; Humphrey and Schmitz, 2002b). A vivid way to illustrate these ideas has led several authors to write that upgrading within a value chain implies "going up the value ladder," moving away from activities in which competition is of the "low road" type and entry barriers are low. The use of a different terminology would lead us to equally effectively describe functional upgrading as a process of acquiring and deepening "technological capabilities" (TCs) at any stage of a value chain (Bell and Pavitt, 1993; Lall, 1992). This would not necessarily imply going up the value ladder, but certainly moving to higher skills and more complex capabilities that are in turn likely to provide larger benefits to local SMEs.[3]

Moreover, our focus on upgrading requires moving a step forward and away from Ricardo's static concept of "comparative advantage" (CA).

---

[3] For a discussion on the relationships between upgrading and technological capabilities see Morrison, Pietrobelli, and Rabellotti (2006).

While comparative advantage registers ex post gaps in relative productivity that determine international trade flows, success in firm-level upgrading enables the dynamic acquisition of competitiveness in new market niches, sectors, or phases of the productive chain (Lall, 2001; Pietrobelli, 1997). In sum, the logic goes from innovation, to upgrading, to the acquisition of firm-level competitiveness (i.e., competitive advantage).[4]

In this chapter we argue that the concept of competitive advantage increasingly matters. In the theory of comparative advantage what matters is relative productivity, determining different patterns of interindustry specialization. According to this theoretical approach, with perfectly competitive markets, firms need only to target production efficiency. In fact, this is not enough, and competitive advantage is the relevant concept for analyzing SMEs' performance, both because of the existence of forms of imperfect competition in domestic and international markets and because of the presence of different degrees of (dynamic) externalities in different subsectors and stages of the value chain.

More specifically, in imperfectly competitive markets, rents and niches of "extranormal" profits often emerge, and this explains the efforts to enter specific segments selectively rather than simply focusing on efficiency improvements, regardless of the prevailing productive specialization (as advocated by the theory of comparative advantage). Moreover, different stages in the value chain and different variety and depth of technological capabilities offer different scope for dynamic externalities. Thus, for

[4] The macroeconomic dimension of competitiveness is often confused with the microeconomic definition, which is embedded in the competitiveness literature. This confusion generated an extensive debate among international trade economists rejecting the notion of "competitiveness" as essentially wrong and misleading, in comparison with the clear concept of "comparative advantage" (Krugman, 1996). Following the concept of comparative advantage, all economies benefit from any international specialization, provided that it is consistent with their pattern of comparative advantage. However, insofar as we admit the possibility of interfirm (intrasector) differentials (e.g., those related to market imperfections, information asymmetries, firm-specific learning and capabilities) that are ruled out by the (macro) theories of comparative advantage, then competitiveness becomes a meaningful, and indeed relevant, concept (Lall, 2001). Further, the comparative advantage approach allows consideration of "dynamic" comparative advantage, that is, that which is acquired through the purposeful efforts of enterprises, and in sectors different from those enjoying static comparative advantage (Pietrobelli, 1997).

example, in traditional manufacturing, the stages of design, product innovation, marketing, and distribution may all foster increases in competitiveness in related activities and sectors. The advantage of functional upgrading is in reducing the fragility and vulnerability of an enterprise's productive specialization. Competition from new entrants—firms from developing countries with lower production costs, which can crowd out incumbents—is stronger in the manufacturing phases of the value chain than in other more knowledge- and organization-intensive phases (e.g., product design and innovation, chain management, distribution, and retail). Therefore, functional upgrading may bring about more enduring and solid competitiveness.

For all these reasons, the concept of production efficiency is encompassed within the broader concept of competitiveness. Efforts to upgrade functionally and intersectorally (and the policies to support these processes) are justified in order to reap larger rents and externalities emerging in specific stages of the value chain, market niches, or sectors.

Sectoral Specificities in Upgrading and Innovation: A Classification for Latin American Countries

An additional element that crucially affects the upgrading prospects of firms and clusters is the "sectoral dimension," that is, the specific characteristics of the industrial sector of the firm. Insofar as we have defined upgrading as innovating to increase value added, then all the factors influencing innovation acquire a new relevance. The sectoral dimension is often overlooked in studies on clusters, perhaps because most of these studies are not comparative but rather detailed intra-industry case studies.

In order to take into account the sectoral dimension and the effect that sector characteristics may have on firms' pattern of innovation and learning, we need to introduce the concept of *tacit knowledge*. This notion was first introduced by Polanyi (1967) and then discussed in the context of evolutionary economics by Nelson and Winter (1982). It refers to the observation that some aspects of technological knowledge are well articulated, written down in manuals and papers, and taught. Other aspects of knowledge are largely tacit, mainly learned through practice and practical examples. In essence, this is knowledge that can be used freely by its owners but that cannot be easily expressed or explicitly communicated to anyone else. The tacit component of technological knowledge makes the transfer and application of such knowledge costly and difficult. As a result, the mastery of technology may require an organization to be active in the earlier stages of its development and a close and continuous interaction between the user and the producer—or transferer—of such knowledge. Interfirm relationships are especially needed in this context. Tacit knowledge is an essential characteristic by which to define a useful grouping of economic activities, as we do in this section.

The impact of collective efficiency and patterns of governance on the capacity of SMEs to upgrade may differ across sectors. This claim is based upon the consideration that industrial sectors differ in terms of technological complexity and in the modes and sources of innovation and upgrading.[5] As innovation studies have shown, in some sectors vertical relations with suppliers of inputs may be particularly important sources of product and process upgrading, as in the case of textiles and most traditional manufacturing. However, in other sectors, the major stimuli for technical change may be provided by technology users, organizations such as universities or the firms themselves, as, for example, with software or agro-industrial products (von Hippel, 1987; Pavitt, 1984).

Consistent with this approach, the properties of *firm knowledge bases* differ across sectors (Malerba and Orsenigo, 1993)[6] and may affect the

---

[5] In order to observe the variety of innovative processes across sectors, Nelson and Winter (1977, 1982) introduced the crucial concept of "technological regime," which they broadly define as a technological condition that defines the boundaries and the direction of the innovative and problem-solving activities of technicians (see also Dosi, 1982, 1988). More recently, other authors have attempted to differentiate technological regimes on the basis of the combination of concepts such as technological opportunity, appropriability of knowledge, cumulativeness of learning, and nature of the knowledge base (Malerba and Orsenigo, 1993; Breschi, Malerba, and Orsenigo, 2000).

[6] The properties of the knowledge base are tied to the nature of knowledge and its degree of specificity, tacitness, complexity, and independence (Breschi, Malerba, and Orsenigo, 2000).

strategic relevance of collective efficiency for the processes of upgrading in clusters. Thus, for example, in traditional manufacturing sectors, technology has important tacit and idiosyncratic elements, and therefore upgrading depends heavily on the intensity of technological externalities and cooperation among local actors (e.g., firms, research centers, technology and quality diffusion centers). In other words, we expect upgrading to depend on the degree of collective efficiency in traditional manufacturing. In other sectors, such as complex products or large natural-resource-based firms, technology is more codified, and access to external sources of knowledge (such as transnational corporations or research laboratories located in developed countries) becomes more critical for upgrading.

Furthermore, differences across sectors raise questions about the role of global buyers in fostering (or hindering) upgrading in different sectors' clusters. Thus, for example, global buyers are expected to be more involved and interested in their providers' upgrading if the technology required is mainly tacit and requires intense interaction. Moreover, in traditional manufacturing industries, characterized by a low degree of technological complexity, firms are likely to be included in global value chains even if they have very low technological capabilities. Therefore, tight supervision of and direct support to suppliers becomes a necessary condition for global buyers who rely on the competencies of their local suppliers and want to reduce the risk of suppliers' noncompliance (Humphrey and Schmitz, 2002b). The situation is likely to be at the opposite extreme in the case of complex products sector firms, in which technology is often thoroughly codified and the technological complexity requires that firms already have internal technological capabilities in order to be subcontracted, or else large buyers would not contract them at all.

Here we develop a sectoral classification that takes into account all of the above-mentioned factors, adapting existing taxonomies to the Latin American case.[7] On the basis of Pavitt's (1984) seminal work, we identify

[7] Starting from seminal contribution of Keith Pavitt (1984), different attempts have been made to identify and understand patterns of innovation (Marsili and Verspagen, 2001), and a number of

several key characteristics of the Latin American economy. In Latin America, in-house R&D activities are very low in both domestic and foreign firms (Archibugi and Pietrobelli, 2003), domestic intersectoral linkages have been displaced by trade liberalization (Cimoli and Katz, 2002), and university–industry linkages appear to be still relatively weak (Arocena and Sutz, 2001).[8] Furthermore, in the past 10 years, Latin America has deepened its productive specialization in resource-based sectors and has weakened its position in more engineering-intensive industries (Katz, 2001), reflecting its rich endowment of natural resources, relative to human and technical resources (Wood and Berge, 1997). Hence, we retain Pavitt's key notions and identify four main sectors for Latin America on the basis of the way learning and upgrading occur and on the related industrial organizational structure that most frequently prevails:[9]

- *traditional manufacturing*, mainly labor-intensive and "traditional" technology industries such as textiles, footwear, tiles and furniture;
- *natural-resource-based sectors (NR-based)*, implying the direct exploitation of natural resources (copper, marble, fruit, etc.);
- *complex products industries (COPs)*, including, among others, automobile, auto components and aircraft industries, ICT, and consumer electronics;
- *specialized suppliers*, which are, in our Latin American cases, essentially suppliers of software.

---

different studies have adopted and refined the taxonomy to analyze the Latin American context (e.g., Guerrieri, 1994; ECLAC, 1996; Ferraz, Kupfer, and Haguenauer, 1996).

[8] University–industry linkages have historically been very poor in Latin America (Plonsky, 1993). During the import substitution period, there was little interest in cooperation because protected market conditions did not encourage firms to innovate. At the same time, universities had little incentive to transfer technologies to business because research was financed mainly by the government. Since the 1990s, the situation has shown signs of change, with some new policies focusing specifically on university–industry linkages.

[9] The risk of "freezing" a classification that may be outdated by changes in technology over the years has been acknowledged by several authors (Freeman, 1994); to this aim, we have adapted the taxonomy to fit our empirical case studies.

Each of these sectors tends to have sector-specific predominant learning and innovating activities. Types of learning and innovation are distinguished in terms of the main sources of technical change, dependence on basic or applied research, modes of in-house innovation (e.g., "routinized" versus large R&D labs), tacitness or codified nature of knowledge, scale and relevance of R&D activity, and appropriability of innovation (Table 1.1).

The traditional manufacturing and natural-resource-based sectors are by far the most prevalent in Latin America and therefore especially important for our present aim of assessing SMEs' potential for upgrading within clusters and value chains. Traditional manufacturing is considered to be supplier-dominated, because major process innovations are introduced by producers of inputs (e.g., machinery, materials). Indeed, firms have room to upgrade their products and processes by developing or imitating new products' designs, often by interacting with large buyers that increasingly play a role in shaping the design of final products, and hence the specifics of the process of production (timing, quality standards, and costs).

Natural-resource-based sectors rely crucially on advances in basic and applied science, which, because it is difficult to appropriate, is most often undertaken by public research institutes, sometimes in connection with producers (farmers, breeders, etc.) (Pray and Umali-Deininger, 1998; Echeverría, Trigo, and Byerlee, 1996). In these sectors, applied research is carried out mainly by input suppliers (of chemicals, machinery, etc.) which can achieve economies of scale and appropriate the results of their research through patents.

Complex products are defined as "high cost, engineering-intensive products, subsystems or constructs supplied by a unit of production" (Hobday, 1998).[10] In these sectors the local network is normally anchored

---

[10] In this study, the definition of COPs does not coincide entirely with that given by Hobday (1998) for complex products systems. He distinguishes COPs from mass-market, commodity-type industries. The former—which include telecommunications exchanges, flight simulators, aircraft engines, and mobile phone network equipment—would be characterized by high component customization, a hierarchical architecture, and small batch production. The latter—which include cars, semiconductors, and consumer electronics—are instead characterized by a higher degree of interface and components standardization (modularity) (Ulrich, 1995), which allows for mass

Table 1.1. Patterns of Learning and Innovation in Different Sectors in Latin America

Sectors	Industries	Learning patterns	Description
1. Traditional manufacturing	Textile and garments, footwear, furniture, tile	Mainly supplier dominated	• Most new techniques originate from machinery and chemical industries. • Opportunity for technological accumulation mainly from improvements in production methods and associated inputs and on product design. • Most of technology is transferred internationally, embodied in capital goods. • Low appropriability, low barriers to entry.
2. Natural-resource-based	Sugar, tobacco, wine, fruit, milk, mining	Supplier dominated	• Importance of basic and applied research led by public research institutes because of low appropriability of knowledge. • Innovation is spurred also by suppliers (machinery, seeds, chemicals, etc.). • Increasing importance of international sanitary and quality standards and of patents. • Low appropriability of knowledge.
3. Complex products	Automobile and auto components, aircraft, consumer electronics	Scale-intensive firms	• Technological accumulation is generated by design, building, and operation of complex production systems or products. • In-house R&D is critical for innovation. • Process and product technologies develop incrementally. • In consumer electronics, technological accumulation emerges mainly from corporate R&D labs and university skills. • Appropriability is medium; high barriers to entry.
4. Specialized suppliers	Software	Specialized suppliers	• Important user-producer interactions. Learning from advanced users. • Low barriers to entry and low appropriability. • High in-house R&D for development of edge technologies.

Source: Based on Pavitt (1984); Bell and Pavitt (1993); Malerba (2000).

to one "assembler," which operates as a leading firm and is characterized by high design and technological capabilities. For our purposes, the relationships of local suppliers with these leading firm "anchors" may be crucial to fostering (or hindering) firms' upgrading through technology and skills transfers (or lack thereof). Scale-intensive firms typically lead complex products sectors (Bell and Pavitt, 1993), in which the process of technical change is realized within an architectural set (Henderson and Clark, 1990) and is often incremental and modular.

Within the specialized suppliers sector, we consider only software, which is typically client-driven. Specialized suppliers are an especially promising sector for developing countries' SMEs, because of the low transport and physical capital costs and the high information intensity of the sector, which moderate the importance of proximity to final markets and extend the scope for a deeper international division of labor. Moreover, the disintegration of some productive cycles, for example, telecommunications, opens up new market niches with low entry barriers (Torrisi, 2003). However, at the same time, the proximity of the market and of clients may crucially improve the development of design capabilities and thereby foster product and process upgrading. Thus, powerful pressures for clustering and globalization coexist in the specialized suppliers sector.

The Research Question and the Methodology of the Study

The research question we address in this book is complex and multifold: we explore the hypothesis that enterprise upgrading is simultaneously affected by firm-specific efforts and actions and by the environment in which firms operate. More specifically, we use detailed and extensive empirical evidence to question how SMEs' upgrading is affected by the collective efficiency of the cluster in which SMEs operate, by the pattern of governance of the value chain in which SMEs participate, and by the peculiar features that

---

production. In the present work, consistently with Bell and Pavitt (1993), the definition given to COPs will include both the above-mentioned types of industries, although the former is rarely encountered in Latin America.

characterize the patterns of learning and innovation in specific sectors. We acknowledge the close interdependence of all these factors, which do not represent alternative explanatory factors, but are rather complementary dimensions that are likely to influence upgrading prospects and strategies. We exploit many rich and original field studies from Latin America and use them to carry out an extensive theory-generating exercise to inspire more rigorous theory building and quantitative testing. Finally, this book also aims to offer *policy lessons* on how to support SMEs' upgrading in the global market.

The following questions are central to the present analysis:

- Is SMEs' upgrading facilitated by the degree of collective efficiency of clusters?
- How does the insertion of clusters into global value chains impact local upgrading strategies?
- Do sectoral differences affect the roles of clustering and value chains for enterprise upgrading?
- What can be done to support SMEs' upgrading in the global market?

This three-dimensional analysis is based on the collection of original data from 12 new cluster studies in Latin America (Table 1.2) and on an extensive review of studies available in the literature. The empirical analyses were carried out between September 2002 and June 2003, with the support of the Inter-American Development Bank. An international team of 12 experts took part in the collection and review of the empirical data. The field studies were undertaken with the same methodology, including field interviews with local firms, institutions and key informants, foreign buyers, and transnational corporations located in the clusters investigated. Field studies were supplemented with secondary sources such as publications and reports.

According to the purposes of this study, case studies were selected that fulfilled the following conditions: (1) *agglomeration:* all cases show

Table 1.2. New Field Studies on Selected Latin American Clusters: Basic Characteristics

Cluster	Country	Date of creation	Number of firms	Production 1995 (US$ millions)	Production 2002 (US$ millions)	Exports 1996 (US$ millions)	Exports 2002 (US$ millions)	Direct jobs	Indirect jobs
1 Salmon–Región Austral[a]	Chile	1978	65 + 150	500.0	1,005.0	480.0	970.0	29,000	12,500
2 Milk and dairy–Boaco, Chontales	Nicaragua	mid-1990s	10,605	25.4	31.8	2.9	12.7	15,624	6,544
3 Mangoes–Petrolina-Juazeiro[bc]	Brazil	1980s	330	8.0	37.0	22.0	51.0	17,400	11,600
4 Grapes–Petrolina-Juazeiro[b]	Brazil	1980s	250	45.0	56.0	10.0	34.0		
5 Melons–Rio Grande do Norte[bc]	Brazil	1980s	120	19.0	13.0	25.0	38.0	19,000	12,500
6 Apples–Santa Catarina[b]	Brazil	1960s	750	23.3	51.7	6.0	31.0	23,500	6,800
7 Furniture–Chipilo, Puebla[d]	Mexico	1987	146	17.5	6.7	17.1	7.0	5,400	n.a.
8 Metalworking–Espírito Santo[e]	Brazil	1988	66	23.3	33.3	1.1	1.7	12,000	48,000
9 Software–Aguascalientes	Mexico	2000s	13	n.a.	4.3	n.a.	n.a.	121	n.a.
10 Software–D.F.	Mexico	1980s	130	n.a.	57.5	n.a.	n.a.	2,000	n.a.
11 Software–Guadalajara[f]	Mexico	1990s	152	n.a.	n.a.	n.a.	n.a.	1,040	n.a.
12 Software–Monterrey	Mexico	1982	76	n.a.	120.0	n.a.	51.1	2,000	n.a.

Source: Field studies carried out for the present study.
Note: n.a. = not available.
[a] 65 firms in main value chain, 150 additional local providers. 40 percent of direct jobs are seasonal.
[b] For Brazilian fruit clusters, sources are IBGE (www.ibge.gov.br) for production and SECEX (www.aliceweb.desenvolvimento.gov.br) for exports.
[c] These figures are incompatible since value of exports exceeds value of production.
[d] Figures for 1996.
[e] Only figures on enterprises associated with the Center for the Development of the Capixaba Metalworking Industry (CDMEC).
[f] In Jalisco only 60 firms are formally registered.

some degree of geographical clustering of SMEs; (2) *upgrading:* the clusters selected have experienced some degree of upgrading, of whatever nature (i.e., product, process, functional, intersectoral); (3) *value chains:* all clusters are inserted in some form of value chain with other firms (and eventually institutions); and (4) *policy lessons:* all cases offer relevant policy lessons for future experiences in terms of either successes or failures.

According to these criteria, additional studies from the literature were analyzed, yielding a total of 40 case studies that were included in this analysis (Table 1.3). The list of cases, while necessarily incomplete, is the largest available—to our knowledge—on which comparative exercises have been carried out. The list provides a good representation of the range of clusters and value chains present in Latin America. Thus, although our sample cannot claim to cover the universe of clusters in the region, it represents a broad sample that allows reasonable generalizations.

Table 1.3. Case Studies

Case study	Country	Source
Traditional manufacturing sector		
Footwear, Sinos Valley	Brazil	Bazan and Navas-Aleman (2004); Vargas (2000); Schmitz (1995, 1999b)
Footwear, Guadalajara	Mexico	Rabellotti (1997, 1999c)
Footwear, León	Mexico	Rabellotti (1997, 1999c)
Footwear, Campina Grande	Brazil	Lemos and Palhano (2000)
Textile, Jalisco	Mexico	Bair and Gereffi (2001)
Textile, Medellín	Colombia	Pietrobelli and Olarte (2002)
Garment, Bucaramanga	Colombia	Pietrobelli and Olarte (2002)
Textile, Itaji	Brazil	Campos, Ferraz Cário, and Nicolau (2000)
Garment, Gamarra	Peru	Visser (1999)
Furniture, Serra Gaúcha	Brazil	Vargas and Alevi (2000); Meyer-Stamer (1998a)
Furniture, Espírito Santo	Brazil	Villaschi and Bueno (2000)
Furniture, Ubá	Brazil	Crocco and Horacio (2001)
Furniture, Segusino-Chipilo	Mexico	Zepeda (Chapter 5 in this volume)
Tile, Santa Catarina	Brazil	Meyer-Stamer, Maggi, and Siebel (2001); Meyer-Stamer (1998a, 1998b); Campos, Nicolau, and Ferraz Cário (1998)

(continued on next page)

Table 1.3. Case Studies (continued)

Case study	Country	Source
Natural-resource-based sector		
Tobacco, Rio Pardo	Brazil	Vargas (2001a, 2001b)
Wine, Colchagua	Chile	Giuliani (2002, 2003)
Wine, Serra Gaúcha	Brazil	Vargas (2001a)
Sugar, Valle del Cauca	Colombia	Millan (2002)
Marble, Espírito Santo	Brazil	Villaschi and Sabadini (2000)
Copper, Cuajone-Toquepala	Peru	Torres-Zorrilla (2000, 2001)
Salmon, Región Austral	Chile	Maggi (Chapter 4 in this volume)
Milk, Boaco, Chontales	Nicaragua	Artola and Parrilli (Chapter 2 in this volume)
Mangoes and grapes, Petrolina-Juazeiro	Brazil	Gomes (Chapter 3 in this volume)
Melons, Rio Grande do Norte	Brazil	Gomes (Chapter 3 in this volume)
Apples, Santa Catarina	Brazil	Gomes (Chapter 3 in this volume)
Complex products industries sector		
Aeronautics, SJC, São Paulo	Brazil	Bernardes and Pinho (2002), Marques (2004)
Automotive, Nova Serrana	Brazil	Lemos et al. (2000), Santos, Crocco, and Lemos (2002)
Metalworking, Espírito Santo	Brazil	Villaschi, Cassiolato, and Lastres (Chapter 6 in this volume); Villaschi and Limas dos Santos (2000)
Automotive, Caxias do Sul, RGS	Brazil	Calandro and Campos (2002)
Automotive, Juárez	Mexico	Dutrénit, Vera-Cruz, and Gil (2002); Carrillo and Hualde (2000)
Audio-visual equipment, Baja California	Mexico	Gerber and Carrillo (2002); Alonso, Carrillo, and Contreras (2000); Buitelaar, Padilla, and Urrutia (1999); Carrillo, Mortimore, and Estrada (1998)
High tech, Campinas–São Paulo	Brazil	Garcia and Roselino (2002)
Intel ICT, San José	Costa Rica	Vargas and Lindegaard (2002)
Electronics, Jalisco	Mexico	Dussel (1999)
Specialized suppliers sector (software)		
Software, Joinville	Brazil	Bercovich and Swanke (2003)
Software, D.F.	Mexico	Ruiz Durán (Chapter 7 in this volume)
Software, Guadalajara	Mexico	Ruiz Durán (Chapter 7 in this volume)
Software, Aguascalientes	Mexico	Ruiz Durán (Chapter 7 in this volume)
Software, Monterrey	Mexico	Ruiz Durán (Chapter 7 in this volume)

The results of the analyses integrating the original case studies (Chapters 2 through 7) and the case studies from the literature are reported in Chapter 9 .

The analysis consists of a systematic attempt to quantify, using Likert scales, each of the clusters studied on the two dimensions that are the objects of analysis: degree of collective efficiency and levels of upgrading. Clusters are also categorized according to the type of value chain to which they are connected.

To quantify the degree of collective efficiency, we carefully assessed its main components, external economies and joint action. A value ranging from absent (0) to high (3) was assigned to each of the following components: for external economies, specialized labor market, local availability of inputs, and ease of access to information and markets; for joint action, backward and forward vertical linkages, and horizontal, bilateral, and multilateral linkages. The indices of external economies and joint action are computed by summing the ratings for each of the indices' components. Then, the index of collective efficiency is the simple average of the scores for external economies and joint action.[11] Similarly, for our assessment of upgrading, a value ranging from absent (0) to high (3) was assigned to each of the four types of upgrading: product, process, functional, and intersectoral. The assigned values were determined either during the original field study, or, in the cases reviewed from existing literature, from the context and specific wording of papers. Finally, we identified the number and mode of governance (market, network, quasi hierarchy or hierarchy) of the value chains in which each cluster participates. Whenever evidence was derived from the literature, with the collaboration of the team of experts, we carefully tried to minimize the occurrence of bias and misinterpretations by complementing and cross-referencing information in many ways.

The empirical analysis is inevitably affected by some limitations in the availability of reliable data. Even when updated firm-level statistics

[11] The indices of external economies and joint action are computed by summing the figures obtained in each component. Then, the index of collective efficiency is the simple average of the two.

are available, which seldom is the case for developing countries, they are available usually at the national or sometimes at the local level, but they are never gathered at the cluster level or to take account of the relationships within the same value chain. However, the richness of the original field studies undertaken for this volume partly offsets these data limitations. The final aim of this study is not to identify causal relationships but rather to explore rich and newly gathered empirical evidence on Latin American clustered SMEs.

The Structure of the Book

The book is structured in three parts. Parts I and II present the new cluster studies, organized according to their sectoral specialization. Part III concludes by exploring complementary methodological approaches and proposing some policy implications.

Part I presents three studies on clusters and value chains in the natural-resource-based sector. In Chapter 2, Artola and Parrilli focus on the recent development of the dairy cluster in the provinces of Boaco and Chontales in Nicaragua, where about 10,000 small producers and 500 large dairy companies operate. They document the shift from a traditional sector, with 80 percent of the production directed to the internal market, toward an industrial production system targeting international markets. This shift started at the beginning of the 1990s with the implementation of a development project funded through international cooperation. Since the mid-1990s there has been a remarkable development of the cluster, as local producers have invested in upgrading the quality of product, process, and organization of their firms. The authors analyze the role of collective efficiency in the upgrading process and investigate how the different patterns of governance of the many value chains operating in the cluster have also influenced upgrading.

In Chapter 3, Gomes examines how small and medium-sized Brazilian fruit growers have managed to meet the rising demands of globalization, particularly through engagement in local institutions. Her analysis is based on three cases: mango and grape production in Petrolina-Juazeiro, apple production in Santa Catarina, and melon production in Rio Grande do Norte. These three clusters differ in terms of public sector involvement in the process of adoption and upgrading of fruit production. At one extreme is mango and grape production in Petrolina-Juazeiro, which is the result of concerted planning by a federal institution; at the other extreme is melon production in Rio Grande do Norte, which is mostly the result of private entrepreneurship, with only minimal public support. Somewhere in between is apple production in Santa Catarina, in which the state was particularly active with support to research and extension services.

In Chapter 4, Maggi studies the cluster of salmon farming and processing in southern Chile. The core of the cluster is composed of more than 500 farming centers, 34 processing companies, and nearly 150 direct suppliers. The expansion of the cluster has been possible because of interenterprise and public–private cooperation efforts. Nevertheless, the pattern of development and cooperation has varied substantially over time. During the first stage (initial learning), between 1978 and 1985, numerous initiatives were encouraged to exploit the comparative advantages around which the industry began to establish itself. During the second stage (maturation), the imperative became the acquisition of productive capacities to maintain competitiveness in an industry whose profit margins were quickly shrinking. Some of the challenges during this phase were confronted by means of collective actions, with impacts at different levels in the value chain. The third phase (globalization) marks a rupture with the previous phases. During this phase larger companies with better insertion in the world market become predominant with rising vertical integration; the larger companies are generally associated with foreign equities and operate simultaneously in several production processes, such as farming, processing, and distribution. In terms of upgrading, the Chilean case offers a wide variety of examples of product, process, and functional upgrading, and even some intersectoral upgrading, with the recent development of the biotechnology sector.

In Part II we present the case of wooden furniture in Mexico, as well as a case from the complex products sector (a metalworking cluster in Brazil) and one from the specialized suppliers sector (software clusters in Mexico). In Chapter 5, Zepeda analyzes the rise and fall of the furniture cluster of Chipilo, near Puebla, Mexico. The cluster emerged during the 1990s, following the amazing export boom of one company that discovered a new niche market in the production of rustic Mexican furniture. Rapidly, in the village of no more than 5,000 inhabitants, many of Italian origin, and traditionally specialized in cattle rearing and craft dairy industries, many cattle sheds were turned into carpenter's shops, and many farmers learned how to produce furniture, in most cases as subcontractors of the leading firm. Unfortunately, in 2000, the cluster entered a crisis, and in 2003 the leading firm closed its plants and declared bankruptcy. Several reasons explain this decline: (1) micro inefficiencies, including excessive employment, huge increases in wages without adequate productivity increases, and bad financial management, and (2) macro factors, including increased internal and external competition (success attracted new local producers and Chinese firms began to produce Mexican country-style furniture at competitive prices), the global recession and a general decline in demand, and the real appreciation of the peso, which raised costs of wood and other imported inputs. The crisis quickly spread to many firms in the cluster. The chapter investigates how product and process upgrading took place rapidly and diffused to most cluster firms and then describes what happened during the cluster's crisis.

In Chapter 6, Villaschi, Cassiolato, and Lastres examine a metalworking cluster in the Brazilian state of Espírito Santo. Their analysis concentrates on the interactions between a few large enterprises competing in the global market and a cluster of SMEs that supply them with intermediate parts and services. Special attention is given to specific characteristics of these interactions, such as the way cooperation between large exporters of low-value-added commodities and their small local suppliers have enhanced the suppliers' industrial capabilities in a very short period of time. These relations—mostly, but not exclusively, informal—have been fostered by several policy interventions, with a particularly important role played by a center for the development of local industry.

In Chapter 7, Ruiz Durán analyzes the cases of software clusters in Mexico City, Monterrey, Nuevo León, Guadalajara, and Aguascalientes. All these clusters are demand-driven, and all of them are located in areas characterized by a strong concentration of economic activities. In some cases the growth process has also been sustained by the strong participation of large transnational companies (Microsoft, IBM, Oracle, SAP) and especially by the spin-off of skilled people from locally based high-tech transnational companies. The process of cluster formation has been induced in most of the cases by the market, and enterprises' commitment has motivated local and federal governments to intervene and encourage this process, creating a favorable local environment and, above all, endowment of an educated labor force. Ruiz Durán explores this fertile combination of collective initiatives.

Part III presents examples of positive and normative approaches and draws some lessons from the extensive empirical evidence. In Chapter 8, Amighini examines the evidence of some upgrading experiences in Latin America during the 1990s. Her focus is on a particular type of upgrading, vertical product differentiation in the traded sector, and her analyses are based on very disaggregated international trade statistics. The goal is to assess the competitive position of a single country in a particular market with respect to its major world competitors. Amighini proposes a method for analyzing export performance at the product level that takes into account the evolution of world demand for a given product, the evolution of market shares for major world exporters of the product, and the trend in export unit value. Countries are classified as upgrading in a particular market during the 1990s if they shifted to higher segments of the market (i.e., to higher-value products) with nondecreasing market shares in that product. Her empirical evidence confirms some of the findings of the case studies, which were obtained with a trade-based perspective, particularly with regard to the fish sector in Chile, the fruit sector in Brazil, and the dairy sector in Nicaragua.

In Chapter 9, Pietrobelli, Rabellotti, and Giuliani present and discuss the main findings of all the field studies, complementing their results with empirical evidence derived from an extensive survey of the literature on clusters in Latin America. They show that the sectoral dimension matters in explaining why clustering and participation in global value chains offer different opportunities for upgrading in different groups of sectors.

In Chapter 10, Pietrobelli and Rabellotti conclude by deriving strategic policy implications from the rich empirical evidence collected in the book. The chapter proposes a menu of actions to support cluster development, targeting three main objectives: the development of external economies, the promotion of linkages between firms, and the strengthening of the local position within value chains. Given the remarkable sectoral differences emerging from the empirical evidence presented in the book, the general lesson is that policy priorities are different according to sectoral specificities. In traditional manufacturing clusters there is a need for interventions aimed at sustaining the development of collective efficiency and at favoring access to additional chains. In natural-resource-based clusters, governments should actively seek to raise local quality, sanitary, and environmental standards through regulation, at the same time helping SMEs fulfill the requirements increasingly imposed in the international markets. Besides, in these clusters the promotion of public-private collaboration in research and efforts in disseminating findings to SMEs are key policy priorities. The identification of the right incentives to get large corporations involved in their local suppliers' upgrading is the decisive policy objective in complex products sector clusters. Finally, in the software clusters it appears that governmental efforts to invest in educational institutions and specialized human capital provide high returns.

References

Albaladejo, M. 2001. The Determinants of Competitiveness in SME Clusters: Evidence and Policies for Latin America. In *Small-Scale Enterprises in Developing and Transitional Economies*, ed. H. Katrack and R. Strange. London: Macmillan.

Alonso, J., J. Carrillo, and O. Contreras. 2000. *Trayectorias tecnológicas en empresas maquiladoras asiáticas y americanas en México.* Working Paper no. 72, Serie Desarrollo Productivo, ECLAC, United Nations, Santiago, Chile.

Archibugi, D., and C. Pietrobelli. 2003. The Globalisation of Technology and Its Implications for Developing Countries: Windows of Opportunity or Further Burden? *Technological Forecasting and Social Change* 70:861–883.

Arocena, R., and J. Sutz. 2001. Changing Knowledge Production and Latin American Universities. *Research Policy* 30(8):1221–1234.

Bair, J., and G. Gereffi. 2001. Local Clusters in Global Chains: The Causes and Consequences of Export Dynamism in Torreón's Blue Jeans Industry. *World Development* 29(11):1885–1903.

Bazan, L., and L. Navas-Alemán. 2004. The Underground Revolution in the Sinos Valley: A Comparison of Upgrading in Global and National Value Chains. In *Local Enterprises in the Global Economy: Issues of Governance and Upgrading*, ed. Hubert Schmitz. Cheltenham, U.K.: Elgar.

Becattini, G. 1987. *Mercato e forze locali: Il distretto industriale.* Bologna: Il Mulino.

Bell, M., and K. Pavitt. 1993. Technological Accumulation and Industrial Growth: Contrast between Developed and Developing Countries. *Industrial and Corporate Change* 2(2):157–211.

Bercovich, N., and C. Swanke. 2003. *Cooperação e competitividade na indústria de software de Blumenau.* Working Paper No. 138, Serie Desarrollo Productivo, ECLAC, United Nations, Santiago, Chile.

Bernardes, R., and M. Pinho. 2002. *Aglomeração e aprendizado na rede de fornecedores locais da Embraer*. Nota Técnica, Instituto de Economia, Universidade Federal do Rio de Janeiro. www.ie.ufrj.br/redesist.

Breschi, S., F. Malerba, and L. Orsenigo. 2000. Technological Regimes and the Schumpeterian Patterns of Innovation. *Economic Journal* 110:388–410.

Buitelaar, R. M., R. Padilla, and R. Urrutia. 1999. Industria maquiladora y cambio técnico. *Revista de la CEPAL* no. 67 (April):133–152.

Calandro, M. L., and H. S. Campos. 2002. O setor de autopeças de Caxias do Sul e Região: diagnóstico para a implementação de política de apoio ao desenvolvimento de SLPs. In *Programa de apoio aos sistemas locais de produção: a construção de uma política pública do RS*, ed. C. C. Chiappino. Porto Alegre, Brazil: Fundação de Economia e Estatística.

Campos, R. R., S. A. Ferraz Cário, and J. A. Nicolau. 2000. *Arranjo produtivo têxtil-vestuário do Vale do Itajaís/SC*. Nota Técnica No. 20, Instituto de Economia, Universidade Federal do Rio de Janeiro.

Campos, R. R., J. A. Nicolau, and S. A. Ferraz Cário. 1998. *Sistemas locais de inovação: um estudo preliminar de casos selecionados no estado de Santa Catarina*. Nota Técnica No. 10, Instituto de Economia, Universidade Federal do Rio de Janeiro. www.ie.ufrj.br/redesist.

Carrillo, J., and A. Hualde. 2000. Existe un cluster en la maquiladora electrónica en Tijuana. In *¿Aglomeraciones locales o clusters globales? evolución empresarial e institucional en el Norte de México*, ed. J. Carrillo, 99–139. Tijuana: Fundación Ebert and El Colegio de la Frontera Norte, Universidad Autónoma de Ciudad Juárez.

Carrillo, J., M. Mortimore, and J. A. Estrada. 1998. *El impacto de las empresas transnacionales en la reestructuración industrial de México: el caso de las industrias de partes para vehículos y televisores*. Working Paper no. 50, Serie Desarrollo Productivo, ECLAC, United Nations, Santiago, Chile.

Cimoli, M., and J. Katz. 2002. *Structural Reforms, Technological Gaps and Economic Development: A Latin American Perspective*. Serie Desarrollo Productivo No. 129, ECLAC, United Nations, Santiago, Chile.

Crocco, M., and F. Horacio. 2001. *Industrialização descentralizada: sistemas industriais locais. O arranjo produtivo moveleiro de Ubá.* Nota Técnica No. 38, Instituto de Economia, Universidade Federal do Rio de Janeiro. www.ie.ufrj.br/redesist.

Dosi, G. 1982. Technological Paradigms and Technological Trajectories. *Research Policy* 11:147–162.

———. 1988. Sources, Procedures and Microeconomic Effects of Innovation. *Journal of Economic Literature* 26:1120–1171.

Dosi, G., C. Freeman, R. R. Nelson, G. Silverberg, and L. Soete, eds. 1988. *Technical Change and Economic Theory.* London: Pinter.

Dussel, E. 1999. La subcontratación como proceso de aprendizaje: el caso de la electrónica en Jalisco (México) en la década de los noventa. Red de Reestructuración y Competitividad, ECLAC, United Nations, Santiago, Chile.

Dutrénit, G., A. O. Vera-Cruz, and J. L. Gil. 2002. *Desafíos y oportunidades de las Pymes para su integración a la red de proveedores: el caso de la maquila automotriz en Ciudad Juárez.* Nota Técnica, Instituto de Economia, Universidade Federal do Rio de Janeiro. www.ie.ufrj.br/redesist.

Echeverría, R. G., E. J. Trigo, and D. Byerlee. 1996. *Institutional Change and Effective Financing of Agricultural Research in Latin America.* Technical Paper No. 330, World Bank, Washington, D.C.

Economic Commission for Latin America and the Caribbean (ECLAC). 1996. *Panorama de la inserción internacional de América Latina y el Caribe.* Edición 1996. ECLAC, United Nations, Santiago, Chile.

Edquist, C. 2002. Systems of Innovation for Development. Background paper for UNIDO World Industrial Development Report, 2002–3. Unpublished. www.unido.org.

Ferraz, J., D. Kupfer, and L. Haguenauer. 1996. El desafío competitivo para la industria brasileña. *Revista de la CEPAL* no. 58:145–173.

Freeman, C. 1994. The Economics of Technical Change. *Cambridge Journal of Economics* 18:463–514.

Garcia, R., and J. E. Roselino. 2002. Critical Evaluation of the Results of the "Informatics Law" and Its Reflexes on the Electronic Complex.

Paper presented at the Sixth EUNIP Conference, Turku, Finland, 5–7 December.

Gerber, J., and J. Carrillo. 2002. Are Baja California's Maquiladora Plants Competitive? Paper presented at San Diego Dialogue Fronterizo "The Future of Manufacturing in Baja California: The Electronics and Auto Part Sectors," July 18.

Gereffi, G. 1994. The Organization of Buyer-Driven Global Commodity Chains: How U.S. Retailers Shape Overseas Production Networks. In *Commodity Chains and Global Capitalism*, ed. G. Gereffi and M. Korzeniewicz. London: Praeger.

———. 1999. International Trade and Industrial Upgrading in the Apparel Commodity Chain. *Journal of International Economics* 48:37–70.

Gereffi, G., and R. Kaplinsky. 2001. The Value of Value Chains [Special Issue]. *IDS Bulletin* 32.

Giuliani, E. 2002. Beyond Static Comparative Advantage in Wine Production: The Case of the Colchagua Valley, Chile. Unpublished.

———. 2003. Knowledge in the Air and Its Uneven Distribution: A Story of a Chilean Wine Cluster. Paper presented at the DRUID Winter Conference, Aalborg, Denmark, January 16–18. www.druid.dk.

Giuliani, E., C. Pietrobelli, and R. Rabellotti. 2005. Upgrading in Global Value Chains: Lessons from Latin American Clusters. *World Development* 33(4):549–573.

Guerrieri, P. 1994. International Competitiveness, Trade Integration and Technological Interdependence. In *The New Paradigm of Systemic Competitiveness: Toward More Integrated Policies in Latin America*, ed. Colin I. Bradford, Jr. Paris: Organisation for Economic Co-operation and Development.

Guerrieri, P., S. Iammarino, and C. Pietrobelli. 2001. *The Global Challenge to Industrial Districts: SMEs in Italy and Taiwan*. Cheltenham, U.K.: Elgar.

Guerrieri, P., and C. Pietrobelli. 2004. Industrial Districts' Evolution and Technological Regimes: Italy and Taiwan. *Technovation* 248(11):899–914.

Henderson, R. M., and K. B. Clark. 1990 Architectural Innovation: The Reconfiguration of Existing Product Technologies and the Failure of Established Firms. *Administrative Science Quarterly* 35:9–30.

Hobday, M. 1998. Product Complexity, Innovation and Industrial Organization. *Research Policy* 26:689–710.

Humphrey, J., ed. 1995. Industrial Organization and Manufacturing Competitiveness in Developing Countries [Special Issue]. *World Development* 23(1).

Humphrey, J., and H. Schmitz. 2000. *Governance and Upgrading: Linking Industrial Cluster and Global Value Chain Research.* Working Paper No. 120, Institute of Development Studies, University of Sussex, Brighton, U.K.

———. 2002a. How Does Insertion in Global Value Chains Affect Upgrading Industrial Clusters? *Regional Studies* 36(9):1017–1027.

———. 2002b. *Developing Country Firms in the World Economy: Governance and Upgrading in Global Value Chains.* INEF Report No. 61, University of Duisburg, Duisburg. http://www.ids.ac.uk/ids/global/vwpap.html.

Kaplinsky, R. 2000. Globalisation and Unequalisation: What Can Be Learned from Value Chain Analysis? *Journal of Development Studies* 37(2):117–146.

Kaplinsky, R., and J. Readman. 2001. How Can SME Producers Serve Global Markets and Sustain Income Growth? University of Brighton and University of Sussex, Brighton. Unpublished. http://www.ids.ac.uk/ids/global/valchn.html.

Katz, J., ed. 1987. *Technology Generation in Latin American Manufacturing Industries.* London: Macmillan.

———. 2001. Structural Reforms and Technological Behaviour: The Sources and Nature of Technological Change in Latin America in the 1990s. *Research Policy* 30:1–19.

Krugman, P. 1996. Making Sense of the Competitiveness Debate. *Oxford Review of Economic Policy* 12(3):17–25.

Lall, S. 1992. Technological Capabilities and Industrialization. *World Development* 20(2):165–186.

———. 2001. Competitiveness Indices and Developing Countries: An Economic Evaluation of the Global Competitiveness Report. *World Development* 29(9):1501–1525.

Lemos, C., and A. Palhano. 2000. *Arranjo produtivo coureiro-calçadista de Campina Grande/PB*. Nota Técnica No. 22, Instituto de Economia, Universidade Federal do Rio de Janeiro. www.ie.ufrj.br/redesist.

Lemos, M. B., C. C. Diniz, F. Teixeira dos Santos, M. A. Crocco, and O. Camargo. 2000. *O arranjo produtivo da Rede Fiat de Fornecedores*. Nota Técnica No. 17, Instituto de Economia, Universidade Federal do Rio de Janeiro. www.ie.ufrj.br/redesist.

Malerba, F., ed. 2000. *Economia dell'Innovazione*. Rome: Carocci Editore.

Malerba, F., and L. Orsenigo. 1993. Technological Regimes and Firm Behaviour. *Industrial and Corporate Change* 2(1):74–89.

Markusen, A. 1996. Sticky Places in Slippery Space: A Typology of Industrial Districts. *Economic Geography* 72:293–313.

Marques, R. A. 2004. Evolution of the Civil Aircraft Manufacturing System of Innovation: A Case Study in Brazil. In *Innovation, Learning, and Technological Dynamism of Developing Countries*, ed. S. Mani and H. Romijn, 77–106. Tokyo: United Nations University Press.

Marshall, A. 1920. *Principles of Economics*. 8th ed. London: Macmillan (1st ed. 1890).

Marsili, O., and B. Verspagen. 2001. *Technological Regimes and Innovation: Looking for Regularities in Dutch Manufacturing*. Paper No. 150, Produced for the Nelson and Winter Conference, Danish Research Unit for Industrial Dynamics, Copenhagen.

McCormick, D. 1999. African Enterprise Clusters and Industrialization: Theory and Reality. *World Development* 27(9):1531–1551.

Meyer-Stamer, J. 1998a. Avoiding Collective Efficiency: Growth and Crises in the Furniture Cluster in São Bento do Sul (Santa Catarina, Brazil). Unpublished. www.meyer-stamer.de/1998/sbs.moveis.htm.

———. 1998b. Towards Knowledge-Driven Development? Upgrading to Face the Challenges of an Open Economy: Experience from Industrial Clusters in Santa Catarina, Brazil. Paper presented at the Conference on Globalisation and Industrial Competitiveness in Brazil, Oxford, June 11.

Meyer-Stamer, J., C. Maggi, and S. Siebel. 2001. *Improving upon Nature: Creating Comparative Advantage in Tile Clusters in Italy, Spain and Brazil*. Report no. 54, Institut für Entwicklung und Frieden (INEF) der Gerhard-Mercator-Universität, Duisburg, Germany.

Millan, F. 2002. El conglomerado del azúcar del valle del Cauca: cien años de construcción social. In *Aglomeraciones agroindustriales en América Latina*, ed. ECLAC. Santiago, Chile: ECLAC, United Nations.

Morrison A., C. Pietrobelli, and R. Rabellotti. 2006. Global Value Chains and Technological Capabilities: A Framework to Study Industrial Innovation in Developing Countries. CREI, University of Rome 3. Unpublished.

Nadvi, K. 1999. The Cutting Edge: Collective Efficiency and International Competitiveness in Pakistan. *Oxford Development Studies* 27(1):81–107.

Nadvi, K., and H. Schmitz, eds. 1999. Industrial Clusters in Developing Countries [Special Issue]. *World Development* 27(9).

Nelson, R. R. 1995. Recent Evolutionary Theorizing about Economic Change. *Journal of Economic Literature* 33(March):48–90.

———. 1998. The Co-evolution of Technology, Industrial Structure, and Supporting Institutions. In *Technology, Organization, and Competitiveness*, ed. G. Dosi, D. J. Teece, and J. Chytry. Oxford: Oxford University Press.

Nelson, R. R., and B. Sampat. 2001. Making Sense of Institutions as a Factor Shaping Economic Performance. *Journal of Economic Behavior and Organization* 44(1):3–54.

Nelson, R. R., and S. Winter. 1977. In Search of a Useful Theory of Innovation. *Research Policy* 6:36–76.

———. 1982. An *Evolutionary Theory of Economic Change.* Cambridge, Mass.: Harvard University Press.

Paniccia, I. 2002. *Industrial Districts: Evolution and Competitiveness in Italian Firms.* Cheltenham, U.K.: Elgar.

Pavitt, K. 1984. Sectoral Patterns of Technical Change: Towards a Taxonomy and a Theory. *Research Policy* 13:343–373.

Peres, W., and G. Stumpo. 2000. Small and Medium-Sized Manufacturing Enterprises in Latin America and the Caribbean under the New Economic Model. *World Development* 28(9):1643–1655.

———, eds. 2002. *Pequeñas y medianas empresas industriales en América Latina y el Caribe.* Buenos Aires and Mexico City: Siglo XXI and ECLAC/United Nations.

Pietrobelli, C. 1997. On the Theory of Technological Capabilities and Developing Countries' Dynamic Comparative Advantage in Manufactures. *Rivista Internazionale di Scienze Economiche e Commerciali* 44(2):313–338.

———. 1998. *Industry, Competitiveness and Technological Capabilities in Chile: A New Tiger from Latin America?* London: Macmillan.

Pietrobelli, C., and B. T. Olarte. 2002. Enterprise Clusters and Industrial Districts in Colombia's Fashion Sector. *European Planning Studies* 10(5):541–562.

Plonsky, A. G., ed. 1993. *Cooperación empresa-universidad en Iberoamérica.* São Paulo: CYTED.

Polanyi, M. 1967. *The Tacit Dimension.* Garden City, N.Y.: Doubleday-Anchor.

Porter, M. 1990. *The Competitive Advantage of Nations.* London: Macmillan.

Pray, C. E., and D. Umali-Deininger. 1998. The Private Sector in Agricultural Research Systems: Will It Fill the Gap? *World Development* 26(6):1127–1148.

Putnam, D. 1993. *Making Democracy Work: Civic Traditions in Modern Italy.* Princeton: Princeton University Press.

Pyke, F., G. Becattini, and W. Sengenberger, eds. 1990. *Industrial Districts and Interfirm Cooperation in Italy*. Geneva: International Institute for Labour Studies, International Labour Organization.

Rabellotti, R. 1997. *External Economies and Cooperation in Industrial Districts: A Comparison of Italy and Mexico*. Basingstoke, U.K.: Macmillan.

———. 1999. Recovery of a Mexican Cluster: Devaluation Bonanza or Collective Efficiency? *World Development* 27(9):1571–1585.

Santos, F., M. Crocco, and M. B. Lemos. 2002. *As MPMEs em espaços industriais periféricos: os casos de Nova Serrana e da Rede de Fornecedores da Fiat*. Nota Técnica, Instituto de Economia, Universidade Federal do Rio de Janeiro. www.ie.ufrj.br/redesist.

Schmitz, H. 1995. Collective Efficiency: Growth Path for Small-Scale Industry. *Journal of Development Studies* 31(4):529–566.

———. 1999a. Increasing Returns and Collective Efficiency. *Cambridge Journal of Economics* 23(4):465–483.

———. 1999b. Global Competition and Local Co-operation: Success and Failure in the Sinos Valley, Brazil. *World Development* 27(9):1627–1650.

Torres-Zorrilla, J. 2000. *Una estrategia de desarrollo basada en recursos naturales: análisis cluster del complejo de cobre de la Southern Perú*. Working Paper no. 70, Serie Desarrollo Productivo, ECLAC, United Nations, Santiago, Chile.

Torres-Zorrilla, J. 2001. El complejo de cobre de la Southern Peru. In *Aglomeraciones mineras y desarrollo local en América Latina*, ed. R. Buitelaar. Santiago, Chile: ECLAC, United Nations–Alfaomega.

Torrisi, S. 2003. Imprenditorialità, nuovi modelli di business e distretti tecnologici: Un confronto tra India ed Irlanda. In *Distretti industriali e distretti tecnologici*, ed. F. Cesaroni and A. Piccaluga. Milan: Franco Angeli.

Ulrich, K. 1995. The Role of Product Architecture in the Manufacturing Firm. *Research Policy* 24:419–440.

United Nations Industrial Development Organization (UNIDO). 2002. *Industrial Development Report* 2002–03. Vienna: United Nations.

Vargas, L., and K. Lindegaard. 2002. New Economies and Innovation for Developing Countries. The Case of Intel in Costa Rica. Paper presented at the DRUID Summer Conference, "Industrial Dynamics of the New and Old Economy: Who Embraces Whom?" Copenhagen, June 6–8. www.druid.dk.

Vargas, M. A. 2000. *Arranjo produtivo coureiro-calçadista do Vale dos Sinos.* Nota Técnica No. 21, Instituto de Economia, Universidade Federal do Rio de Janeiro. www.ie.ufrj.br/redesist.

———. 2001a. Local Systems of Innovation in Developing Countries: A Study of Technological Learning in Local Productive Arrangements in Brazil. Paper presented at the DRUID Winter Conference, Aalborg, Denmark, January 16–18. www.druid.dk.

———. 2001b. *Forms of Governance, Learning Mechanisms and Upgrading Strategies in the Tobacco Cluster in Rio Pardo Valley-Brazil.* Working Paper No. 125, Institute of Development Studies, University of Sussex, Brighton, U.K.

Vargas, M. A., and R. M. Alevi. 2000. *Competitividade, capacitação tecnológica e inovação no arranjo moveleiro da Serra Gaúcha.* Nota Técnica No. 39, Instituto de Economia, Universidade Federal do Rio de Janeiro. www.ie.ufrj.br/redesist.

Villaschi, A., and F. O. Bueno. 2000. *Elementos dinâmicos do arranjo produtivo Madeira/Movéis no Nordeste de Capaixaba.* Nota Técnica No. 24, Instituto de Economia, Universidade Federal do Rio de Janeiro. www.ie.ufrj.br/redesist.

Villaschi, A., and M. de Souza Sabadini. 2000. *Arranjo produtivo ornamentais (marmore, granito) no Estado do Espírito Santo.* Nota Técnica No. 15, Instituto de Economia, Universidade Federal do Rio de Janeiro. www.ie.ufrj.br/redesist.

Villaschi, A., and E. Limas dos Santos. 2000. *Arranjo produtivo metalmecânico, Espíritu Santo.* Nota Técnica No. 14, Instituto de Economia, Universidade Federal do Rio de Janeiro. www.ie.ufrj.br/redesist.

Visser, E.-J. 1999. A Comparison of Clustered and Dispersed Firms in the Small-Scale Clothing Industry of Lima. *World Development* 27(9):1553–1570.

von Hippel, E. 1987. Cooperation between Rivals: Informal Know-How Trading. *Research Policy* 16:291–302.

Williamson, O. E. 2000. The New Institutional Economics: Taking Stock, Looking Ahead. *Journal of Economic Literature* 38(September):595–613.

Wood, A. 2001. Value Chains: An Economist's Perspective. *IDS Bulletin* 32(3):41–45.

Wood, A., and K. Berge. 1997. Exporting Manufactures: Human Resources, Natural Resources and Trade Policy. *Journal of Development Studies* 34(1):35–59.

Part I

Upgrading in Clusters and Value Chains in Natural-Resource-Intensive Sectors

CHAPTER 2

The Development of the Dairy Cluster in Boaco and Chontales, Nicaragua

Ner Artola and Mario Davide Parrilli

In this chapter, we examine a dynamic dairy products cluster in Boaco and Chontales, Nicaragua, which underwent significant growth in the 1990s and is now the most developed cluster in the country. However, its dynamism is still below other well-known international clusters because Nicaragua is one of the slowest-growing countries in Latin America. Nicaragua has an enduring tradition as a producer and exporter of agricultural goods, a target recently reinforced by policymakers who are trying to revive the idea of making Nicaragua the "Central American granary," as it was in the 1960s (Parrilli, 1998). This study presents evidence on the relevance and development potential of clustering in the least developed countries. In the Nicaraguan context, the concept of cluster assumes a broad meaning. Within the government agenda, cluster is often used without a clear focus on geographical proximity, which is a feature strongly emphasized in the international literature on clustering (Schmitz, 1995; Pietrobelli and Rabellotti, Chapter 1 in this volume). Instead, in this case study, cluster is used as a broader analytical framework that includes the conglomerate of producers, suppliers, clients, and other economic agents within the national production chain (Porter, 1990; INCAE, 1999a). Therefore, the cluster in-

---

The authors would like to thank Carlo Pietrobelli, Roberta Rabellotti, Marco Dini, Pablo Angelelli, and Juan José Llisterri for their valuable comments regarding earlier versions of this chapter.

vestigated here is not geographically concentrated in a limited number of municipalities but covers a bigger region, Boaco and Chontales, extending to an area of between 5,000 and 10,000 square kilometers. Moreover, due to the country's specialization in dairy products and their processing, this cluster tends to blur into an even wider national framework, as the analysis of value chains will make clear.

The initial dynamism of the dairy cluster can be traced back to the arrival in the early 1990s of Salvadoran entrepreneurs who sought to capitalize on Nicaragua's comparative advantage to produce cheese for export to Central America and the United States.The cluster comprises a large number of producers, which has grown in recent years in both the primary and the industrial processing sectors. Table 2.1 presents some information about the size of the dairy industry in the country and in this specific cluster. This study examines the primary strengths of the Nicaraguan dairy cluster in terms of external economies and joint actions, identifies the main productive and commercial channels using a value chain perspective, analyzes upgrading processes undertaken by the cluster in these years, and, finally, focuses on the policy lessons that may be drawn from this successful experience.

Table 2.1. Dairy Production Chain in Nicaragua and in Boaco and Chontales, 2000

	Nicaragua	SMEs in Boaco-Chontales	Large companies in Boaco-Chontales
Number of livestock companies	100,000	10,000	540
Total production (millions of gallons/yr)	60–90	20–25	10–15
Number of industrial enterprises	1,200	70–100	0
Total processing (millions of gallons/yr)	60–90	20–30	0
Exports (US$ millions)	24	10	0

Sources: Central Bank of Nicaragua (2001) for production and export values; INEC (2001) for the number of livestock companies; INCAE (1999a) for the number of companies; *La Prensa* [Managua], Suplemento Económico para el Sector Lácteo, February 7, 2002, for production for each territory.

Collective Efficiency in the Dairy Products Cluster

Drawing on the concept of collective efficiency as a core element of the level of competition in clusters, we will examine its two key features: external economies and joint actions (Pietrobelli and Rabellotti, Chapter 1 in this volume; Schmitz, 1995).

External Economies

A growing literature suggests that external economies are among the primary strengths of small and medium-sized enterprise clusters (Ghani and Stewart, 1991; Schmitz, 1995; Rabellotti, 1997). In considering the geographic environment of Boaco and Chontales, we are able to identify a number of external economies that are particularly significant. These include clients' access to the cluster, the local availability of factors of production, and a free flow of information and innovations. These externalities, which contribute to the local process of growth, are nevertheless still at an incipient stage and do not involve all enterprises, but only those firms in the cluster having access to the externalities and the capabilities to internalize them.

Having access to a region with a large number of clients is a great advantage. The region is close to the capital and has good road access, at least to the main urban centers where the cheese manufacturers are located. This is why a large number of clients, including large firms, purchase milk from producers, buyers, and some of the region's factories. However, road infrastructure outside of the urban centers is generally poor, which hinders interaction between livestock producers and cheese manufacturers. Milk often arrives too late at factories and due to the high level of acidity is then rejected and must be sold locally.

Both workers and management possess a high level of technical ability with regard to the traditional methods used at the majority of companies. But few companies are able to manage and understand cutting-edge technology and specific skills, such as the composition and properties of milk and quality assurance procedures and standards.

In recent years, some of the leading local businesses have made efforts to improve processes and products, which has given rise to a widespread awareness of the importance of quality. The presence of foreign industries has sparked a radical transformation in the production process and an increase in local competence. As a result, small businesses in the region have begun hiring chemists and food technologists to control the quality of raw and processed milk.

Ample supplies of intermediate inputs are available for both on-farm dairy production (e.g., fodder, medicine, aluminum containers) and industrial processing (e.g., machine parts, lab tools). The latter are more easily acquired in the capital city, but this does not adversely affect production efficiency. Machinery, however, is often a problem because of a shortage of machine-manufacturing companies, and so machinery must be purchased abroad, often at high cost.

With regard to information and innovation, flows of knowledge, although basic, promote consistent and sustained development of the dairy manufacturing sector in Boaco and Chontales. These flows of knowledge are based on informal exchanges, imitation of techniques, and a search for similar markets. They are also a result of the arrival of medium-sized Salvadoran and Honduran businesses in the early 1990s, which began to stockpile milk, process it, and export it to their countries. This practice has generated a similar trend among local businesses, which have started manufacturing and marketing their products and taking them to supermarkets in the capital city.

Unlike in other clusters in the country, in Boaco and Chontales the local concentration of the cheese companies is, by and large, well received. Livestock and industrial producers have managed to form positive clustering relationships and have thereby avoided recurrent conflicts to attract the same clients, which has allowed the producers to benefit from agglomeration. These positive relationships also increase the incentive to develop joint actions.

Joint Actions

Milk producers are aware of the opportunities and threats related to the new context of globalization. They know that competitiveness is also derived from alliances aimed at improving the quality of products, with a view to selling in the international market. Consequently, joint actions have recently increased: business groups have been formed to process and market milk, and business associations have been created to defend corporate interests.

In recent years, cooperatives have also emerged in the industrial and trade sectors. Livestock producers combine efforts and set up their own processing facilities, which are administered independently of farming activities. The cooperative plant buys milk from producers, while supplying them with milk collection and storage services, as well as road improvement. Cooperatives may also provide producers with credit and manage investment funds offered by development agencies. Lastly, they provide sanitary and health services for cattle, such as artificial insemination and other services, including the sale of supplies and marketing of the final product.

One interesting example of joint action is the case of Cooperativa de Cantores, a group of 37 cheese manufacturers from the city of Boaco. They joined together to purchase land and relocate outside of the city in order to resolve the environmental problems they had been causing in a nearby site (e.g., with water waste). Thanks to the Finnish-sponsored Livestock Development Project (PRODEGA) and support from other organizations, this cooperative has managed to improve the quality of its product significantly (e.g., by adopting the "dry salting" technique).

Another noteworthy joint initiative is an alliance formed among nine livestock producers in Chontales, Alianza Amerrisque. In 2002, this alliance joined forces with the National Union of Farmers and Cattle Ranchers (UNAG) to seek funding to build a dairy product processing facility. This joint alliance, Grupo Empresarial Chontales, includes 2,350 producers and stockbreeders. To acquire the funding, Grupo Empresarial Chontales would need the support of PRODEGA, which would finance the technical and economic feasibility study for the installation of the processing plant. From a commercial standpoint, the project, backed by the governmental Institute for Rural Development (IDR), will focus on the U.S. market, with an aim to export premium products, such as *morolique* cheese[1] (*La Prensa* [Managua], November 4, 2002).

A second type of joint action is of a political nature. The most noteworthy example is the Nicaraguan Chamber of Dairy Products (CANISLAC), which emerged in 2000. The chamber is comprised of milk producer representatives and representatives of small, medium-sized, and large businesses. The role of CANISLAC is to pressure government officials to defend its interests. For example, a few years ago, CANISLAC reacted to the impending closing of the Salvadoran border to Nicaraguan dairy products by pressing the government to maintain looser Salvadoran border restrictions for an additional time period, thereby giving national producers an opportunity to attempt to meet the required standards.

CANISLAC is also driving the discussion of how best to integrate Central American and U.S. customs (in the free trade agreement with the United States) in an effort to control imports of powdered milk, which negatively impact national producers. As a result, the government has increased customs barriers on imports by 40–60 percent.

For the same reasons, the chamber is requesting that the country's Labeling Law be enforced. This law stipulates that product containers must specify whether milk is whole or reconstituted. It is also requesting, among other things, that the government promote programs aimed at increasing national milk consumption, such as the "Glass of Milk for Students" program, which would be offered to school children up to the sixth grade, with funds that would be provided by the Ministry of Education.

The importance of CANISLAC's campaign is such that it has gained a high level of acceptance and is even supported by large companies. For example, Parmalat, a transnational company specialized in dairy products,

---

[1] *Morolique* is a cheese typically consumed in southern San Salvador. It ferments for 24 hours and then matures for a few days (becoming "hard young cheese" or *queso duro blando*) or up to three months (becoming "hard old cheese" or *queso duro viejo*).

has reduced its powdered milk purchases since first arriving in the country and has significantly increased its liquid milk purchases from producers. Eskimo, a large ice cream manufacturer, also affirms that it has reduced the amount of powdered milk it uses.

In sum, in the dairy cluster joint actions take two main forms: the development of cooperatives aimed at improving the production process and sales strategy of small local firms, and the role played by business associations in lobbying at local and national levels. In both cases, there is a strong commitment of local producers who are increasingly aware of the potential benefits of cooperation.

Institutional Setting

Since the 1990s, sectoral development has also been carried out with the support of international agencies and the government. For example, PRODEGA, the Finnish project, has played a key role in the development of the dairy sector in Boaco, and more recently in Chontales. Together with the IDR, PRODEGA has worked to support private investments for the creation of summer roads and is also promoting a business-oriented cooperative model for milk collection and conservation, as well as for processing and marketing dairy products. Another organization that has supported the cluster is the United Nations Industrial Development Organization (UNIDO), through its business networks project, in cooperation with the Institute of Small and Medium-Sized Enterprises (INPYME). Recently, UNIDO has been organizing a series of activities aimed at promoting a culture of quality among milk producers and cheese factories, with assistance from the Nicaraguan Institute of Business Development (INDE), the National University of Engineering (UNI), PRODEGA, and other national institutions.

For all of these reasons, the National Competitiveness Program, assigned to the Office of the Vice President of the Republic, has recently identified the dairy sector as being among the sectors with the greatest development potential in Nicaragua. As a result, activities to promote the sector have been carried out that have helped to improve relations between the public and private sectors. For example, the government has decided to redirect public investment toward roads, electrification, and the setting up of 20 milk collection centers.

The role played by these institutions has been central to sustaining the growth of individual local enterprises as well as cooperatives. The funds, the support provided to cooperatives, and the efforts to promote and increase awareness of the benefits of joint action have all been and still are key factors increasing local competitiveness in the national and international markets.

The Value Chains of the Dairy Products Cluster

As in other sectors and clusters, numerous value chains have emerged in the dairy cluster of Boaco and Chontales that involve the grouping of small and medium-sized enterprises (Boomgard et al., 1992; Bourgeois and Herrera, 1996; Artola, 2000; Barahona and Parrilli, 1999; Parrilli, Barahona, and Narváez, 1999; Parrilli, 2000). These chains are characterized by their distinct forms of organization, which affect the development of relations among the various actors in the dairy chain: milk producers, cheese manufacturers, and sales companies. The main value chains are described below and illustrated in detail in Figure 2.1.

- *Chain 1:* Periurban livestock owners with milk farms supply raw milk for consumption to the public and to the country's major cities. They sell directly to retail milk distributors and end-consumers.
- *Chain 2: Manteros* collect milk from the most remote areas and, using artisan methods, process it into dairy products such as cheese or curd, and supply the nation's largest popular markets. *Manteros* sell to middlemen or distribute directly to retailers in the cities.
- *Chain 3:* Small Salvadoran enterprises purchase milk directly from producers to make cheeses and purchase cheese from other factories for export and sale to retailers in El Salvador.

Figure 2.1. Value Chains in the Nicaraguan Dairy Industry

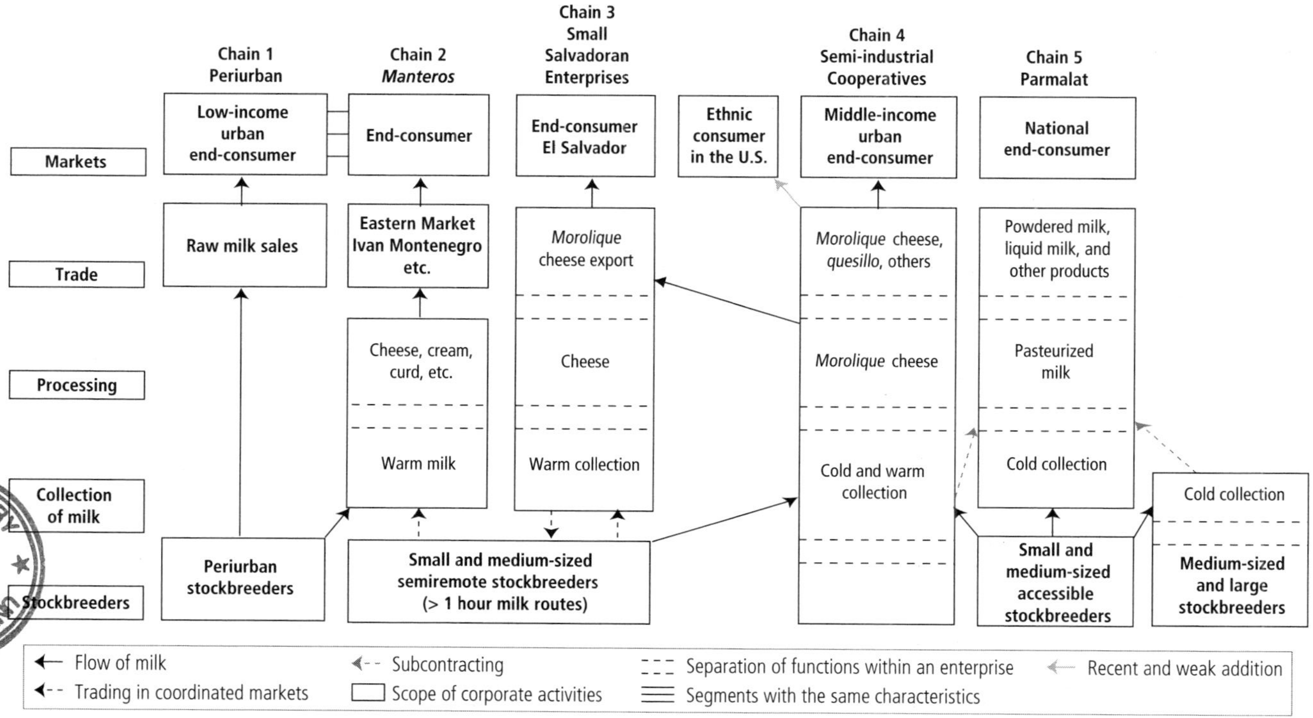

Source: Design adapted from Boomgard et al. (1992). Data taken from various interviews and secondary sources.

- *Chain 4:* Semi-industrial cooperatives comprise small and medium-sized milk producers grouped in cooperatives. Activities include collection, processing and marketing of milk, along with other services (e.g., credit). These cooperatives sell raw milk to industrial plants and cheese to Salvadoran middlemen and national supermarkets and, at times, export cheese directly.
- *Chain 5:* The multinational company Parmalat is connected with various raw milk collection networks set up for the production of pasteurized milk. Parmalat purchases the majority of milk from associated enterprises; its main clients include supermarkets and local stores in the country's major cities.

The remainder of the analyses in this chapter focus on the last three chains listed (Chains 3, 4, and 5) because they are most significant in terms of the sector's export performance and the cluster's upgrading.

The Multinational Company Parmalat[2]

Parmalat arrived in Nicaragua in 1999 when it bought the milk processing plant La Perfecta. Parmalat's presence in Nicaragua may be explained by the importance of the regional Central American market. With 40 million inhabitants, Central America has a large unsatisfied demand, which was

[2] This field study was undertaken before the explosion of the international financial crisis of Parmalat. The future of Parmalat in Nicaragua, as well as in other countries where it operated, is not very clear at the moment. There are strong public and private efforts to sustain its operations in Nicaragua, including with the intervention of some new local partners. In March 2004, Parmalat was going to be sold in pieces by its main creditors (Banco de América Central and Tower Bank of Panama) because of US$5.4 million in unpaid debts. But the government of Nicaragua made serious efforts to prevent the crisis, which would have affected thousands of farmers nationwide and many Nicaraguan consumers, calling for the intervention of national private economic groups to take over or support Parmalat. Finally, a Central American financial company, LAFISE, with the support of a Nicaraguan bank, Bancentro, paid the outstanding debt and bought 49 percent of Parmalat's equity shares. The building of this joint venture indicates the national will to carry on the important role played by Parmalat during the second half of the 1990s. Of course, past marketing plans aimed at expanding to the Central American market should be pursued more cautiously now; nonetheless, our insights on the positive role played by Parmalat for cluster upgrading retain their validity.

met with imports of up to US$146 million in 1997, 95 percent of which came from the European Union, New Zealand, and the United States (FUSADES-IICE, 2000). In this regard, the stockbreeding potential and geographic location of Nicaragua—which allows for savings on transport costs—fits well with Parmalat's export strategy for the Central American market, for some of which (El Salvador and Guatemala) it has already gained the necessary certification.

Until this point, Parmalat's main business activity had been the distribution of pasteurized milk in the national market, which is protected with tariffs of between 40 and 60 percent during the rainy season when there is overproduction. As a distributor, Parmalat is moving forward with two key retail market segments. The first is the most modern supermarkets, where middle- and high-income consumers shop, which are located in the capital and other major cities. They offer a wide variety of dairy products that face competition from imported, high-value-added products. The second targeted retail market is the 15,000 local stores selling the most commonly purchased products (pasteurized milk, cream, etc.) in middle- and low-income neighborhoods and towns, where the strongest competition comes from imported powdered milk. For this activity, Parmalat has its own fleet of refrigerated transport vehicles to distribute products.

The limiting factor continues to be the low per capita milk consumption levels in Nicaragua—40 kilograms per inhabitant per year, much lower than in neighboring Costa Rica, with consumption of 150 kilograms per inhabitant per year (FUSADES-IICE, 2000). This difference is explained largely by the low level of family income, which translates into low purchasing power. In Nicaragua, a small family with a monthly income of US$50 must allot nearly 30 percent of its budget for daily milk consumption of one liter (pasteurized milk costs US$0.51 per liter). Raw milk is a more affordable alternative, costing US$0.34 per liter.

Parmalat's backward linkages are aimed at guaranteeing a steady supply of milk as a commodity for its industrial plant. The company collects 60 percent of the milk it processes (approximately 30,000 gallons daily) from the Boaco and Chontales region. The main method used by Parmalat to monitor the delivery standards of raw material suppliers is a combination of grading and pricing policy. Milk samples are taken from each supplier to the company headquarters for analysis. The laboratory results are used to determine the quality of milk delivered, which in turn determines the price to be paid, with incentives for the best milk. According to Parmalat engineers, 70 percent of the milk received is Grade A, which is purchased at C$3.20 per liter (US$0.22 at the end of 2002); the remainder is Grade B and is purchased at C$2.60 per liter (US$0.18). An additional C$0.90 (US$0.06) is paid for refrigerated milk of either type. Grade C milk is, in principle, rejected.

Parmalat draws on three main sources for its milk supply. First, for a small amount, Parmalat has its own collection centers in the region. These collection centers receive milk from the various transport routes and store it at a temperature of 4°C until it is transferred to the industrial plant. Here, specialists who are knowledgeable about established sanitation standards interact with producers. Specialists visit producers at the farms to inform them of the company's requirements and monitor milking practices. When low-quality milk is delivered, specialists recommend corrective measures. In the case of repeated violations, the purchase of milk may be suspended. The second source, accounting for 70 percent of the milk processed by Parmalat, is cooperatives.[3] However, these cooperatives are gradually reducing deliveries as they progress in the industrial transformation of milk. Parmalat has contracts with these cooperatives regarding milk volume, quality, and pricing, but both parties have launched complaints and accusations of nonperformance as to the agreements entered into. Still, technical collaboration exists with the cooperatives regarding the quality of the raw material supply. Parmalat specialists participate in workshops held by cooperatives, offering technical guidelines on how to produce high-quality milk.

The third source of milk is local medium-sized or large producers or small groups of producers that provide 20 percent of Parmalat's

[3] Interview with Parmalat officials, November 2002.

milk supply. This source of supply is increasing. With these companies, Parmalat usually has an agreement specifying that Parmalat provides the cold storage equipment (cooling tanks) and trains staff on quality control procedures; the local company provides the infrastructure, electricity, and milk collection.

Transport of milk from the farm to the collection center is carried out in two ways: either producers transport the milk using their own means of motorized transportation, or Parmalat has a collection route and contracts small haulers to ship the milk. Transport of milk from cooling tanks to plants is carried out by Parmalat, using trucks with cooling systems.

Small Salvadoran Enterprises

Several small Salvadoran entrepreneurs have been making large investments in cheese factories. These companies are now well integrated with local producers that have limited market access as a result of poor infrastructure conditions. This chain represents 11 percent of artisan milk processors, but it controls 45 percent of the milk collected in winter and 38 percent collected during summer months (López and Castillo, 1999). Collection capacity per factory ranges from 500 to 1,000 gallons per day in the summer, and this amount can be doubled during winter months.

The control of export trade has been key in managing this chain. In addition to being cheese manufacturers, the majority of companies are also retail intermediaries distributing in major Salvadoran markets. Salvadoran entrepreneurs generally have in-depth knowledge of the market and are able to organize legal and illegal cheese marketing circuits. Currently, most export cheese seems to be taking the illegal route, as there are still few certified cheese factories.

With regard to processing, Salvadoran entrepreneurs possess production know-how for *morolique* cheese, for which there is a high demand in the Salvadoran market. They were the first to design and build factories with some level of technology, including larger hoops that allow cheese to be pressed with greater precision and greater collection and storage capacity for products. Artisan-like technology spread rapidly in the region and contributed in large part to the expansion of cheese activities and exports. In addition to cheese manufacturing, Salvadoran entrepreneurs buy from other, smaller-scale plants that process milk from rocky and remote areas.

Taste and aroma have a greater influence on the quality of the product than does compliance with sanitary rules. Thus, current milk quality requirements are not an issue for artisan cheese production. Raw material arrives at the factory unclassified. Milk is accepted even if it has a high level of acidity. There are, however, some plants, especially those targeting the export market, that are improving their infrastructure and manufacturing practices by investing in fully equipped buildings and modern, stainless steel equipment. At the same time, these entrepreneurs are beginning to take the issue of milk quality more seriously. For example, they pay a differentiated price for milk depending on delivery time. Producers that are geographically closer deliver milk that is fresher and with a lower level of acidity and thus are paid more. Furthermore, Salvadoran businessmen contribute to quality control by supplying filters to producers, performing density analyses to control water content, and so on.

Now that other actors, such as local cooperatives and individual producers and Honduran entrepreneurs, are venturing into export cheese manufacturing, the Salvadoran enterprises have been adapting to the new circumstances with different strategies. Salvadorans have increased their intermediary role by exporting cheese produced by local cooperatives and have also improved their relationships with local businessmen, moving from purely market relations to organizational structures that include the provision of services that are scarce in rural areas, such as credit and cattle ranching supplies.

In this chain, the transport of milk from the farm to the plant is carried out in two ways. The first is through contracting one or two carriers, in which case the cheese manufacturer negotiates the price of milk directly with producers. The second method, which is less common, is the purchase of milk from local intermediary carriers who, having worked extensively with the producers, have managed to build a good collection network based on personal and commercial relations.

Semi-industrial Cooperatives

This chain is characterized by three core elements. First, in the early 1990s, groups of small and medium-sized producers came together to resolve the milk marketing problem. Second, the opportunities presented by the demand for raw material from industrial plants and the growth of the foreign cheese market create positive expectations and incentives for new companies to enter the industry. Lastly, the support brought by the presence of international assistance organizations—Finnish and Italian in Boaco and Nueva Guinea, respectively—strengthen the organization process of producers joining together in cooperatives.

In Boaco and Chontales there are 12 cooperatives with a total of approximately 2,000 member producers. In most cases, they are located in small towns that have a certain level of basic infrastructure (water, energy, roads) and an institutional presence (e.g., mayor's offices, nongovernmental organizations [NGOs], health services, education). These businesses generate 30 to 50 permanent jobs each. During winter months, the more advanced businesses tend to contract additional workers at the processing plant. Their strength lies in the organization of milk supply and collection, the first phase of intermediation.

The cooperatives have both member and nonmember suppliers. It is estimated that 30 to 40 percent of national milk production is captured by this group of businesses. The collection strategy combines the purchase of milk with the provision of practical services, such as credit and technical assistance. Collection volumes have continued to increase; for example, the Camoapán plant went from 500 gallons of milk in the winter of 1994 to 5,000 gallons in the winter of 2002.[4] International aid

---

[4] Field interview with Denis Rivera, general manager of the San Francisco de Asís de Camoapa Cooperative, November 2002.

facilitated investments in the cold collection network and in the processing capacity of the plant.

The location of the supplier influences the destination of the milk, as the suppliers located nearest to the plant deliver the highest-quality milk. Milk is conserved in cooling tanks at a temperature of 4°C and is then sold at a higher price to the large plants of Parmalat, Prolacsa, and Eskimo. Suppliers located in more remote areas have lower-quality raw material for cheese manufacturing. The nominal price received by associated suppliers might be less if they were to sell directly to Parmalat, but they also receive compensation in the form of access to the various services offered by the cooperative. It is important to note that members are not always loyal to the cooperative; in fact, there are cases of producers who also sell independently to Parmalat.

In short, there are a variety of patterns of governance in these chains, differing according to the types of actors involved and the actors' ability to upgrade. Cooperatives that have managed to enter the milk processing sector and that have ventured into the cheese export market depend less on the distribution of milk to large industries and have strengthened their ties to networks of small rural entrepreneurs. Producers that have trouble accessing good markets, however, see the large companies as an opportunity for selling cold milk and depend on Salvadoran merchants for cheese sales. In this case, the relationships between large companies and the small local companies are quasi-hierarchical governing structures in which the large companies impose the rules. This relationship is limited in terms of the potential for business expansion in the higher-value-added segments of the chain.

There is also some reciprocal influence among the chains. The Salvadoran chain has provided feedback regarding quality and processing to the *manteros* that supply milk from more remote areas. Parmalat has provided feedback on raw material quality to the cooperatives and private milk collecting enterprises. Parmalat has also provided a certain level of sustainability to a number of cooperatives by buying substantial amounts, thus ensuring the cooperatives' growth, and in some cases, by repaying cooperatives' bank debts. At the same time, the cooperatives supply raw material from various sources to Parmalat at a low cost. All of these connections must be taken into account by the various institutions operating in the territory.

Upgrading Processes in the Dairy Products Cluster

In recent years, the dairy industry in Nicaragua has experienced surprising growth and improvements from the productive and commercial standpoint. Table 2.2 illustrates this growth.

In addition to an increase in production, an upgrading process is also taking place that is dependent on the dynamics of some small enterprises that are moving from artisan production to modern industrial production and, at the same time, from livestock production to industrial production and direct marketing. These major advances are forms of process upgrading (the former) and functional upgrading (the latter), which represent the most noteworthy innovations achieved by the Boaco and Chontales cluster. (For definitions of the different forms of upgrading, see Pietrobelli and Rabellotti, Chapter 1 in this volume.)

One of the immediate effects of these development processes is the emergence of a number of new enterprises, particularly in the Boaco and Chontales region, where the number grew from 18 to 71 in the 1997–98 period alone, contributing to a total of 137 new enterprises nationwide (INCAE, 1999a).

Table 2.2. Production, Collection, and Pasteurization of Milk in Nicaragua
(millions of gallons)

	1995	1996	1997	1998	1999	2000	2001
Production	48	50	53.5	55.8	57.3	59.3	63.2
Collection	13	12.8	12.4	10.5	11.1	11.4	14.2
Pasteurization	7.4	7.2	7.4	8.8	10.4	10.6	13.7
Export (US$ millions)	6.4	9.0	14.2	17.9	15.7	22.7	n.a.

Source: Central Bank of Nicaragua (2000–2002).

Functional Upgrading

Beginning in the early 1990s, producers from the country's interior began selling their products, *morolique* cheese in particular, to the Salvadoran market. This change was brought about by the arrival of Salvadoran investors, who set up factories to produce and export cheese directly.

Although this has been beneficial to some extent, it has also resulted in a strong dependence on foreign exporters. When the Salvadoran government began to block unpasteurized Nicaraguan products, producers in Boaco and Chontales experienced difficulties and sought to resolve the situation. One group of producers developed an underground sales network, while another group worked to achieve the level of quality and technology required to maintain its market share in El Salvador.

The first group of producers took this route out of necessity because it was difficult for them to upgrade cheese factories in the short term and also because the much-sought-after *morolique* cheese loses its flavor once it has been pasteurized. The alternative, established by international standards, is to let the cheese mature for more than 60 days, which is a long time for small enterprises that do not have well-equipped storage facilities or the funds to store large quantities of product. Although the first group of producers is larger, the second group has taken a more positive approach to the new market challenges. They are a group of cooperatives that have become leaders in the cluster and are having a significant catalyzing effect on other enterprises aiming to emulate their success.

Meeting quality standards has pushed small businesses to open new markets not only abroad, but also within Nicaragua. In fact, several cheese cooperatives have managed to move into the country's higher-income segments through supermarkets in the capital and other cities. By using higher-quality producers, they have been able to earn more for their production, which has brought them higher profit margins.

Functional upgrading refers to a whole course of development of the capabilities of dairy SMEs in Boaco and Chontales. The producers have learned how to engage in higher-value-added phases of production by strengthening business management, which enables them to reach a higher level of competitiveness. Livestock owners have started abandoning their own individual practices in order to join together and participate actively in more advanced stages of production. First, they joined together to engage in milk collection activities and to sell refrigerated milk to large companies, and then they became involved in the industrial processing of milk and cheese, having acquired *morolique* cheese manufacturing techniques from the small Salvadoran enterprise group and adapted the techniques to meet their needs. Currently, small cheese businesses are moving into the direct export of cheese in order to reach larger and more dynamic markets (e.g., the U.S. market), which offers greater opportunities for the growth of the dairy cluster in Boaco and Chontales.

Process Upgrading

Process upgrading has been the basis of the dairy industry's transformations. Upgrading has meant improving inadequate hygiene conditions and enforcing more advanced practices, including pasteurization of milk, process certification, and certification of manufactured cheeses.

In Boaco and Chontales, the dairy sector continues to face problems ranging from poor quality control in most artisan factories to Honduran cheese companies' unfair appropriation of typical cheese brands; from poor road and electricity infrastructure to a lack of cold storage for preserving cheese. Despite these problems, there are signs of vitality in this sector, such as new forms of industrialization and marketing that involve international certification. For example, the Hygiene and Epidemiology Institute (SILAIS) of the Local Healthcare System of Chontales performs ongoing monitoring of the 24 cheese companies in that region.[5] Also, the Ministry of Agriculture and Forestry has taken a key role in the inspection and certification process. Together with the Hygiene and Epidemiology

[5] Dr. Magdalena Marín, Director of the Chontales SILAIS, in an interview with *La Prensa*.

Institute, it has enabled 14 cheese factories to reach the levels required by international certifying bodies. These include industrial plants such as Parmalat, Eskimo, and Prolacsa, which produce yogurt, ice cream, liquid milk, cheese, cream, and butter (and powdered milk in the case of Prolacsa), as well as semi-industrial plants that produce cheese for export to El Salvador, Honduras, and, to a lesser extent, Guatemala, Costa Rica, and the United States. Additionally, there are some 30 artisan factories that are under surveillance and have export permits from Honduran and Salvadoran authorities. With regard to the international system (HACCP), Eskimo is certified, while Parmalat and five other semi-industrial plants are currently in the process of becoming certified. Three of these plants are located in the Boaco and Chontales region.

The multinational company Parmalat entered this sectoral reform process in 1999, when it took over the country's leading dairy company, La Perfecta. Parmalat's arrival brought significant changes for the cheese companies and livestock producers. Since its arrival, Parmalat has invested several million dollars in technology to expand its industrial capacity, diversify production, broaden distribution channels, and improve the quality of the milk production process, from milking to distribution. Of these investments, US$1.5 million has gone into technology (mostly for collection tanks and trucks), in addition to investments in 20 milk collection centers in several regions of the country. These collection centers are equipped with refrigeration tanks, emergency power plants, heaters, and in some cases, pasteurizing machines. The municipalities of Boaco, Camoapa, and Juigalpa in the region of Boaco and Chontales, and neighboring regions such as Nueva Guinea, Río Blanco, and Matiguás, are the regions that supply the largest amount of milk to Parmalat. The impact generated by the Italian company can also be seen in the quality of the milk supplied by producers, who are obtaining higher prices for their milk (*La Prensa*, May 22, 2002).

At the same time, small businesses in the region have created some 40 collection centers and have invested in technology and improving milking procedures. To date, the most well-known cooperative (Camoapán) has invested US$250,000 in the plant and will continue investing in order to diversify its products and improve working conditions for on-farm producers. The results have been so positive that currently, only 12 percent of milk collected is of inferior quality (Grade C), while four years ago, 50 percent of all milk was Grade C. This cooperative collects about 5,000 gallons of milk daily, 60 percent[6] of which is processed. Three and a half years ago, 50 percent of milk collected was sold to Parmalat; now sales to Parmalat account for only 10 percent, showing how this enterprise has grown by achieving greater independence from large companies and through its ability to generate greater added value.

All of these improvements have also been driven by collective initiatives, such as the creation of CANISLAC in 2000, the inauguration of the First Nicaraguan Dairy Sector Conference in Juigalpa in 2002, and the 2002 milk fair in Juigalpa. These events demonstrate the business spirit of the producers in this cluster and their progress toward collective development practices.

These advances have captured the attention of the government, which is supporting the dairy sector as a sector with high economic development potential and has listed it among the priorities of the National Competitiveness Program, PROCOMPE (INCAE, 1999b; De Franco et al., 1995; De Franco et al., 1996). The government's new attitude is exemplified by a new comprehensive development program for the dairy sector, with long-term goals aimed at upgrading production, industrialization, and marketing. Moreover, the government has also increased the Import Tariff (DAI) from 40 percent to 60 percent in an attempt to favor the growth of the domestic supply in a temporarily protected market.

Product Upgrading

Because of the structural changes made to processes and functions, cheese companies have started to diversify their products. After producing only

---

[6] Interview with the head of production at Camoapán, November 2002.

the typical mature, dry cheese products, small enterprises have moved into the industrial production of cheeses such as *quesillo* (fresh cheese), smoked cheese, and butter.

More recently, some enterprises have diversified their product offerings even further, producing cheeses such as cheddar, grated cheeses, blue cheeses, and green cheeses. All products are currently under investigation by the Inspection and Certification Department of the Ministry of Agriculture and Forestry.

Policy Lessons

The level of development achieved by this cluster is still relatively low and clearly behind that of other well-known clusters analyzed in the literature and in this book. At present, the dairy cluster in Boaco and Chontales is still in a first stage of development, as the number of processing firms in the area and their overall production and export have the potential to increase much more. Nevertheless, the industry's recent functional, process, and product upgrading have been quite outstanding and deserve serious attention. The recent purchase of an important share of Parmalat by national and Central American private economic groups is an indication of the attractiveness of the sector.

On the basis of the developments in the Nicaraguan dairy sector reported above, some key lessons on agro-industrial development policy can be identified. First of all, collective efficiency matters. In fact, increased cooperation between the various cluster actors has allowed synergies that improve collective efficiency, therefore supporting the upgrading process of the cluster. For example, CANISLAC has achieved a certain level of contractual power with the government and has secured the government's commitment to address important issues such as improving road infrastructure and signing trade agreements with other countries. The emergence of sectoral and regional clusters has made it possible for enterprises to organize in order to address common needs (e.g., negotiate better prices, gain access to more advanced technology). Furthermore, the historically strong tradition of cooperatives in the rural sector has been extended to processing enterprises. Several small artisan firms formed cooperatives for the processing of dairy products, which gave them the opportunity to pull together enough resources to invest in new competitive technology, providing the basis for producing and selling to higher-income segments of consumers domestically and abroad.

From the point of view of external economies, the arrival of Salvadoran entrepreneurs created a critical mass of enterprises, technology, and know-how to enhance the learning process (even by means of imitation) and the overall upgrading of the cluster. This has induced remarkable process and functional upgrading in an environment traditionally dominated by an artisan way of producing and selling dairy products.

In specific locations, the increased integration of milk producers with agro-industrial value chains that have good access to markets is having a positive impact on productivity. In Boaco, for example, the entry of new actors into the market has increased competition for milk, which has provided milk producers with an opportunity to join the cold collection network for the manufacturing of dairy products. This has led to some level of price stability for producers. On cattle-raising farms, genetic dairy and fodder production techniques have been adopted for summer feeding that help to increase milk production yield, and more sanitary milking practices have been implemented that help improve the quality of milk. As a whole, the agro-industrial link has shown improvement with regard to equipment and infrastructure, as well as agro-industrial differentiation and specialization processes. SMEs have increased their pasteurization capacity from 5,000 liters of milk daily in 1999 to 43,000 liters in 2002.

Some observations can be made about the upgrading process promoted by the different value chains. Among the many value chains, three have been growing and steadily sustaining the growth of the cluster. The value chain managed by small national processing cooperative firms appears to have the most interesting governance system because it is controlled by local capital (the other two are controlled by foreign enterprises).[7] In spite of the importance of local control, it is hard to think that this agro-industrial chain could have developed without the big external push from the multinational company chain and the foreign medium-sized enterprises chain. The push has occurred in various ways, including purchasing of refrigerated milk from local producers, assisting them technically in processing, and showing them how to sell to high-income markets. It is more likely that these value chains are interdependent, at least in this first stage of development, although significant changes may take place in the future. The crisis of Parmalat will challenge the existence of its own value chain, while simultaneously pushing the other chains to modify their trajectories, perhaps by trying to control part of the market that was going to be controlled by Parmalat.

Still focusing on the importance of the value chains, it needs to be recognized that the integration of SMEs into international markets is contingent on the formation of alliances between a well-organized agro-industry and national and foreign buyers who understand market demand and opportunities. In fact, there are already groups of national entrepreneurs in the country that act as intermediaries between the agro-industry and the North American market and appear to be actively searching for markets and making arrangements with associated enterprises to export cheese to the U.S. market (e.g., the LAFISE group). Parmalat has also shown interest in exporting cheese to the United States through its own distribution channel. Furthermore, the cooperatives seem to agree on selling through distribution companies, provided they obtain a reasonable price. Finally, some cooperatives have already established contacts with foreign buyers to export to the United States.

International competition and the gradual liberalization of trade have enabled SMEs to adapt better to demand. Compulsory quality and sanitary standards in export markets have placed substantial pressure on local enterprises and cooperatives to invest in their factories and to

---

[7] The recent purchase of 49 percent of Parmalat capital shares by a large national economic group is certainly showing an increased interest among national stakeholders (the government and livestock owners) in the development of this value chain.

search for new alliances with other actors in the dairy products chain. For example, the Salvadoran market demands both pasteurized and unpasteurized cheese, so the import ban imposed by the Salvadoran government on unpasteurized Nicaraguan products represents a discriminatory trade policy. This measure has sparked an increase in cheese smuggling, thus putting formal cheese companies at a disadvantage, as they are faced with higher costs for transport, storage, and so on. This translates into lower prices for the producers or payment delays (or even missing payments), thereby creating greater conflicts between SMEs producing cheese and medium-sized milk producers.

Technical support services for primary production are needed but are not sufficient to enable SMEs to participate competitively in the international market. The provision of technical services is the predominant instrument of development policies. However, this approach does not take into account the linkages between agriculture and the chains of processing and marketing, and the services that improve these linkages, which range from milk transport from the farm to marketing in national and foreign markets.

The role played by international cooperation, providing technical assistance and encouraging suppliers to organize, has supported integration of small and medium-sized enterprises into agro-industrial value chains. Specific investments made by the Finnish cooperation agency in the cold collection network in Comoapa, by the Italian development cooperation in Nueva Guinea, and the promotion of cooperatives of small and medium-sized milk producers have been useful. The investments have enabled local producers to achieve increased negotiation power and economies of scale, which have translated into a business opportunity for milk buyers such as Parmalat, as a result of reduced transaction costs and larger volumes of milk offered by the enterprises.

As a result of all these developments, local enterprises, particularly cooperatives, have been able to advance further and create conditions that enable them to coordinate the collection of quality milk from partners and nonpartners in order to participate in the Parmalat value chain. Local enterprises have also been able to manufacture artisan cheese using lower-quality milk (thus joining the value chain of Salvadoran entrepreneurs), to progress toward process improvements by integrating pasteurization and adopting sanitation standards in line with international standards, and finally, to enter the cheese export business. These are all interesting steps toward an increase in competitiveness of the Nicaraguan dairy cluster.

References

Artola, N. 2000. Small-Scale Producers and Sesame Commodity Chains under Structural Adjustment. In *Rural Development in Central America: Market, Livelihoods and Local Governance*, ed. R. Ruben and J. Bastiaensen. London: Macmillan.

Barahona, T., and M. D. Parrilli. 1999. Análisis subsectorial en la rama madera/muebles: el caso de Las Segovias. Nitlapán-UCA, Managua. Unpublished.

Boomgard, J., S. Davies, L. Haggblade, and D. Mead. 1992. A Subsector Approach to Small Enterprise Promotion and Research. *World Development* 20(2):199–212.

Bourgeois, R., and D. Herrera. 1996. *Cadenas y diálogo para la acción*. San José, Costa Rica: CIRAD/IICA.

Central Bank of Nicaragua. 2000–2002. *Informe anual*. Managua: Central Bank of Nicaragua.

De Franco, M., N. Sacasa, R. Raudes, R. Sevilla, and L. Zúñiga. 1995. *La dinámica del mercado de productos lácteos en Nicaragua*. Análisis Total. Vol. 1. Managua.

De Franco, M., R. Sevilla, H. Downing, and A. Sandino. 1996. *Caracterización y propuesta de estrategia para el sector semi-industrial de productos lácteos en Nicaragua*. Análisis Total. Vol. 2. Managua.

Fundación Salvadoreña para el Desarrollo Económico y Social (FUSADES) and Instituto de Investigación en Ciencias Económicas, Universidad de Costa Rica (IICE-UCR). 2000. *El impacto sectorial del proceso de integración subregional en Centroamérica: sector lácteo y sector metal mecánico*. Buenos Aires: IDB-INTAL.

Ghani, E., and F. Stewart. 1991. How Relevant Are Externalities for Development? *World Development* 19(6):569–594.

Instituto Centroamericano de Administración de Empresas (INCAE). 1999a. *Agenda para la competitividad de Nicaragua hacia el siglo XXI*. Managua: CLACDS-HIID.

———. 1999b. *El potencial del sector lácteo en Nicaragua*. Instituto Centroamericano de Administración de Empresas (INCAE), Managua. Unpublished.

Instituto Nacional de Estadísticas y Censo (INEC). 2001. *Censo agropecuario*. Managua: INEC.

López, N., and S. Castillo. 1999. Diagnóstico de las queseras artesanales y su impacto en el medio ambiente. Proyecto Prevención de la Contaminación Industrial: Subcomponente Industria Alimenticia (Queso y Café), MARENA-PANIF, Managua. Unpublished.

Parrilli, M. D. 1998. El granero de Centroamérica: otra piedra de tropiezo. *Revista Envío* (April).

———. 2000. *Análisis subsectorial en la rama de cuero/calzado de Nicaragua*. Cuaderno de Investigación No. 14, Nitlapán-UCA, Managua.

Parrilli, M. D., T. Barahona, and E. Narváez. 1999. *La cadena maderera: en busca de los eslabones perdidos*. Cuaderno de Investigación No. 6, Nitlapán-UCA, Managua.

Porter, M. 1990. *The Competitive Advantage of Nations*. London: Macmillan.

Rabellotti, R. 1997. *External Economies and Cooperation in Industrial Districts: A Comparison of Italy and Mexico*. London: Macmillan.

Schmitz, H. 1995. Collective Efficiency: Growth Path for Small-Scale Industry. *Journal of Development Studies* 31:529–566.

CHAPTER 3

Upgrading without Exclusion: Lessons from SMEs in Fresh Fruit Producing Clusters in Brazil

Raquel Gomes

Small fruit growers everywhere have been especially hard hit by the global restructuring of food retail because of the production and postharvest management and investments required to ensure consistent supplies of quality fruits (Dolan and Humphrey, 2001; Farina, 2002; Gibbon, 2003; Reardon, Timmer, and Berdegue, 2003; Thrupp, 1994). In light of this exclusive tendency, I was struck by how production by small and medium-sized growers across three fresh fruit clusters[1] in Brazil has remained substantial even in recent years, with small—and especially medium-sized—growers accounting for 30 to 60 percent of production. Given that SMEs channel most of this production via larger growers or directly to buyers, this chapter seeks to explain how SMEs have been resilient and responsive to pressures for upgrading.

This research draws from my doctoral dissertation (Gomes, 2004) in the Department of Urban Studies and Planning at the Massachusetts Institute of Technology, where I am scholar of the Brazilian Ministry of Education (CAPES). Generous funding by the Bank of Northeast Brazil and research fellowships from the Inter-American Foundation and MIT's Industrial Performance Center made this research possible. Interviews with importers in Rotterdam, Holland, were conducted under the auspices of AGORA'2000 for the IDB-MIF Technical Cooperation project on value chains. Carlos Guaipatin provided insightful comments and suggestions.

[1] The term "cluster" is used very loosely throughout to refer to a spatial agglomeration of firms producing the same crop. As Tendler (2001a) notes, these cases are not clusters as formally defined, since they do not share in the underlying assumptions of small-firm dominance and a particular set of interfirm relations.

Researchers often explain the exclusion of smaller growers as a result of the current global restructuring and not as a reflection of local agents and organizations influencing the abilities of smaller firms to acquire the necessary assets to respond to these increasing pressures. The global value chain literature, for example, argues that in buyer-driven value chains, like those of fresh fruits, the final buyer is the actor who drives the decision making in the chain, deciding what needs to be produced, how it should be produced, and by whom (Humphrey and Schmitz, 2000).[2] Buyers therefore squeeze SMEs out of the market because SMEs are unable to meet buyers' requirements for quality, volume, and continuity. In addition, SMEs present relatively high transaction costs for buyers in their interactions with and monitoring of their suppliers.[3]

While recognizing the rising powers of buyers in shaping fresh fruit value chains, in this chapter I argue that SMEs are not necessarily at the mercy of buyers. Rather, government support and joint action among growers and between growers and other local agents, such as local input suppliers and consultants, influence the very way SMEs participate in global value chains in the cases investigated.[4] More specifically, I argue that public sector support influenced the adoption of fruit production by SMEs in earlier decades by shaping the structure of production in each case, influencing the possibilities for SMEs to produce fruit crops and the possibilities for cluster-wide joint action. And more recently, SMEs have managed to remain in these high-value markets through four avenues:

[2] Gereffi (1994) differentiates between buyer-driven and producer-driven commodity chains based on the location of the key barriers to entry along each value chain. In buyer-driven chains, like that of fresh fruits, large retailers and trading companies shape a decentralized network of suppliers. This stands in contrast to producer-driven chains, in which large, usually multinational companies coordinate production networks along backward and forward linkages.

[3] The issue of monitoring is especially relevant given the heightened risks to buyers associated with marketing fruits that may present evidence of food safety problems to consumers, production-related environmental degradation, or labor rights violation.

[4] Nadvi and Schmitz (1999) and others in *World Development* 27(9) dedicated to analyzing the association between joint action and upgrading among firms in a cluster.

Table 3.1. Fruit Production in Santa Catarina, Petrolina-Juazeiro, and Rio Grande do Norte

	Santa Catarina Apples	Petrolina-Juazeiro Mangoes	Petrolina-Juazeiro Grapes	Rio Grande do Norte Melons
Area planted (hectares)[a]	14,162	16,676	5,042	5,012
Share of national production[b]	51%	26%	8%	38%
Value of production ($US millions), 2001	52	37	56	13
Value of production ($US millions), 1995	23	8	45	19
Share of total exports[c]	96%	90%	30%	90%
Value of exports ($US millions),[d] 2002	31	51	34	38
Number of growers	700	150+	400+	100+
Total employment[e]	30,300	29,000	19,000	

[a] Production data from IBGE/Produção Agrícola Municipal (www.ibge.gov.br). Data are average annual values for 1995–2001.

[b] Refers to share in total production of each crop in Brazil. For example, apple production in Santa Catarina accounts for 51% of Brazil's total production of apples.

[c] Refers to the share of exports from each case in total Brazilian exports of that crop. Year to which figures refer and source: PJ: 1997, in Damiani (1999); RN: 1998, in Gomes (1999); SC: 2000, in FIESC (2001).

[d] Data from Ministério da Indústria e Comércio (www.aliceweb.gov.br).

[e] Employment data for SC from Boneti et al. (1999), for PJ from Damiani (1999), and for RN from Gomes (1999).

involvement in public–private research partnerships, ethnic-based cooperatives, subcontracting relations with large grower-exporters, and increased interaction with local input suppliers and consultants that have served as sources of technical assistance and innovation.

My analysis is based on three cases of fresh fruit production in Brazil: apple production in Santa Catarina (SC), mango and grape production in Petrolina-Juazeiro (PJ), and melon production in Rio Grande do Norte (RN), as described in Table 3.1. These are among Brazil's largest clusters of fresh fruit in terms of production, number of growers, and employment. They also represent about half of Brazil's total fresh fruit exports between 1990 and 2000.[5] These cases have been recognized elsewhere as "success stories" because of their outperformance (on average) of other

[5] According to data from SECEX, average annual export values for Brazilian apples, mangoes, grapes, and melons accounted for 52 percent of total fresh fruit exports. In 2000, the combined value of these exports was US$106 million, out of a total of US$169 million.

municipalities in their respective states in terms of agricultural production and the associated increase in quality-of-life indicators.[6]

Santa Catarina is Brazil's leading apple producer, with over 700 growers and 14,000 hectares, employing 30,000 workers and accounting for about half of Brazilian apple exports. Petrolina-Juazeiro is Brazil's largest fresh fruit cluster, with over 100 growers producing 17,000 hectares of mangoes and 600 growers producing 5,000 hectares of grapes, in addition to hundreds of other growers cultivating bananas, coconuts, watermelons, and other crops. The production of mangoes and grapes alone employs over 29,000 workers in producing 90 percent of Brazil's mango exports and 30 percent of its table grape exports.[7] Lastly, melon growers in Rio Grande do Norte produce 5,000 hectares of melons, employing 19,000 workers in producing about 40 percent of Brazil's melon production and 90 percent of its exports.[8]

These clusters started to grow in the 1970s and 1980s and have faced several adverse conditions since the early and mid-1990s: reduced government support compared to that on which growers depended when they began producing in the 1970s and 1980s, an influx of imports from the 1994 stabilization plan, and the rapid restructuring of food retail. Despite these challenges, SMEs remain competitively in the market.

The SMEs in this study are so defined relative to the range in farm size in each case, as reflected in Table 3.2. As such, a grower producing 50 hectares may be considered large in the case of grapes, but small in

---

[6] According to Bonelli (2001), the average annual rate of growth of the primary sector between 1975 and 1996 in SC's apple sector was 8.7 percent, compared to 3.7 percent for the entire state of SC. Similarly, the growth rate for PJ was about 12.7 percent, compared to an average of 3.2 percent for the states of Pernambuco and Bahia, and 4.8 percent for melon producing areas in RN, compared to 1.8 percent for RN as a state. Bonelli further claims these growth rates explain most of the increase in estimated improvements in quality-of-life indicators across the municipalities.

[7] Data from Damiani (1999). Employment figure for 1996, export figure for 1997.

[8] Production is concentrated in the northwest municipalities of Mossoró and Barauna, with some production also in Assu, Carnaubais, and Ipanguacu. According to IBGE, the average annual share of melons produced in RN in total melon production between 1997 and 1999 was 39.8 percent. Export share from own fieldwork, as presented in Gomes (1999).

Table 3.2. Participation of SMEs in Fruit Production in Santa Catarina, Petrolina-Juazeiro, and Rio Grande do Norte *(percent)*

Case—crop	1985	1988/1991	1996/1997	2002
Santa Catarina—apples[a]	48	35	30	n.a.
Petrolina-Juazeiro—all crops[b]	81	66	61	56
Mangoes	n.a.	n.a.	30	40[c]
Grapes	n.a.	n.a.	59	60[d]
Rio Grande do Norte—melons[e]	0	9	27	n.a.

Note: These data reflect the percentage of production of each crop that is produced by SMEs. For example, in 1985, SMEs produced 48% of the all the apples produced in Santa Catarina. The share of production is in terms of area planted in PJ and RN and in tons in SC.

[a] SMEs refer to growers with an annual production of less than 1,000 tons. Data for 1985 and 1996 from Santa Catarina State Census, as cited in Boeing (1998); data for 1991 from Hentschke (1994).

[b] SMEs refer to growers with less than 100 planted hectares. The first row is the share of SMEs in the total irrigated area in PJ, not just for mangoes and grapes. These data are included since no time series are available that pertain specifically to mangoes and grapes. Data are for Senador Nilo Coelho Irrigation Project, the largest among CODEVASF's six projects in PJ. Unless otherwise noted, data for 1985 and 1988 from Miranda (1989), 1996 from Alves da Silva et al. (1996), and for 2002 from www.codevasf.gov.br/produtos/pro_senadornilocoelho.htm.

[c] Data from interview with director of EMBRAPA Semi-Árido.

[d] Data from interview with grape consultant in Petrolina.

[e] SMEs refer to growers with less than 300 planted hectares. Data from own fieldwork, as presented in Gomes (1999).

the cases of melons, because the financial, management, production, and postharvesting requirements per hectare are much greater for grapes than for melons. Generally speaking, SMEs differ from larger growers not only in terms of area planted or produced, but also in terms of fixed capital equipment (such as storage and processing plants), administrative strategy (self-managed versus professionally managed), and the use of labor (self-supervised versus hierarchically supervised). Large growers undertake agricultural production as an activity secondary to construction, transportation, or banking, and many are from traditionally wealthy and politically connected families. Medium-sized growers, in contrast, are usually agronomists or agricultural technicians, fully dedicated to their farms, which tend to focus almost exclusively on fruit crops. Small growers range from well-qualified growers, with the means to eventually expand into medium-sized growers, to others who remain focused on lower-value crops, with only minimal investments in fruits.

In order to look for patterns that may run across these cases on how SMEs have responded to the changing market, I developed detailed case studies and life histories of growers, of grower organizations, and of state-grower relations. The majority of my data came from structured, open-ended interviews with growers of all sizes, researchers and administrators from local and state institutions, state agricultural officials and technicians, rural credit officers, input suppliers, agricultural consultants, university professors, technicians of the U.S. Department of Agriculture (USDA) in Washington, D.C., export field inspectors in Petrolina, and importers of Brazilian fresh fruit in the United Kingdom and Holland.

This chapter is organized as follows. The first section sets the context for this study by describing the impacts of a globalized food market on SMEs. The second section then describes how SMEs first adopted fruit production, particularly through public sector support in earlier decades. Given the rising market pressures and the fall in public sector support over the years, the third section argues that SMEs have more recently benefited from public–private partnerships in agricultural research; the endurance of ethnic-based networks; the rising tendency of larger firms to subcontract production; and the increase in private sources of agricultural extension accessible to SMEs. Finally, the concluding section summarizes the patterns of upgrading by SMEs across the cases and offers a few insights gained from this research on how public sector policies can facilitate participation of and upgrading by SMEs in the fresh fruit sector.

Harvesting in the 1990s: The Rise of Supermarkets and Its Implications for SMEs

Producing fresh fruits in the 1990s has become an even more demanding activity for SMEs when compared to past decades. As is well documented, SMEs have generally faced high barriers to entry in fresh fruits because of investment requirements, insufficient volumes, limited production and marketing knowledge, and insecure access to postharvest and transport services (Carter, Barnham, and Mesbah, 1996; Collins, 1995; Maxwell and

Fernando, 1989). The restructuring of food retail in the past decade has introduced additional challenges to all growers, and especially to SMEs, by imposing a series of norms and standards according to which growers must produce.

The global market for fresh fruits has changed in its consolidation of global retailers, which are gradually replacing national retailers and local vendors.[9] In Brazil, the consolidation of food retail has been especially rapid since the stabilization plan of 1994, which attracted increased foreign direct investment by multinational supermarket chains, such as Carrefour, Ahold, and Wal-Mart (Farina, 2002). As a result, the share of supermarkets in national food retail increased from about 30 percent in 1990 to 75 percent in 2000 (Reardon, Timmer, and Berdegue, 2003). For fresh produce in particular, supermarkets in Brazil now account for about 50 percent of national sales (Reardon, Timmer, and Berdegue, 2003).

The restructuring of food retail has been accompanied by an increase in buyer-driven standards as large retailers seek to differentiate their products on the basis of quality and consumer safety, thus generating additional sources of profit (Reardon and Farina, 2001). This product differentiation has led buyers to shift gradually from demanding product standards alone to imposing a series of process standards as well (Reardon, Timmer, and Berdegue, 2003). The buyers' concern then is in terms of the characteristics not only of the product itself, but also of the production process, including its impact on food safety, labor, and the environment.

The rising competition in the fresh fruit industry and the need to impose these norms and standards has meant a changing relationship between growers and buyers. Whereas previously this relationship was generally segmented with an intermediary, retailers are increasingly shifting away from middlemen and wholesalers to more direct forms of procurement. These alternative strategies include formal and informal

---

[9] This transformation is epitomized by the experience in the United Kingdom in the 1990s, where supermarkets and major retailers increased their market share (in terms of revenues from all final sales) of fresh fruits and vegetables from 44 percent in 1992 to 76 percent in 1997 (Dolan and Humphrey, 2001).

contracts directly with growers and the establishment of their own distribution centers, practices which allow the supermarkets greater leverage in enforcing their quality and safety norms and standards (Farina, 2002). All of this means that growers must now be much more than just price-competitive—they must now meet the mounting demands for better fruits, "better" being whatever the supermarkets define as better: varieties, production methods, postharvesting technologies, packaging and labeling specifications, and acceptable environmental impacts and working conditions.

The Public Roots of SME Production

Much of the research explaining how market forces squeeze out SMEs tends to overlook how these SMEs were historically inserted into this sector. Evidence from my cases suggests that whether or not SMEs participate in these high-value markets depends not only on the more powerful actors along a chain (including importers, buyers, and supermarkets), but also on the scale and scope of public sector support that may facilitate SME adoption of fruit crops in the first place. Evidence from my cases also suggests that public sector policies were especially important in explaining SME's participation and performance in these chains.

In what follows, I illustrate how public sector support influenced SME adoption of fruit crops in the early years of each cluster, especially through its impact on the structure of production and the relationship the state established between SMEs and public sector agricultural research and extension agencies.

In addition to directly influencing SME adoption of these crops, the structure of production also shapes the potential for collective action among growers, a course that scholars repeatedly point to as conducive to firms' upgrading efforts. Therefore, the patterns of collaboration (or lack thereof) observed today reflect interfirm relations set in motion decades ago when state intervention in the 1970s and 1980s determined which growers adopted fruit crops and at what scale. Across my cases, the implications of structure of production for cluster-wide upgrading are reflected in the varying levels to which the larger firms and growers' associations collaborate (or fail to collaborate), especially in terms of establishing ties with public sector agencies that could facilitate the upgrading process.

Instituting a Small-Firm Bias in Santa Catarina

Apple production in the state of Santa Catarina is concentrated in two areas surrounding the cities of Fraiburgo and São Joaquim. Both areas have soils and climate favorable for apple production, but they differ from one another in their terrain and, consequently, pattern of occupation. Fraiburgo and its surrounding areas have vast expanses of gently rolling hills, allowing for large-scale production. The surface in São Joaquim, in contrast, is mountainous and rocky, favoring smaller-scale production instead.

Apple production by SMEs in Santa Catarina began with a group of growers belonging to the former São Paulo–based agricultural cooperative, COTIA. These growers began with very limited knowledge of apple production, living through years of trial and error, toiling with several varieties which ultimately turned out to suffer from pollinization problems, low productivity, and low quality. Two decades later, these same SMEs were producing high-quality apples, investing in modern pack houses and storage facilities, and exporting directly to European buyers. The transformation of this group of growers, although unmatched by any other in the cluster, reflects the general trend toward improved production by other SMEs in São Joaquim. Today, SMEs produce over 30 percent of the state's apples, supplying to large firms in Fraiburgo and also firms in Vacaria in the neighboring state of Rio Grande do Sul, while the former COTIA growers market directly themselves.

That SMEs in Santa Catarina have managed to participate in the apple market is explained primarily by policies of the Santa Catarina state government that supported small-scale production along with larger growers from early on in the formation of the sector. Several factors contributed to this early support: the Santa Catarina state government's long-standing commitment to small-scale enterprises; its timely search for an agricultural activity to replace the production of grains, which was shifting toward Brazil's midwest frontier; and the successful experience of the pioneering firm in Fraiburgo in producing apples. SMEs also benefited from support through the federal government, which promoted domestic production of apples to reduce Brazil's dependency on imported apples.

The role of the pioneering firms in Santa Catarina differed from that in the other cases. In Santa Catarina, the largest firm first experimented, then collaborated with the state in opening its farms to state researchers, and eventually donated its plant collection to the state. Inspired by the successful apple production by this pioneering firm in Fraiburgo, in 1968 the Santa Catarina state government established an uncommonly well-structured program targeted at promoting the production of apples and other temperate fruits. The Programa de Fruticultura de Clima Temperado (PROFIT), administered through the state's Agricultural and Research Agency (EPAGRI),[10] first mapped out regions within the state suited for fruit production and established several regional technical extension offices. Through its support, PROFIT enabled small growers to adopt apple production through a combination of support policies for credit, marketing, research, training, and extension.

This early state support was striking in its aggressive outreach and research efforts, which established a link between SMEs and the state agricultural agency that persisted well into the 1990s. Beginning in the mid-1960s, EPAGRI established extension offices in each of the regions considered favorable for apple production, providing at least one agronomist specializing in temperate fruit production for every 20 growers. EPAGRI also offered training courses and seminars for growers held in EPAGRI training centers throughout the state and helped small growers organize into cooperatives that enabled growers to process and market their apples

---

[10] The SC state agricultural agency that implemented PROFIT was the Association of Credit and Rural Assistance (ACARESC). The state merged ACARESC with the state's agricultural research agency (EMPASC) to create EPAGRI in 1991. I use the acronym EPAGRI throughout this short discussion to avoid confusion.

collectively. Even today, growers recognize the effectiveness of this early support in getting them started.

In addition to agricultural extension, the state's agricultural research system also assured that all growers, regardless of their scale of production, had access to public sector research. EPAGRI distributed the responsibility and resources for apple research across two state research experimental stations, one near Fraiburgo and the other in São Joaquim. This structure allowed state researchers to tailor their work to the particular characteristics of each region, which differ in terms of climate, terrain, and soils, and to the different varieties, with emphasis on Gala in Fraiburgo and Fuji in São Joaquim. At the same time, the state invested heavily in training its cadre of researchers and sought technical expertise and financial resources from several developed countries that had extensive experience with apple production.[11]

As a result of these earlier policies, SMEs have produced apples alongside larger growers for the past three decades. This critical mass of SMEs has enabled growers to forge ties with each other through two large cooperatives, one established by former COTIA members and the other by a group of SMEs assisted by EPAGRI in the mid-1970s. Growers in these cooperatives have collectively overcome the problem of low volume and together produce 10 percent of total apple production in Santa Catarina.[12] At the same time, the state's strategy of reaching out to SMEs established a long-lasting relationship, which continues to benefit growers today directly through the experimental station in São Joaquim and indirectly via SME participation in cluster-wide upgrading efforts coordinated by the sector association (Brazilian Apple Growers Association, or ABPM), along with EPAGRI.

---

[11] These included collaboration with the Israeli Volcanic Center in training in the use of a chemically induced break of dormancy; the establishment of phyto-sanitary alert stations funded by the German GTZ; and collaboration with Cornell University and the experimental station in East Malling in the United Kingdom in the development of apple varieties suitable to the region.

[12] In 1999, the three cooperatives in São Joaquim produced between 1,279 and 1,439 hectares of apples, and total area planted in SC was 14,162 hectares.

The Changing Nature of SMEs in Petrolina-Juazeiro

The booming fresh fruit cluster in Petrolina-Juazeiro is the result of the intervention by the San Francisco River Valley Development Agency (CODEVASF), a parastatal dedicated to the promotion of navigation, irrigation, agricultural and industrial development in the San Francisco River Valley.[13] In Petrolina-Juazeiro, CODEVASF expropriated land to implement public irrigation projects, enlisted different-sized growers and agricultural processing firms in each project,[14] provided incentives for agricultural industries to establish in the region,[15] and supported the creation of a grower association (VALEXPORT) that was key to the formation of export channels. While SMEs in Santa Catarina benefited from a state government historically committed to supporting smallholder production, SMEs in Petrolina-Juazeiro benefited from CODEVASF's explicit policies favoring their incorporation into the irrigation projects along the San Francisco River Valley. In providing different-sized lots, CODEVASF established a structure of production consisting of both large and small growers. Large growers had anywhere from 20 to 200 hectares on which they first produced tomatoes, beans, and melons, prior to switching to mangoes. Small growers, in turn, received from CODEVASF six-hectare irrigation-ready lots (with on-farm pumps, canals, and drainage system installed and ready for use), guidance on what to produce, technical assistance, and facilitated access to credit and buyers. As a result of these early policies, SMEs occupied over 80 percent of the land in the projects until the mid-1980s, then their share gradually declined to nearly 60 percent by 1996 (Table 3.2).

Despite the decline of the total share of SMEs producing in Petrolina-Juazeiro's irrigation projects since the mid-1980s, SMEs today produce as

---

[13] See Chapter 2 in Damiani (1999), "An Overview of Early Government Interventions," for a discussion of the role of CODEVASF in the development of the San Francisco River Valley.

[14] Processing firms were mostly dedicated to processing tomato paste.

[15] Government incentives for large farms in Petrolina-Juazeiro included subsidizing 50 percent of their irrigation infrastructure and ensuring investment capital for the remaining 50 percent through the Bank of the Northeast and the Bank of Brazil (Damiani, 1999).

much as 40 percent of the cluster's mangoes and 60 percent of its grapes. This decline is the result of two events. First, small growers were largely replaced by medium-sized growers, who increased farm size and diversified into fruit production. The small growers that first settled in Petrolina-Juazeiro's public irrigation projects produced mostly annual crops, especially tomatoes, for which they had contracts with tomato paste processing industries that CODEVASF helped establish in Petrolina-Juazeiro. The tomato paste industry collapsed in the late 1980s and, unable to diversify into other crops, up to 70 percent of small growers abandoned their farms.[16] In their place, dozens of medium-sized growers, mostly agronomists, agricultural technicians, and liberal professionals, merged small farms to produce mangoes, grapes, and other fruits. By the mid-1990s, the majority of SMEs in the projects were producing perennial fruit crops, many of them supplying large exporting firms, while others exported directly to foreign clients. In addition, medium-sized growers in Petrolina-Juazeiro have also benefited from the almost tripling in the number of pack houses certified to export mangoes to the United States, from 5 in 1997 to 14 in 2001.[17] Though the sources of these changes were different, their outcomes were reinforcing because the expansion of postharvesting capacity with these new pack houses opened the marketing channels for the new medium-sized growers to enter the market.

SMEs in Petrolina-Juazeiro thus benefited from CODEVASF's explicit policies favoring their incorporation into the irrigation projects along the San Francisco River Valley. Yet the state–SME relationship in Petrolina-Juazeiro differed from that in Santa Catarina in important aspects that influenced the long-term viability of smallholder production.

---

[16] These original occupants were also hurt by CODEVASF's withdrawal of free water and technical assistance. See Alves da Silva et al. (1996), Gomes (1996), and Cavalcanti (1999).

[17] This surge in pack houses certified to export to the United States in only four years is partly explained by the now-lower cost associated with the thermal bath equipment needed as a requirement of the USDA preclearance program for mangoes. Initially, this equipment was imported from the United States and cost anywhere from $750,000 to $1 million per firm (Damiani, 1999). Now firms can purchase this equipment domestically for a fraction of the cost.

While early on, SMEs in both cases benefited from abundant support with credit, training, research, extension, and marketing (cooperatives in Santa Catarina, link to agro-industries in Petrolina-Juazeiro), SMEs in Santa Catarina produced the same crops as the larger growers, while SMEs in Petrolina-Juazeiro focused initially on annual crops and switched to perennial fruits only in the 1990s. As a result, SMEs in Santa Catarina benefited from the learning process all along. SMEs in Petrolina-Juazeiro instead first learned how to produce irrigated annual crops, only later adopting perennials.

This sequencing of easier to more difficult crops in Petrolina-Juazeiro largely explains how numerous SMEs with limited agricultural experience eventually succeeded in adopting fruit crops. At the same time, this sequencing was accompanied by the replacement of as many as 70 percent of smallholders with medium-sized growers.[18] This second wave of SMEs in Petrolina-Juazeiro—dominated by medium-sized growers—was thus an unintentional and costly outcome of CODEVASF's policies toward SMEs. In other words, CODEVASF facilitated SME adoption of fruit crops not intentionally, but as a byproduct of an initial strategy for SMEs that failed.

This sequencing in Petrolina-Juazeiro also influenced the research agenda of the Center for Research of the Tropic Semi-Arid (CPATSA), the main public sector agricultural research agency acting locally.[19] Early on, CPATSA focused almost exclusively on annual crops, generating a rift between it and growers already producing perennials in the 1980s. It was only in the late 1990s, with mounting pressures from large growers, that CPATSA shifted its agenda toward fruit crops. Such tension and disconnect never occurred in the case of apple growers in Santa Catarina, who worked continuously with the state agricultural agency, EPAGRI.

---

[18] This 70 percent figure reflects the turnover among the original occupants of CODEVASF's largest project in PJ, the Senador Nilo Coelho Irrigation Project. See Alves da Silva et al. (1996).

[19] CPATSA is one of the regional research centers of the Brazilian Agricultural Research Agency (EMBRAPA).

The Piecemeal Approach to SMEs in Rio Grande do Norte

In contrast to the other cases, SMEs did not participate in the early phase of the melon industry in Rio Grande do Norte. Instead, early government support primarily induced a few very large firms to produce, with only piecemeal support to SMEs. Unlike the concerted government intervention through EPAGRI in Santa Catarina and in Petrolina-Juazeiro through CODEVASF, government support in Rio Grande do Norte was instead limited to the more conventional provision of highly subsidized credit during the 1980s, a reflection of the regional development strategy undertaken by SUDENE, the BNB, and the Bank of Brazil.[20] Although firms in the other cases also benefited from subsidized credit when they began producing, the form in which this credit was allocated in Rio Grande do Norte led to a very different structure of production. Instead of a deliberate policy promoting a dual structure with both large and small growers, SUDENE, the Bank of the Northeast (BN), and the Bank of Brazil channeled credit to two very large firms. As a result, while CODEVASF reduced the possibility of land concentration by establishing limits to land size, inducing the creation of several 100–200 hectare firms, with only a few larger firms (with up to 400 hectares), these federal agencies created a highly concentrated structure in Rio Grande do Norte. In fact, at its peak production, the pioneering firm in Rio Grande do Norte had over six times as much irrigated area as the largest firm in Petrolina-Juazeiro. The provision of abundant and highly subsidized venture and investment capital in the early years enabled these pioneering firms to test new varieties of melons and learn the best production practices for the local conditions, establish

---

[20] In the case of the western municipalities surrounding Assú, growers also benefited from the construction of the Armando Ribeiro Dam. The majority of melon production is concentrated around the easternmost municipalities in the state, around Mossoró, where irrigation water is drawn from underground aquifers and not from the dam. It is important to note, however, that DNOCS did not build the dam as part of a strategy for irrigated agriculture. Instead, it built this dam as part of its broader strategy to distribute water through the semiarid northeast. Without it, however, irrigation in Assú would have remained limited to the Assú River banks, prone to periodic flooding.

domestic and foreign export channels, and build a recognized name for locally produced melons. However, in contrast to the joint efforts among large firms observed in Santa Catarina and Petrolina-Juazeiro, larger firms in Rio Grande do Norte remained largely antagonistic toward each other and the rest of the cluster. They were politically strong individually, directly accessing and benefiting from government support. These same firms eventually went bankrupt in 2001–2002, unable to adjust to the new realities of the Brazilian economy and the world market. Nevertheless, the problems of collective "inaction" they generated persisted.

SMEs nevertheless benefited from several public sector initiatives in Rio Grande do Norte, including a public irrigation project in the subregion of Assú,[21] federal agrarian reform settlements of the National Institute for Colonization and Agrarian Reform (INCRA) throughout the state, and a BN-sponsored program that subsidized land for recently graduated agronomists. Although each of these initiatives ultimately helped SMEs adopt melon production, their impacts were minimized because they did not count on a politically backed agency like CODEVASF or a committed state government as in Santa Catarina. Instead, large growers appropriated much of the benefit of the public dam to the exclusion of smallholders,[22] and the agrarian reform settlements failed to account for local peculiarities that could have signaled the possibility of smallholder production of irrigated crops sooner.[23] As for the BN-sponsored program for agronomists, it imposed a production system on growers incompat-

[21] Only a minority of melons produced in RN depend on irrigation water from this dam. Most of the state's melon production, around the municipalities of Mossoro and Barauna, draws water from underground.

[22] Although DNOCS originally designed the dam with a redistributive component through a public irrigation project, the redistributive effects in Assú have been minimal because the state (1) failed to inform local inhabitants of its planned project for the region, (2) delayed the settling of growers, (3) did not provide appropriate technical assistance, and (4) redistributed project properties from SMEs to larger growers (Gomes da Silva, 1992; Gomes da Silva et al., 1997).

[23] The federal agrarian reform settlements enabled growers to produce melons, but only after intervention in the mid-1990s by NGOs that helped growers access special lines of credit, provided technical assistance, and served as initial liaison between the large firms and growers.

ible with the realities of the local economy.[24] In addition, SMEs in Rio Grande do Norte never counted on research or extension support like SMEs in the other cases.

Despite the absence of the kinds of public sector support and growers' associations present in Santa Catarina and Petrolina-Juazeiro, SMEs in Rio Grande do Norte entered the market in the early 1990s and rapidly increased their participation, reaching 27 percent of the area planted by 1997 (Table 3.2). SMEs' increased presence is largely explained by the relatively easy nature of melon production and the changing market environment that has forced larger firms to subcontract since the mid-1990s.

Melons are relatively easier to produce because they require considerably less capital to produce than apples, mangoes, and grapes. The per hectare cost of simply planting these other crops, covering the first three or four years, during which they do not bear fruit (but not the maintenance cost once they are actually producing), ranges from about US$3,000 for mangoes to US$15,000 for grapes.[25] The production cost of melons, from planting to harvesting, amounts to US$4,710 per hectare. This means that the risk involved in trying something new with the production of melons is considerably lower than that involved in experimenting with the other crops.

In addition, the production of melons differs from that of mangoes, grapes, and apples in an important way: melons are an annual crop harvested in 60 days; mangoes, grapes, and apples are perennials, taking at least three years until their first harvest. This means that within two short months, melon growers see the results of a new variety or the outcomes

---

[24] Through BNB's PRODESA (Programa de Apoio Creditício à Reorientação da Pequena e Média Unidade Produtiva Rural do Semi-Árido Nordestino), qualified agronomists received bank loans for the purchase of land in the semiarid region, investments, technical assistance, vehicles, farm machinery, and other expenses associated with starting an agricultural enterprise. In turn, participants acted as extension workers to neighboring growers. The main problem with PRODESA was that it required growers to produce a variety of crops, including rain-fed crops, and also small animal husbandry. Participants complained of the diverse requirements which economically made no sense and kept them from expanding (BNB/IICA, 1997).

[25] Production costs from Carvalho (1996).

of modifications to the production process, such as spacing, weeding, irrigation, or fertilizer and pesticide use. Growers of the other, perennial crops, in contrast, must wait at least three years to observe any comparable results, making the learning process longer and more expensive in terms of both the actual research costs and the opportunity cost of having to wait years before arriving at some conclusion about improved production technologies. These characteristics of melon production facilitated adoption by SMEs and enabled them to take advantage of an expanding market when large growers began subcontracting.

As a result of these differences, growers are more likely to act collectively and in collaboration with the state when they produce perennial crops (such as mangoes, grapes, and apples), whose upgrading often calls for complex and long-term R&D, too costly for individual growers to undertake. Growers of annual, short-term crops (such as melons), in contrast, can usually carry out much of the R&D independently or with guidance from local input suppliers, consultants, and their buyers and thus have fewer incentives to collaborate with other growers or government agencies.[26]

In sum, SMEs first managed to adopt fruit production in Santa Catarina and Petrolina-Juazeiro largely because of a combination of public sector policies that enabled them to overcome problems of access to land, credit, and agricultural research and extension. This early support was especially favorable to SMEs in Santa Catarina, who benefited from investments in the apple sector along with larger growers. In Petrolina-Juazeiro, CODEVASF generated two waves of SMEs, with the second wave—mostly medium-sized growers—benefiting from the failure of the first. SMEs in Santa Catarina and Petrolina-Juazeiro also benefited from active and effective sectoral associations that were led by larger growers but generated externalities that facilitated upgrading by SMEs as well. SMEs in Rio

---

[26] For other discussions on the impacts of crop characteristics on how growers organize and which activities they undertake collectively, see Attwood and Baviskar (1987), Perry et al. (1997), and Tendler (1984).

Grande do Norte, in contrast, had comparatively limited and truncated public sector support and no comparable grower association. They nevertheless managed to produce melons because of the crop's relatively easier nature, along with the rising tendency of larger firms to subcontract since the mid-1990s.

Resilience through Joint Action in Upgrading

The above policies and events explain how SMEs adopted fruit production but fall short in explaining how SMEs have managed to survive in today's globalized market. As reflected in Table 3.2, SMEs have remained in the market in more recent years, despite mounting pressures from buyer-driven demands that result from the restructuring of global food retail and the demise of the kinds of public sector support they received in earlier decades.[27]

The value chains literature claims that global buyers are likely to engage with their suppliers in efforts to upgrade, actively supplying information and monitoring the implementation of the recommended innovations. This explanation, however, does not always hold for value chains of agricultural products, in which retailers are not concerned with backward or forward integration, preferring to reallocate the risks in food procurement and quality maintenance to other actors in the chain (Humphrey and Oeter, 1999; Humphrey and Schmitz, 2000; Marsden, 1997). The intermediaries in these chains relay market information on to their suppliers, but they are less likely to engage in the actual process of upgrading than would be the case in buyer–producer relations in other sectors (see Pietrobelli, Rabellotti, and Giuliani, Chapter 9 in this volume).

[27] The reduced scope of public sector support over the decades is reflected in falling expenditures for agricultural research and extension. Expenditures by the Brazilian Agricultural Research Agency (EMBRAPA), Brazil's largest and most important agency in the field, peaked in 1996 then dropped by 1999 (Beintema, Dias, and Pardey, 2001), while federal expenditures on agricultural extension fell from 21 percent of total government spending in agriculture in the early 1980s to 5.5 percent by the late 1990s (Gasques, 2001). See Olinger (1996) for an insider's view of the rise and fall of the national agricultural extension system and its impacts on agricultural extension in the state of SC.

This implies that growers must acquire the knowledge and skills needed to upgrade themselves.

In this section I argue that SMEs' capabilities to participate in the market today and to upgrade are largely a function of joint action among growers and between growers and other local actors. In particular, the resilience of SMEs across these cases is associated with public–private research partnerships inclusive of SMEs, the endurance of ethnic-based networks based on SMEs, a rising tendency for larger firms to subcontract production from SMEs, and finally, the increase in private sources of agricultural extension on which SMEs now depend.

Public–Private Partnerships in Agricultural Research

Growers across the cases investigated, and especially in Petrolina-Juazeiro and Santa Catarina, have turned to the public sector for support in their upgrading efforts, particularly with identifying improved varieties (as demanded by global buyers), implementing fruit-fly-free zones (as required by the U.S. Department of Agriculture), and defining integrated production practices (as required by the European Union). Meeting these norms and standards involves activities which by their very nature demand public sector action, including adaptive research, specific improvements in farming practices, and biological control of pests and pathogens, along with other research products that have public good characteristics. As such, results from research, once disseminated, become freely available (i.e., nonexcludable), and one grower's use of this knowledge does not reduce its supply to others (i.e., nonrival). Public sector involvement in these activities is also justified on the grounds of risk and uncertainty associated with research, as well as its economies of scale, both of which would keep the private sector from taking on these kinds of activities itself (Pray and Umali-Deininger, 1998; Hayami and Ruttan, 1985; Jarvis, 1994).

Public sector support in these areas has increasingly been provided in conjunction with growers associations, largely as a result of federal government policies promoting the creation of public–private partnerships.[28] Although the larger growers in each cluster dominate these associations, SMEs have also benefited from their efforts both directly and indirectly. As larger growers upgrade through these partnerships, many SMEs benefit directly via participation in sectoral associations, including the ABPM in Santa Catarina and VALEXPORT in Petrolina-Juazeiro. Indirectly, SMEs also benefit from these efforts when they are subcontracted by larger growers who transfer the knowledge and skills obtained through these partnerships to their suppliers.

In addition, public sector agencies have implemented mechanisms to ensure SME access to these efforts. In Petrolina-Juazeiro, for example, CPATSA often collaborates with the Brazilian Agency for Small and Micro Enterprise (SEBRAE), where SEBRAE contributes to funding research that ultimately benefits SMEs, such as research on seedless grape varieties. In Santa Catarina, the state agency EPAGRI carries out apple research in its experimental station in São Joaquim, easily accessible to local growers. In both cases, government agencies also included SMEs in their field trials for the design of integrated production practices.

The Strength of Ethnic Ties

Of particular importance in explaining the resilience of SMEs across my cases is COTIA, the now-extinct agricultural cooperative of Japanese immigrants to São Paulo which spread its experience and opened production frontiers throughout Brazil between 1945 and 1994.[29] Intent on helping immigrant families become economically active in Brazil through agricultural production, COTIA established hundreds of agricultural colonies throughout Brazil, becoming the largest agricultural cooperative in Latin America, with 200 branch offices staffed by 22,000 employees throughout

---

[28] The National Research Council (CNPq), in coordination with the Ministry of Agriculture, implemented several competitive grant programs for fruit research in the 1990s (such as the BIOEx and Agronegocio) requiring researchers to submit proposals endorsed by growers' organizations.

[29] COTIA shut down in 1994 as a result of an overextended bureaucracy and financial commitments.

Brazil and over 21,000 members.[30] COTIA provided technical assistance and marketed products produced by its members as well as those from nonmembers through extensive channels with domestic supermarket chains and a permanent office in Rotterdam, the port of entry for most fresh fruits into Europe (Damiani, 1999).

Through its members, COTIA spread information on crop varieties and provided a model of planting techniques for many crops throughout Brazil. In the context of the three cases investigated, COTIA turned out to play an important role in the development of each of the clusters by providing local growers with a competent production and marketing network, as well as a model of collective action. Even following its closure in 1994, former COTIA members continued playing an important role in the development of the fresh fruit industry through the formation of independent cooperatives in Santa Catarina and Petrolina-Juazeiro and a marketing group in Rio Grande do Norte.

COTIA established a colony of six families in São Joaquim in 1964, through which growers benefited from the state's rising interest in promoting apple production. Growers learned about apple production and obtained investment and working capital through PROFIT. With the closure of COTIA, apple growers in São Joaquim organized themselves into the Cooperativa Agrícola de São Joaquim (SANJO). Today, SANJO produces about 37 percent of the apples produced in São Joaquim and 5 percent of the state production, marketing through many clients it "inherited" from COTIA as well as newer clients it has established itself.

Almost two decades after COTIA began producing apples in São Joaquim, it accepted CODEVASF's invitation to establish a colony in the newly opened irrigation projects in Petrolina-Juazeiro.[31] In 1984, COTIA established a colony with 36 members across 1,927 hectares and opened

---

[30] Interview with directors of Cooperativa Agrícola de Juazeiro (CAJ) in Juazeiro.

[31] This "delay" reflects the unrealistically favorable economic environment surrounding these fruit clusters until the 1990s, in which abundant cheap credit and secure demand ensured high profit margins despite administrative inefficiencies.

a branch office in Juazeiro to provide technical assistance and coordinate purchases. COTIA growers in Petrolina-Juazeiro introduced the production of melons and table grapes to the region and helped other growers break into exports by lending one of their export managers to the newly established Petrolina-Juazeiro grower cooperative, VALEXPORT; providing contacts in Europe; and allowing the use of COTIA's office in Rotterdam (Damiani, 1999). Moreover, COTIA purchased and exported melons and grapes from other growers, in the process teaching these other growers about the norms and standards of the export market, and established the Brazilian Grape Marketing Board (BGMB), a group within VALEXPORT focused on the joint sales of table grapes. As in Santa Catarina, growers in Petrolina-Juazeiro also created their cooperative once COTIA collapsed. The Cooperativa Agrícola de Juazeiro (CAJ) consists of 45 growers, each with an average of 10–12 hectares of grapes, in addition to production of mangoes, passion fruit, and other fruit crops.

COTIA's agricultural expertise also reached melon growers in Rio Grande do Norte. Although COTIA never established a colony in Rio Grande do Norte, as it did in Santa Catarina and Petrolina-Juazeiro, it nevertheless influenced the melon industry through the transfer of technology via a consultant to the pioneering firm, the subsequent move of several former COTIA growers to the region, and the establishment of COTIA-based marketing channels. As a result, melon growers in Rio Grande do Norte also benefited from COTIA's extensive experience in production and marketing.

Benefiting from Contractual Ties with Grower-Exporters

Many SMEs have also managed to participate in these markets by engaging in subcontractual arrangements with large grower-exporters. With few exceptions in Santa Catarina and grape growers in Petrolina-Juazeiro, large firms increased their practice of subcontracting only in the mid-1990s, as they faced increased pressures for efficiency in light of growing competition and falling profit margins, while no longer having access to subsidized public credit.[32] Subcontracting enabled larger growers to maintain or even expand their volumes, while reducing per unit costs by relaying production risks and labor costs to their SME suppliers.[33]

SMEs, in turn, benefited from these relationships in receiving clear standards by which to produce; input packages equivalent to that which large firms themselves use, with grace periods extending to the harvest season; and technical assistance from production through postharvesting. Contractual ties with larger growers thus enabled many SMEs to participate in markets that are more demanding than the local, lower-niche markets SMEs tend to use initially.

It may be useful to add that not all SMEs benefit from these contractual ties in the same way, however, since large firms establish a variety of contracts. These range from annual contracts inclusive of inputs, technical assistance, soil analysis, harvesting, transportation, processing, and marketing, with a minimum assured base price, to informal verbal arrangements limited to marketing. This argument holds for the select group of growers which the large firm finds reliable in terms of responsiveness to its demands for volume, quality, or a specific variety.

Central to my argument is the evidence that many SMEs have managed to use these contractual ties with larger firms as a springboard for establishing direct ties with buyers themselves (Tendler, 2001a). This was typical for several medium-sized growers in Rio Grande do Norte, who initially supplied the pioneering firms with melons and subsequently, when contacted by a foreign buyer familiar with the quality of their melons,

---

[32] According to Albuquerque (2001), labor costs up to 55 percent of total production costs for grapes in PJ, 18 percent for apples in SC, 10 percent for melons in RN, and 8 percent for mangoes in PJ. An important component of this wage labor which motivates firms to subcontract is the *encargos sociais*. As a result, production by large firms can cost twice as much as that by SMEs. In the case of melons in RN, for example, production by the large firms in 1996 was between R$3,500 and R$6,000 per hectare, for medium-sized growers between R$2,500 and R$3,000, and for small growers between R$1,800 and R$2,500. In the case of grapes in PJ, overall costs for smaller growers in 1993 were 45 percent lower than those for larger growers (Collins, 1995).

[33] Gertler, Wolfe, and Garkut (2000) summarize the main views on the importance of local embeddedness in explaining innovation. Schmitz (1995) analyzes the role of these "noneconomic ties" between local firms in a Brazilian shoe cluster in the "diffusion and innovation of ideas."

switched from subcontracting to direct source. The same was done by an association of medium-sized mango growers in Petrolina-Juazeiro. After having sourced one of the leading mango exporters for several years, this association is now establishing direct contacts with an importer in Rotterdam.

When Agricultural Extension Goes Private: Input Suppliers and Consultants

In trying to identify sources of innovation among growers, my interviewees repeatedly reminded me of the importance of the social milieu—how growers continuously interact and exchange views on production technologies.[34] Growers meet formally, including at associational meetings and those coordinated by federal or state agencies, such as a training course on fruit flies by EMBRAPA in Rio Grande do Norte or an HACCP training by the FDA in Petrolina-Juazeiro. They also congregate at the countless seminars and presentations given by the multinational agricultural input suppliers and the field days sponsored by the input stores. Growers meet socially and informally throughout town, while waiting for service in banks, shopping for agricultural inputs, and having drinks at the bar. Engagement in this broader context has undoubtedly contributed to upgrading by SMEs. Absent the evidence on the formation and impact of these ties on local upgrading, this section presents two drivers of innovation for which there is (limited) evidence: input suppliers and consultants.

The expansion of fruit production across the cases has been accompanied by an increase in the number of agricultural input stores and in investments from national and multinational agricultural input suppliers. The number of stores dedicated to serving fruit production have multiplied: in Petrolina-Juazeiro, the number of stores increased from 5 in the 1980s to 20 in 2000; in Rio Grande do Norte, the increase was from 2 stores in

---

[34] For discussions on the problems of voice in associations, see Biggs and Smith (1998), Locke (1995), and Tendler (1999).

the 1980s to 7 in 2000. Increased competition has induced stores to offer a greater variety of services to growers. In addition to selling agricultural inputs and implements, stores now serve as important providers of technical assistance and, occasionally, of financial support.

In Petrolina-Juazeiro, for example, stores organize workshops on main crops in each project, choose growers for field trials, to whom they provide technical assistance throughout the cycle, then host field days in each trial area through which store agronomists review recommended production practices. In addition, store agronomists visit growers on demand to suggest possible solutions to technical problems growers may face with production. As a result, a visit through the irrigation projects will reveal the presence of logo-marked vehicles driven by store extension workers where once the motorcycle or downtrodden vehicle of the public extension worker was found.

In Rio Grande do Norte, the technical assistance provided by input suppliers has been particularly important in the absence of stronger public sector support as the dealers themselves have helped growers identify the most suitable melon varieties to produce. Input suppliers in this case serve as the main liaison between growers (including SMEs) and multinational seed distributors. Agronomists from the stores essentially choose several growers to carry out field trials with particular varieties and provide them with assistance throughout the growing cycle. At harvest time, store agronomists evaluate the outcomes and pass the information on to the multinational seed distributors, who then market successful varieties and continue their variety improvement program for the region. Input suppliers in Rio Grande do Norte also serve as financial institutions by providing melon growers with payment plans with grace periods longer than the melon cycle, allowing growers to pay for their inputs with their sales revenues.

For their part, national and multinational agricultural input suppliers have also been increasingly engaged with growers. Across the cases, these suppliers hold seminars to showcase new products, at times in local auditoriums, at times at local bars and restaurants. Each of these meetings provides a forum for growers to exchange experiences and impressions on the use of particular inputs and technologies.

The growth of these clusters has also been accompanied by an increase in the number of agronomists providing consulting services to growers. These consultants are often from other states and move to the clusters to take advantage of the increasing number of growers. Others are former employees of larger firms who either lose their jobs as these firms downsize or leave on their own to start their own consulting business or farm. They have turned out to be important conduits of information and drivers of dissemination across the clusters. These consultants developed their expertise from years of working for the large firms, where they learned about optimal production practices and established contacts with researchers, seed and input companies, and buyers. Like the input stores, these consultants also maintain tight relations with several multinational agricultural input providers.

Although many firms have always counted on consultants, they usually hired outside consultants for visits to the farms. The difference now is that most consultants have either settled down in the fruit producing areas from elsewhere or are from the clusters themselves, meaning they are better acquainted with local varieties and local conditions, as well as with the resources available to growers locally as they strive to upgrade. Aside from passing information directly on to their clients, consultants contribute to a broader dissemination of technological information indirectly, as the information they pass on to their clients reaches their clients' neighbors and acquaintances.

In sum, the available empirical evidence suggests that the new market demands have raised the returns to joint action, both strengthening already existing associations and generating new ones among SMEs and other local actors. Whereas SMEs always needed to sell their products jointly in order to overcome the individual problem of low volume, they now face the additional challenge of upgrading their production and postharvesting technologies, as well as collectively ensuring compliance with buyer-driven norms and standards.

Policy Implications

Throughout this chapter I have emphasized the different ways public sector policies influenced the participation and upgrading of SMEs over time. These experiences were not flawless, as reflected, for instance, in the high turnover of small growers originally settled in the irrigation projects in Petrolina-Juazeiro. Nevertheless, the experiences offer a series of lessons on what the public sector can do to support SME participation in the fresh fruit industry and on industrial policy in general. In what follows, I draw from Santa Catarina and Petrolina-Juazeiro, the cases with explicit government policies for SMEs, in highlighting the forms of support that seemed most effective in helping SMEs adopt fruit production in earlier decades and upgrade in more recent years.

On Implementing Effective SME-Based Policies

Early government support in both Santa Catarina and Petrolina-Juazeiro were central to SME adoption of fruit crops. In general terms the approach was very similar in both cases, with a government agency facilitating SME access to land, credit, inputs, and agricultural research and extension. Yet the form in which this support was provided resulted in very different outcomes for SMEs. In Santa Catarina, SMEs began producing apples early on and have generally continued to do so to the present day, improving their production and marketing capabilities. In Petrolina-Juazeiro, the earlier policies enabled hundreds of SMEs to adopt irrigated annual crops but were ultimately ineffective in helping these growers diversify into fruit crops. As a result, the majority of the original smallholders abandoned their farms, opening the way for medium-sized growers to purchase their farms, beginning in the mid-1990s. Medium-sized growers thus ultimately benefited from the earlier policies that established areas for small-scale production of irrigated crops, yet at the substantial economic and social cost incurred by the turnover of hundreds of smallholders.

These different outcomes may be partly explained by comparing the rise and fall of the local tomato pulp processing industry in Petrolina-Juazeiro, on which the majority of SMEs in Petrolina-Juazeiro first depended, to the growing demand for national apples, which certainly facilitated the continuity of apple growers in Santa Catarina. Yet these outcomes also suggest something favorable about the form in which this support was supplied in Santa Catarina versus that in Petrolina-Juazeiro. In particular, there are at least two aspects underlying the effectiveness of policy support in Santa Catarina that could be promoted elsewhere. First, the Santa Catarina state government established an uncommonly strong institutional relation with SMEs by having an experimental station easily accessible to SMEs and through its agricultural extension program. Locating the experimental station in the vicinity of SMEs meant that state researchers could focus on improved production technologies for the physical specificities of the local region and of direct relevance to SMEs. Just as important, this proximity also facilitated the interaction between state researchers and growers, creating formal and informal networks which outlasted the eventual reduction of state support for the sector in the 1990s. SMEs in Petrolina-Juazeiro initially interacted with multiple public sector agencies, including CPATSA and CODEVASF's own extension services, but none of these relationships endured. Second, along with its SME-based strategy, the Santa Catarina state government also supported apple production among larger growers, especially through R&D. By promoting the production of the same crop by large growers and SMEs, the state enabled SMEs to benefit from the positive externalities generated by the larger growers. As such, SMEs benefited from the establishment of phyto-sanitary alert stations, pest monitoring programs, and a hail control system, in addition to the development of a variety of research efforts on apple production technologies over the past four decades. In Petrolina-Juazeiro, these kinds of large-grower-generated spillovers to SMEs have occurred only recently because large growers and SMEs have historically produced different crops, thus sharing few common problems.

Promises and Perils of Public–Private Research Partnerships

As noted earlier, the public sector support of agriculture is much different today than when growers first began producing. Overall federal funding for agriculture research fell, and many state agricultural extension agencies shut down. In adjusting to this new scenario, the Brazilian federal government devised new funding mechanisms for agricultural research, seeking to improve the efficiency and effectiveness of public funding by complementing it with private sector participation in the funding and design of agricultural research through public–private partnerships.

In principle, these alternative mechanisms should increase the efficiency of public research by giving growers greater leverage in defining the research agenda (thus making research more applicable and useful for growers) while providing additional funds for public sector agencies (Alston, Pardey, and Roseboom, 1998; Echeverría, 1998; Portugal and Contini, 1997). This effectiveness, however, is partly based on the assumption that grower groups or associations involved in these partnerships are actually representative of a majority of growers involved in a given activity. While these associations may in effect represent the majority of volume produced, they do not always reflect the voices (and therefore needs) of the majority of growers, including SMEs.[35] This crowding-out problem may even be worsened with these new funding mechanisms, which essentially increase the attraction of public sector agencies to larger, more modern firms which are more likely to secure funding for public research than the medium-sized newcomers.[36]

Across the cases analyzed, public–private partnerships in agriculture research have been most effective in benefiting SMEs in Santa Catarina because of their participation in the well-organized and effective ABPM, which represents about 80 percent of the apples produced in Brazil. Despite

---

[35] Tendler (2001b) notes a similar attraction between professionals in training and technical assistance centers, including agricultural research and extension workers, and their more "modern" clients.

[36] This argument is further developed in Gomes (2004).

complaints about the dominance of larger firms, SMEs readily recognize how they have benefited from ABPM's collaborative efforts with government agencies, including the establishment of integrated production practices and the improvement of research infrastructure across the state's experimental research stations focusing on apple research.

Like the ABPM in Santa Catarina, the growers association in Petrolina-Juazeiro, VALEXPORT, has also participated in and benefited from several partnerships, in this case with CPATSA. But benefits to SMEs have been less direct because of VALEXPORT's relative exclusion of SMEs in favor of the larger mango growers who control VALEXPORT. The discontent of SMEs with VALEXPORT led at least two groups of medium-sized mango and grape growers (the latter having participated in VALEXPORT for over a decade) to want to break away from the association. Among other problems, these growers want to coordinate their research agendas directly with CPATSA, eliminating the intermediation of VALEXPORT, which traditionally set the research agenda and charged its members accordingly. During my most recent visit to Petrolina-Juazeiro, the mango growers had succeeded in establishing direct ties with CPATSA, with which they were working on implementing integrated production practices.

In times of reduced public sector support for agriculture, whether SMEs continue benefiting from public agriculture research will depend on the extent to which they have a voice before government agencies. This voice may be embedded institutionally, as in the enduring structure of research and extension in Santa Catarina. Or it may come about as government agencies recognize the possible gains of working directly with these groups of growers, as has been the experience of CPATSA and SEBRAE with SMEs in Petrolina-Juazeiro, which have already proven their capabilities of competing in these demanding markets.

References

Albuquerque, Lessandro. 2001. The Current and Future Prospects of the Brazilian Fruit Suppliers to the EU: Opportunities, Challenges, and Sustainability. Report written for Capespan International.

Alston, J. M., P. G. Pardey, and J. Roseboom. 1998. Financing Agricultural Research: International Investment Patterns and Policy Perspectives. *World Development* 26(6):1057–1071.

Alves da Silva, José Maria, Alberto Martins Rezende, and Carlos Arthur Barbosa da Silva. 1996. Avaliação dos pólos agroindustriais do semiárido brasileiro: condicionantes críticos do desenvolvimento do Pólo Petrolina-Juazeiro. Ministry of the Environment, Water Resources, and the Legal Amazon and the Arthur Bernardes Center of the Federal University of Viçosa, Brasília. Unpublished.

Attwood, Donald, and B. Baviskar. 1987. Why Do Some Cooperatives Work but Not Others? *Economic and Political Weekly Review of Agriculture* 22(26):A38–A55.

Banco do Nordeste and Inter-American Institute for Cooperation in Agriculture (BNB/IICA). 1997. *Programa de Apoio Creditício à Reorientação da Pequena e Média Unidade Produtiva Rural do Semi-Árido Nordestino (PRODESA): Avaliação global e proposta de aperfeiçoamento.* Fortaleza, Brazil: Banco do Nordeste.

Beintema, Nienke M., Antonio Flavio Dias Avila, and Philip G. Pardey. 2001. *Agricultural R&D in Brazil: Policy, Investments, and Institutional Profile.* Washington, D.C.: International Food Policy Research Institute.

Biggs, Stephen, and Grant Smith. 1998. Beyond Methodologies: Coalition-Building for Participatory Technology Development. *World Development* 26(2):239–248.

Boeing, Guido. 1998. *Informe conjuntural: maçã.* Florianópolis, Brazil: Instituto CEPA.

Bonelli, Regis. 2001. *Impactos econômicos e sociais de longo prazo da expansão agropecuária no Brasil: revolução invisível e inclusão social.* Texto para Discussão No. 838, Instituto de Pesquisa Econômica Aplicada (IPEA), Rio de Janeiro.

Boneti, José Itamar da Silva, Jorge Dotti Cesa, José Luiz Petri, and Roque Hentschke. 1999. *Cadeias produtivas do Estado de Santa Catarina: maçã.* Boletim Técnico No. 105, Empresa de Pesquisa Agropecuária e Extensão Rural de Santa Catarina S.A. (EPAGRI), Florianópolis, Brazil.

Carter, Michael R., Bradford Barnham, and Dina Mesbah. 1996. Agricultural Export Booms and Rural Poor in Chile, Guatemala, and Paraguay. *Latin American Research Review* 31(1):33–65.

Carvalho, José Márcio. 1996. Comercialização de frutos de qualidade: a importância dos tratamentos pós-Colheita. Master's thesis, Departamento de Administração e Economia, Universidade Federal de Lavras (UFLA), Lavras, Minas Gerais, Brazil.

Cavalcanti, Josefa Salete Barbosa. 1999. Globalização e processos sociais na fruticultura de exportação do Vale do São Francisco. In *Globalização, trabalho, e meio ambiente: mudanças socioeconômicas em regiões frutículas para exportação,* ed. Josefa Salete Barbosa Cavalcanti. Recife, Brazil: Editora Universitária da Universidade Federal de Pernambuco.

Collins, Jane L. 1995. Farm Size and Non-traditional Exports: Determinants of Participation in World Markets. *World Development* 23(7):1103–1114.

Damiani, Octavio. 1999. Beyond Market Failures: Irrigation, the State, and Non-traditional Agriculture in Northeast Brazil. Ph.D. dissertation, Department of Urban Studies and Planning, Massachusetts Institute of Technology, Cambridge, Mass.

Dolan, Catherine, and John Humphrey. 2001. Changing Governance Patterns in the Trade of Fresh Vegetables between Africa and the United Kingdom. Unpublished paper, Institute of Development Studies, University of Sussex, Brighton, U.K.

Echeverría, Ruben G. 1998. Agricultural Research Policy Issues in Latin America: An Overview. *World Development* 26(6):1103–1111.

Farina, Elizabeth M. M. Q. 2002. Consolidation, Multinationalisation, and Competition in the Supermarket and Processing Sectors in Brazil:

Impacts on Horticulture and Dairy Products. *Development Policy Review* 20(4):317–334.

Federação da Indústria do Estado de Santa Catarina (FIESC). 2001. *Cultura da maçã brasileira*. Florianópolis, Brazil: FIESC.

Gasques, José Garcia. 2001. *Gastos públicos na agricultura*. Texto para Discussão No. 782, Instituto de Pesquisa Econômica Aplicada (IPEA), Brasília.

Gereffi, Gary. 1994. The Organization of Buyer-Driven Global Commodity Chains: How US Retailers Shape Overseas Production Networks. In *Commodity Chains and Global Capitalism*, ed. Gary Gereffi and Miguel Korzeniewicz. Westport, Conn.: Praeger.

Gertler, Meric S., David A. Wolfe, and David Garkut. 2000. No Place like Home? The Embeddedness of Innovation in a Regional Economy. *Review of International Political Economy* 7(4):688–718.

Gibbon, Peter. 2001. Upgrading Primary Production: A Global Commodity Chain Approach. *World Development* 29(2):345–363.

———. 2003. Value-Chain Governance, Public Regulation and Entry Barriers in the Global Fresh Fruit and Vegetable Chain into the EU. *Development Policy Review* 21(5–6):615–625.

Gomes, Raquel. 1996. Socioeconomic, Management, and Institutional Determinants of Technical Efficiency: The Case of Small Producers in Irrigated Agriculture in Northeast Brazil. Master's thesis, Department of Agricultural Economics, University of Arizona.

———. 1999. Unexpected Growth and Unintended Spillovers: The Making of the Melon Industry in Mossoró-Assú, Northeast Brazil. First-year doctoral paper, Department of Urban Studies and Planning, Massachusetts Institute of Technology, Cambridge, Mass.

———. 2004. Farming for Supermarkets: Its Collective Good Problems and What Brazilian Growers Have Done about Them. Doctoral dissertation, Department of Urban Studies and Planning, Massachusetts Institute of Technology, Cambridge, Mass.

Gomes da Silva, Aldenôr. 1992. *A parceria na agricultura irrigada no Baixo Açu*. Natal, Rio Grande do Norte RN: Centro de Ciências Humanas, Letras e Artes, Universidade Federal do Rio Grande do Norte (UFRN).

Gomes da Silva, Aldenôr, Joaquim Araújo, Kelly Soares, Robson Braga, and Olga Moura. 1997. Agroindústria e identidade de classe no pólo da fruticultura irrigada do Rio Grande do Norte. Núcleo de Estudos Rurais, Universidade Federal do Rio Grande do Norte.

Hayami, Yujiro, and Vernon W. Ruttan. 1985. *Agricultural Development: An International Perspective.* Baltimore: Johns Hopkins University Press.

Hentschke, Roque. 1994. *Maçã: estudo da situação catarinense frente ao MERCOSUL.* Documento No. 148, Empresa de Pesquisa Agropecuária e Extensão Rural de Santa Catarina S.A. (EPAGRI), Florianópolis, Brazil.

Humphrey, John, and Antje Oeter. 1999. Strategies for Diversifying and Adding Value to Food Exports: A Value Chain Perspective. Institute of Development Studies, University of Sussex, Brighton, U.K. Unpublished.

Humphrey, John, and Hubert Schmitz. 2000. *Governance and Upgrading: Linking Industrial Cluster and Global Value Chain Research.* Working Paper No. 120, Institute of Development Studies, University of Sussex, Brighton, U.K.

Jarvis, Lovell S. 1994. Changing Private and Public Roles in Technological Development: Lessons from the Chilean Fruit Sector. In *Agricultural Technology: Policy Issues for the International Community,* ed. Jock R. Anderson. Wallingford, U.K.: CAB International.

Locke, Richard. 1995. *Remaking the Italian Economy.* Ithaca, N.Y.: Cornell University Press.

Marsden, Terry. 1997. Creating Space for Food: The Distinctiveness of Recent Agrarian Development. In *Globalizing Food: Agrarian Questions and Global Restructuring,* ed. David Goodman and Michael Watts. London: Routledge.

Maxwell, Simon, and Adrian Fernando. 1989. Cash Crops in Developing Countries: The Issues, the Facts, the Politics. *World Development* 17(11):1677–1708.

Miranda, Frederico Cristino, ed. 1989. *Project de irrigação Vale do Massangano (Senador Nilo Coelho): relatório de avaliação ex-post.* Brasília: Companhia de Desenvolvimento do Vale do São Francisco (CODEVASF).

Nadvi, Khalid, and Hubert Schmitz. 1999. Clustering and Industrialization: Introduction. *World Development* 27(9):1503–1514.

Olinger, Glauco. 1996. *Ascensão e decadência da extensão rural no Brasil.* Florianópolis, Brazil: Empresa de Pesquisa Agropecuária e Extensão Rural de Santa Catarina, S.A. (EPAGRI).

Perry, Martin, Richard Le Heron, David J. Hayward, and Ian Cooper. 1997. Growing Discipline through Total Quality Management in a New Zealand Horticulture Region. *Journal of Rural Studies* 13(3):289–304.

Portugal, Alberto Duque, and Elísio Contini. 1997. O público e o privado na pesquisa agropecuária brasileira. In *Resumo dos Anais do XXXV Congresso Brasileiro de Economia e Sociologia Rural.* Brasília: Sociedade Brasileira e Economia e Sociologia Rural.

Pray, Carl E., and Dina Umali-Deininger. 1998. The Private Sector in Agricultural Research Systems: Will It Fill the Gap? *World Development* 26(6):1127–1148.

Reardon, Thomas, and Elizabeth Farina. 2001. The Rise of Food Quality and Safety Standards: Illustrations from Brazil. Paper presented at the International Food and Agribusiness Association Food and Agribusiness Symposium, Sydney, June 27.

Reardon, Thomas, C. Peter Timmer, and Julio A. Berdegue. 2003. The Rise of Supermarkets in Latin America and Asia: Implications for International Markets for Fruits and Vegetables. In *Global Markets for High Value Food Products,* ed. Anita Regmi and Mark Gelhars. Washington, D.C.: USDA/ERS.

Schmitz, Hubert. 1995. Small Shoemakers and Fordist Giants: Tale of a Supercluster. *World Development* 23(1):9–28.

Tendler, Judith. 1984. The Well-Tempered Capitalist: Profiles from Bolivian Coops. *Journal of the Inter-American Foundation* 8(2):37–47.

———. 1999. Thoughts for a Research Agenda. Paper presented at the Workshop on Public–Private Partnerships, University of Michigan, Ann Arbor, Mich., June 25.

———. 2001a. Comments on "Governance and Upgrading" paper, Part 3, for Workshop on Local Upgrading in Global Chains, Department of Urban Studies and Planning, Massachusetts Institute of Technology, Cambridge, Mass.

———. 2001b. *Transforming Local Economies: Lessons from the Northeast Brazilian Experience*. Working Paper No. 4, Joint Massachusetts Institute of Technology (MIT)/Development Bank of Northeast Brazil (BNB) Research Project on Rethinking Regional Policy in Northeast Brazil, Department of Urban Studies and Planning, Massachusetts Institute of Technology, Cambridge, Mass.

Thrupp, Lori Ann. 1994. New Harvests, Old Problems: Feeding the Global Supermarket. *NACLA Report on the Americas* 23(3):22–27.

CHAPTER 4

The Salmon Farming and Processing Cluster in Southern Chile

Claudio Maggi Campos

The recent expansion of industrial salmon farming in Chile has had a significant impact on the production, labor, and socioeconomic conditions of the Tenth Region (or Lake Region), providing more than 40,000 direct and indirect jobs today. More than 85 percent of national salmon production is concentrated in this area and, because of the geographic possibilities for expansion, which include the neighboring northern Aysén region, that percentage could increase to 98 percent. The southern salmon industry is devoted mostly to exports. Between 2001 and 2002, the industry's annual exports totaled nearly US$1 billion. Salmon and trout products accounted for more than 70 percent of the total value of exports of the regions of Los Lagos and Aysén (ProChile, 2000). According to available production data, in 2001 the region produced more than 25 percent of the world's pond-farmed salmon and trout (Infante, 2002, using statistics from SalmónChile).

The purpose of this chapter is to examine the development, challenges, and prospects of the salmon farming and processing cluster in Chile's southern region. The first section offers a general history of the cluster and the stages it has gone through to reach its current level of development. The second section describes the value chain that is at the heart of the cluster. Then we examine the main sources of external economies, collective efficiency, governance models, and types of upgrading at the various stages of cluster development. Finally, policy guidelines are proposed to stimulate the competitive development of the SMEs that comprise the cluster.

General History of the Salmon Cluster

The salmon and trout farming and processing industry is concentrated in the southern part of the Los Lagos region (Tenth Region, provinces of Llanquihue and Chiloé), located about 1,000 kilometers south of Santiago, and, to a lesser extent, in the northern part of Aysén region. More than 500 salmon farming centers currently operate in an area of about 200 square kilometers between latitude 42° and 43°30′ South. The area includes lakes, shores, and the inland sea of the island of Chiloé. The main city and regional capital is Puerto Montt, with a population of 210,000 and population growth of nearly 50 percent between 1992 and 2002.

The boom of salmon farming has brought new life to the local economy, which was based on traditional fishing, mollusk farming and harvesting, traditional agriculture, and summer tourism. According to estimates from SalmónChile, the salmon industry supports about 28,000 direct jobs and more than 12,500 indirect jobs in the region. The direct jobs are located in processing plants (50 percent), fattening farms (33 percent), and hatcheries (15 percent). The indirect jobs are in direct supply businesses located around the hatcheries, farming centers, and processing plants. In the last decade, there has been significant expansion of both commercial and personal services, established mostly in the cities of Puerto Montt, Puerto Varas, and Isla Grande de Chiloé.

The industry has grown rapidly, reaching an average annual expansion rate of 25 percent in the last 10 years, as shown in Table 4.1.

Evolution of Global Supply and Demand

The salmon farming production boom in Chile's southern region is part of a global trend of continuous growth in seafood production, which in

Table 4.1. Chile and Tenth Region: Evolution of Farmed Salmon and Trout Production
(weight of eviscerated product)

Year	Production of farmed salmon and trout in Chile (thousands of tons)	Chile's percentage of world farmed salmon production	Tenth Region estimated production (thousands of tons)	Total export value (US$ millions FOB)
1987	2	1.5%	1	8.0
1990	26	7.9%	20	140.0
1993	69	17.1%	60	291.4
1996	165	24.4%	150	525.0
1999	201	22.1%	180	817.8
2001	405	32.4%	350	964.3

Source: Infante (2002), using statistics from SalmónChile.

the last three decades has become the world's fastest-growing food production sector.

Only in 1997 did farmed salmon come to represent the largest share of the worldwide supply of salmon and trout. While wild-salmon fishing has remained stable at 600 to 800 gross tons per year, the global production of farmed salmon increased 70-fold between 1981 and 2000, when production exceeded one million tons.

The three main producers, Norway, Chile, and Scotland, generate 80 percent of the world's supply of farmed salmon. While Norway increased its production 160 percent between 1990 and 2000, Chilean production increased more than 900 percent.

According to international estimates for the 1995–2000 period, salmon consumption increased at an annual average rate of 14 percent in the European Union and 20 percent in the United States. For the 2000–2005 period, slightly lower market rates were expected, which should continue into 2005–2010. The Japanese market would at 2010 be at the peak of its demand and therefore should not show significant consumption increases in the future.[1]

[1] The Japanese market is the main destination of trout and Coho salmon, which today represent slightly over 50 percent of the volume of Chilean salmon exports.

Cluster Development Stages

The quick expansion of the salmon industry in this region can be attributed to a combination of natural and acquired external economies. First, this region has favorable natural conditions, including optimal hydrographic conditions for salmon farming and seasons opposite to those of the main producing countries and consumption centers, which initially stimulated the export of fresh products. Secondly, the environment offers unpolluted waters, and natural light is available even during winter months, because of a more equatorial latitude than production centers in Northern Europe. Third, critical supplies, including energy and food supplies needed for farming—mainly flour and fish oil from the Eighth Region, 500 kilometers away—are readily available by sea and land from nearby supply centers. A fourth advantage of this region is its human resources: entrepreneurial, university-educated professionals who are ready to participate in medium-risk projects were initially attracted from the central region of the country.[2] And, since the start of fish farming activities, a labor force familiar with the fishing trade in the region[3] and competitive in terms of cost/productivity has been available. Fifth, the region offers a coherent institutional framework. The judicial, administrative, and economic structure, from the outset, have not interfered with the development of activities such as the awarding of coastal concessions by public authorities and with overall "light" regulations. Since the mid-1980s, public support has increased in the areas of health, commercialization, and technology transfer. In terms of technology transfer, two fundamental initiatives were those of Fundación Chile and its affiliate Salmones Antártica, as well as the setting up of the experimental fish farm by the Fishery Development

---

[2] The majority of the first generation of investors in the Chilean salmon industry (1982–1986) were entrepreneurs or national business groups; some were already established in the region, but most were from Santiago. They allocated excess funds from other areas of business (industry, construction, forestry, industrial fishing), attracted by a combination of promising prospects and an undeniable attraction for the region, with its promise of a better quality of life.

[3] On the island of Chiloé alone there were 103 fishing villages and more than 5,500 traditional fishermen.

Institute (Instituto de Fomento Pesquero, or IFOP) in the Aysén region (Pietrobelli, 1998).

Three stages in the life cycle of the cluster have been identified (Table 4.2). The first stage, cluster formation (or the initial learning period) corresponds to the time when initial efforts were made to exploit the comparative advantages that made the establishment of the business possible. The success of this stage was confirmed when, in 1985, the first 1,000 tons for export were produced, and a year later when the Association of Salmon and Trout Producers was formed. In Chile, the initial push for salmon farming was supported by state organizations, but an actual government policy was never established. Rather, the initial development of salmon farming was the result of a collective learning process initiated by the pioneering actions of a public–private institution and supported by foreign demand factors and a horizontal development policy on exports.[4]

The pioneering industrial activities that date back to the mid-1970s were of an experimental nature. In 1974, the North American company Union Carbide, through its affiliate Domsea Farms Chile, launched production with imported eggs. This first attempt, made on the island of Chiloé, was a ranching system, or ocean ranching. The volatility of earnings, along with a series of climatic misfortunes, discouraged further investments in this production system. In 1981, Fundación Chile purchased the facilities of Domsea Farms and created Salmones Antártica, which in 1998 was the first company to exceed production of 1,000 annual tons.

In 1986, 17 national producers formed the Chilean Association of Salmon and Trout Producers.[5] In its early years, the association addressed two basic issues: marketing and a quality seal. Because initial exports were mostly fresh products, the trading price varied depending on the producers' urgency to sell, especially since this was an "exotic" supply in

[4] In the case of Chile, the milestones that mark the beginning of this phase are, between 1982 and 1983, the creation of the Export Promotion Office, the devaluation of the peso, and the sustained adoption of a high exchange rate.

[5] Now known as the Chilean Salmon Industry Association (SalmónChile). It has 32 affiliated production companies, which combined represent more than 70 percent of the industry's production.

Table 4.2. Life Cycle Stages of the Chilean Salmon Cluster

	Initiation **From 1978 (50 tons)** **to 1985 (900 tons)** **Price: US$9–10/kg.**	**Maturity** **From 1986 (1,350 tons)** **to 1995 (143,000 tons)** **Price: US$4–5/kg.**	**Globalization** **From 1996 (150,000 tons)** **to present (400,000 tons)** **Price: US$2.8–4.5/kg.**
Primary objective	• Survival of fish and sale of product	• Increase production volumes	• Increase productivity
Distribution channels	• Direct sales and cooperatives	• Brokers • Association of national producers (Salmoexport)	• Wholesalers (supermarkets) • Strategic alliances or integration with end-markets
Technological channels	• Experimental fish hatchery • Fattening expertise	• Backward linkages (fish hatchery) • Quality certification • Increase production scale	• Domestic production of eggs • Forward linkages (process) • Control on production cycle of salmon • Automated control systems of parameters (water, light, etc.) • Vaccines and food • Sustainability of the system
Public policy	• Regulation • Technology transfer • Precompetitive investment and research	• Infrastructure • Marketing and promotion • Supplier technological development and innovation (cages, nets, and food)	• Environmental management • Increase productivity and technology transfers • Biotechnology (diseases and genetic management)
Type of business at core of cluster	• Small- and medium-sized enterprises	• Small- and medium-sized enterprises • Presence of foreign groups	• Large enterprises (integration and concentration)
Type of supply companies in cluster	• Few and unstable; businesses tend to self-supply to meet their needs	• Increase outsourcing; local businesses become more specialized	• Specialized, local SMEs • Significant presence of highly specialized international companies
Social capital framework	• Public and private pioneering efforts	• Association among producers	• Production system inserted in the global chain of production–marketing

Source: Adapted and updated from Maggi, Montero, and Parra (2000).

a market that was traditionally dominated by producers in the Northern Hemisphere. The association managed to coordinate the trading process by regulating the quality standards of export shipments, using a seal that was voluntarily accepted by all producers, as was done in other producing countries such as Norway and Scotland. The quality seal made it possible for Chilean production to be approved based on its quality, because a minimum quality limit was established for all producers, independent of whether or not they were affiliates of the association. Fundación Chile was the organization in charge of defining the standards and strictly implementing the requirements (Pietrobelli, 1998).

The sector entered a second phase of maturity, in which the challenge was no longer to successfully achieve the fattening of salmon, but to achieve the higher levels of production required by the new conditions of the global market. This involved significant changes to the installed capacity of farming centers, as well as the establishment of distribution channels. In 1990, a group of national producers joined to create Salmoexport, an export company that managed to bring together 13 national salmon companies,[6] which at the time represented 30 percent of Chilean production. The company's main objective was to launch a more intense marketing effort by promoting products and opening up new markets. During this period, the foreign companies present in the region enjoyed import royalties and special subsidies and had already more or less consolidated their market position, since their products were being sold by the parent companies to which they belonged.[7] Although Salmoexport was in business for only three years, it brought visibility to national enterprises and contributed to increasing the professionalism of the marketing activities of Chilean companies. The development phase ended with two external impacts: the Asian crisis and dumping accusations made by Alaskan producers.

The third phase—globalization of the cluster—marks a departure from the previous cycles, with the larger companies surviving, generally

---

[6] These include Tecmar, Cultivos Marinos Chiloé, Robinson Crusoe, Aucar, and Salmones Andes.

[7] These companies include Nishiro (Japanese), Salmones Antártica, Marine Harvest, and Mares Australes.

getting external funds, and participating in the farming, processing, and commercial phases.

The Value Chains

The structure of the salmon cluster production chain is comprised of three subsystems: the "core" of the chain, the supply company subsystem, and the subsystem of support institutions (Figure 4.1). What we call the "core" of the chain includes the three fundamental stages of the production process. First is the production of eggs, fry, and smolts, which is the fresh water production stage. The stage lasts an average of one year and concludes when the fish reach the smolt stage (juveniles between 85 and 100 grams). The fattening and harvest production stage takes place in seawater, in the farming centers. The stage lasts approximately 9 months for Pacific salmon (specimens of 2.8 to 3 kilograms) and between 15 and 18 months for Atlantic salmon (4.5 to 5 kilograms).The third processing stage corresponds to the development of the final product in processing plants.

The support industry subsystem consists of suppliers of salmon feed; equipment, supplies, and fish farming infrastructure; equipment for processing plants; pharmacological supplies and ichthyopathology services; loading, transportation, and maintenance services; and packing and crating.

Finally, the institutional subsystem encompasses regulatory bodies (Sernapesca, Conama, Environmental Health Service, Directemar, Labor Inspection); development institutions (Corfo, Sence, ProChile, etc.); universities (Austral, Los Lagos) and other R&D and technology transfer centers, such as the Instituto Tecnológico del Salmón (Salmon Technology Institute, or INTESAL);[8] financial services; and organizations in the category that includes transportation and maritime logistic services, such as SalmónChile and Arasemar.

---

[8] Owned by SalmónChile.

Figure 4.1. Production Chain of the Salmon Cluster in Southern Chile

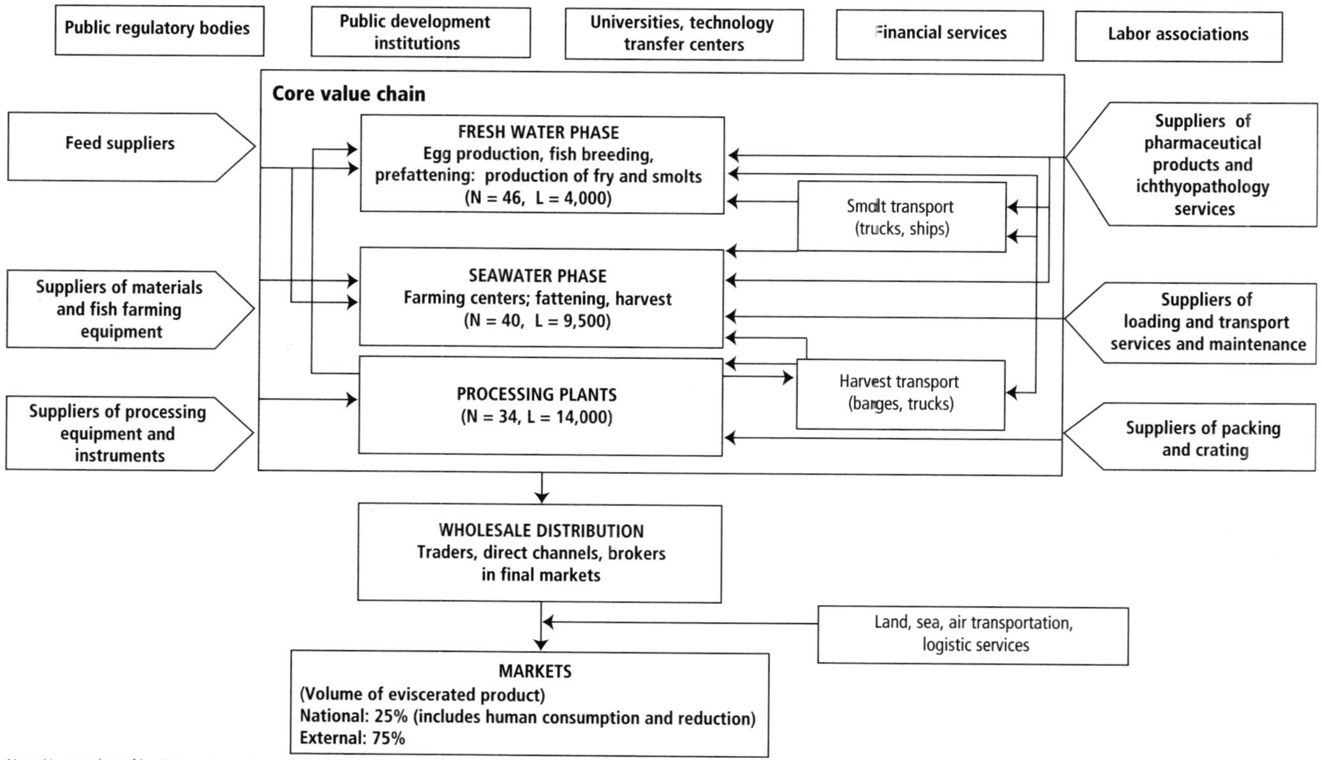

Note: N = number of businesses; L = estimated direct employment.

Figure 4.2. Production Cost Structure of Fresh Atlantic Salmon Filet

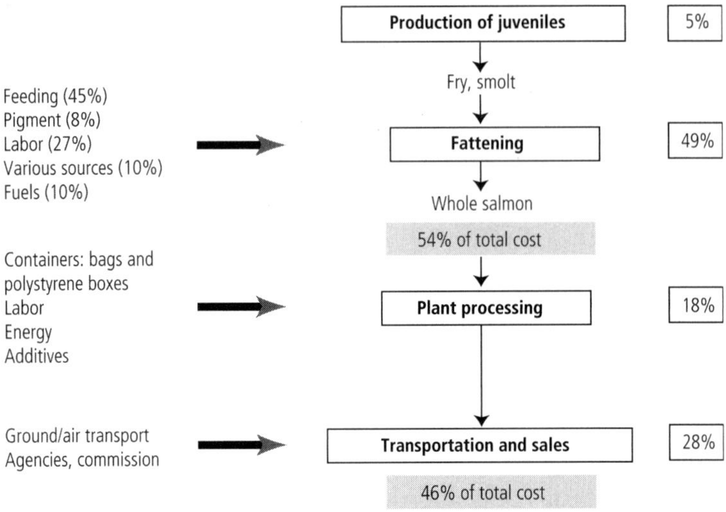

Source: Vidal (2002).
Note: Fresh Atlantic salmon filets represent about one-third of the total value of exports of the cluster.

Figure 4.2 shows the typical structure of production and distribution costs of a representative product supplied by the cluster. It shows the dominance of the fattening stage, or seawater farming, which accounts for almost 50 percent of the total cost. Within that stage, feed represents 45 percent of the cost, that is, 22 percent of the total cost, including wholesale distribution.

Considering the number of businesses and jobs created, the Chilean salmon cluster groups together account for more than 210 businesses distributed through the core of the value chain and the subsystem of supply industries. In addition, there are at least another 100 goods and services firms in the area that offer occasional or partial services to the cluster. Table 4.3 shows the predominance of firms vertically integrated along the core of the cluster's value chain. Vertical integration has grown over the last six years, as the cluster has entered the globalization stage.

Table 4.3. Number of Firms and Jobs in Cluster

Subsystem	Industry	Number of independent firms	Number of integrated firms[a]	Total	Jobs (estimated, December 2001)
Core of production chain	Fish farming (hatchery)	5	19	24	4,000
	Prefattening, lake center,	10	31	41	9,500
	cultivation centers	9	31	40	14,000
	Processing	6	28	34	1,000
	Subtotal	30	36[a]	66[a]	28,500
Direct supply industries (estimate)	Feed suppliers	3	2	5	800
	Equipment, farming materials	50		50	3,300
	Pharmaceuticals, ichthyopathology	20		20	900
	suppliers	30		30	3,200
	Suppliers of processing equipment	12		12	1,000
	Packing, crating, harvesting, transportation, maintenance suppliers	30		30	3,300
	Subtotal	145	2	147	12,500

Sources: Number of firms: Elaborated by the author with information from SalmónChile, Sernapesca, and Aguilar (2002); Employment: Estimates derived from information in Infante (2002) and Vidal (2002).

[a] Integrated firms are those that comprise at least 2 percent of the processes in the core of the value chain. Affiliate businesses are also included in this category, even if they operate under different corporate names in each phase of the chain. Therefore, the numbers under "Integrated firms" and "Total" are less than the total of those participating in each phase of the value chain core.

With regard to professional qualification, it is interesting to note that, according to estimates from Fundación Chinquihue,[9] 76 percent of the workforce employed in the processing plants is either completely unqualified or possesses a low level of qualification. According to the same source, the ratio of professionals to specialized technicians in the

[9] A training and industrial services facility created with Japanese cooperation.

local salmon industry is six to one, which is the exact inverse of the current ratio for Norwegian or Scottish industries (one to six). Also, despite advances in productivity, much of the businesses' competitiveness is still based on pyramidal labor structures, with the base receiving very low salaries. According to our sources, over the last three years the reduction of operational margins in the industry has resulted in wage stagnation and even erosion for professionals, technicians, and operators.

Size Distribution and Foreign Capital Participation

In the mid-1990s there were more than 100 businesses operating in the region in the farming and sea fattening phases alone. Since then, the tendency to increase the average size of nurseries has led to a process of constant mergers and acquisitions that has brought the number of businesses down to 40.

Most of the larger companies have incorporated the different production phases into their firms, whether through acquisition or association with existing businesses or by investing directly in earlier or later phases of the process. This trend toward consolidation is taking place at a global scale. Thus, of the nearly 600 businesses operating worldwide in 1994, fewer than 280 remained in 1999.[10]

According to recent estimates, foreign capital accounts for about 36 percent of the total investment value of the core of the chain (Infante, 2002). However, if we take into consideration the supply industries, that percentage would most likely be significantly higher. Most notably, in the feed supply industry, four of the five businesses in operation belong to Dutch and Norwegian groups. The presence of foreign capital in the cluster increases mainly because of the need for greater financial capacity required to operate in the industry. Similarly, the demand for greater operational efficiency attracts foreign suppliers of equipment and technologies, which set up subsidiaries and representatives in the region.

---

[10] Statistics obtained from the Nutreco Web site (www.nutreco.com).

Three types of production industries can be observed in the cluster's core (Table 4.4). The first group is comprised of six businesses with annual production of more than 25,000 tons and sales over US$50 million per year. These businesses are fully vertically integrated from egg production to marketing at the final destination. They also have personnel devoted to R&D. In the last few years, the largest firm, which was originally Scottish, was acquired by the Dutch group Trouw-Nutreco; three others have incorporated key U.S., Japanese, and Norwegian partners in recent years, while the remaining two are open corporations, with majority ownership by national conglomerates.

The second group corresponds to six firms with majority ownership by national (generally not regional) capital that reach production levels that are considered high by international standards, between 15,000 and 25,000 tons per year, with yearly sales between US$20 million and US$40 million. Typically, they belong to multisector consortia, which provide them with working capital and important financial backing to undertake investment expansions and technology acquisitions.

A third group consists of 20 businesses of medium size by global standards, family owned, mostly from the southern region, which have grown gradually and faced the need to expand their capital structure in order to meet investment demands of the industry. Many businesses in this group have been bought out by larger ones. Like the larger businesses, these firms have become vertically integrated in the last few years, and thus their average size is considerably larger today than 5 or 10 years ago.

Until 5 years ago, the fish farms were held by independent businesses. However, despite the high level of specialization this phase requires, these farms have been gradually bought out by medium-sized and large businesses that own hatchery centers and maintain the farms as independently operating centers. Of the 46 firms that operate in the development of eggs and the fresh water phase today, only 15 are not forwardly integrated.

The high level of specialization of salmon feed producers must be emphasized. Over the past six years, they have undergone a process of

Table 4.4. Main Businesses in Salmon Cluster in Southern Chile

Name of business/group	Product (location)	Value of exports 2001 (US$ millions FOB)	Capital structure/recent changes
GrupoTrouw–Chile (Nutreco–Holland)	Feed (Osorno). Fish-farming, processing, commercialization (Lgo. Llanquihue, Puerto Montt, Chiloé).	240.0	Multinational corporation with Dutch capital. Trades on the Amsterdam Stock Exchange. Deals with sales to Trouw-Chile (feed) and Marine Harvest (salmon). Has acquired production businesses in Norway, Scotland (Marine Harvest), and Chile (Mares Australes).
Ewos–Chile (Norway)	Feed (Chiloé and Coronel, Eighth Region).	115.0	Multinational corporation with mostly Norwegian capital. Operates an R&D experimental station in Chiloé.
Grupo Aqua Chile (Chile–United States)	Fish breeding, farming and processing, commercialization (Gala, Puerto Cisnes, Chiloé, Puerto Montt).	100.0	Holding consisting of Chilean and U.S. capital. Initially a joint venture between Pacífico Sur (Chile) and Aquafarms (United States). Incorporated Piscicultura AquaChile in 1998 and bought Salmopack (processing plant) in 2000.
Camanchaca S.A.	Fish breeding, farming and processing (Puerto Montt, Chiloé).	75.0	Firm associated with industrial fishing. Chilean capital. Publicly traded corporation.
Multiexport S.A. (Chile–Japan)	Fish breeding, farming, processing, commercialization (Puerto Montt, Chiloé).	60.0	Holding. National capital. Recent strategic partnership with Grupo Mitsui Co. Ltd. (Japan).
Salmofood S.A.	Feed (Chiloé).	60.0	Created in 1993 with support from farming companies: Aguas Claras, Invertec, Aucar, and Tecmar. Invertec is principal shareholder today.
Mainstream S.A.	Fish breeding, farming, processing (Chiloé).	56.3	National, S.A. Publicly traded. Eblen Fly. controls 70% of ownership. Bought assets from Aucar.

(continued on next page)

Table 4.4. Main Businesses in Salmon Cluster in Southern Chile (continued)

Name of business/group	Product (location)	Value of sales/ export 2001 (US$ millions FOB)	Capital structure/recent changes
Fjord Seafood Chile (Norway–Chile)	Fish breeding, farming, processing, commercialization (Aysén, Chiloé, Puerto Montt).	53.6	Norwegian capital. Recently acquired by Tecmar Ltda. and Linao Ltda.
Alitec (Holland)	Foodstuffs (Pargua, Chiloé).	50.0	Belongs to the Dutch corporation Provimi.
Salmones Antártica (Japan)	Farming, processing (Aysén, Chiloé).	45.0	Created by Fundación Chile in 1981, sold to a Japanese corporation at the end of the 1980s.
Biomar S.A. (Chile–Norway)	Foodstuffs (Puerto Montt).	42.0	Mainly Norwegian capital. Publicly traded.
Cultivos Marinos Chiloé	Farming, processing (Chiloé, Aysén).	40.0	Belongs to a national holding with investments in the real estate and hotel sectors. Group began in 1980s thanks to Corfo loans.
Aguas Claras S.A.	Fish breeding, farming, processing (smoked).	37.0	Acquired by Antarfish (Chilean holding). Founding partner of Salmofood.
Invertec–Mar de Chiloé	Fish breeding, farming, processing (Chiloé).	35.0	National capital, family owned (Montanari family). Founding partner of Salmofood. Holding structure. Sole of the larger ones not associated with SalmónChile.
Los Fiordos Ltda.	Fish breeding, farming, hatchery, processing, commercialization (Chiloé, Aysén).	35.0	Part of an agricultural industry national holding, Agrosuper. Part of its production targets national market. Commercializes the "Super salmón" brand.
Ventisqueros	Fish breeding, farming, processing (Puerto Montt).	25.0	National capital.
Trading Unimarc	Farming, processing, commercialization (Chiloé).	25.0	National, Errázuriz family.

intense concentration and control by foreign capital. In the early 1990s, there were 22 firms, of which only five survive today as a result of various mergers and bankruptcies. Of these five, only one is held by national investors, while the remaining four belong to transnational corporations from Norway and the Netherlands. The integration strategies of these enterprises differ regardless of whether they are nationally or foreign-owned. For example, the multinational corporation Trouw-Nutreco integrated all the production phases when it acquired the Scottish firm Marine Harvest in a global deal that included all of the facilities in the Tenth Region. Salmonfood pursued an initiative that began as an association with national producers in an attempt to ensure supply and quality of the input that most affected production costs; today, Invertec controls the majority of shares of Salmonfood. Alitec, which was acquired by the Dutch corporation Provimi, followed a different strategy, specializing in the niche of feeds for the fresh water phase.

Value Chain Suppliers

In the early 1980s, when salmon farming at a commercial scale was in its early stages, there was a lack of specialized inputs available in the local market. Facilities were rudimentary: wooden tubs for the fish farms (which today are made of fiberglass or polyvinyl chloride [PVC]), small cages for fattening were built by local carpenters under the supervision of technicians (nowadays cages are made of PVC and conform to complex design specifications), and a large number of people were involved in the operation's logistic support.

By the end of the 1980s, businesses often specialized in one of the central phases of the production chain (egg production, fish farming, salt water fattening, or processing plant), managing most of the direct support activities (logistics, transportation, laboratory, vaccines) within the firm.

Today, the structure is the opposite. The firms have been integrated along the production chain, but they have also outsourced most of the support services, as their supply has become more consolidated in the region. The change is reflected in the fact that in 1993, there were 21 suppliers of goods and services located in the region, while by 2001, this number had risen to 237.[11] It is estimated that the salmon hatchery and processing industry is the primary client of nearly 150 of these businesses.

These tendencies have altered the structure of interbusiness relationships within the cluster. With integrated, larger firms dominating the cluster, the relationship between them and local suppliers—particularly small and medium-sized businesses—now involves increased irregularity and business discontinuation, pressuring the operating margins of local suppliers and discouraging investment in training, technological upgrading, and in some instances, professionalization of services. This has opened a space for opportunistic practices by free riders, who have secured a demand for services through cost advantages reached through noncompliance with standards, usually related to labor regulations.

That is not the case in the relations that predominate between salmon producing firms and international suppliers of goods, food, and specialized equipment, because in those instances negotiation tends to be more balanced. In the case of food suppliers and small producers, the relationship tends to be the opposite, because the feed producers offer loans in exchange for the sale of the supplies, to be paid after the harvest. Such financial dependency grants the feed supplier some influence over the client firm's production and marketing decisions.

Cluster Sales and Exports

More than 95 percent of the production of the salmon cluster goes to foreign markets. Currently, more than 60 countries are export destinations, but with a strong concentration in the United States and Japan, markets

[11] Data from Fundación Chile (1994–2002). Data include businesses with parent companies or affiliates located in the Lake Region.

which together represent more than 80 percent of the value of Chilean exports. Exports to the United States are more processed and have higher value added (boneless fillets, portions), which is reflected in their value per unit.

The development of strategies to diversify markets is an explicit objective undertaken by the Asociación de Industrias del Salmón (SalmónChile), which is headquartered in Puerto Montt and Santiago. In order to achieve market diversification, SalmónChile receives support from the state for export promotion from ProChile, but there is consensus that value-added marketing is not enough to position a product/country image (Infante, 2002). An annual investment of some US$10 million (1 percent of exports) would be needed in order to achieve that goal, an amount that is comparatively low at the international level, compared with other food products. However, it is estimated that the total investment in marketing does not exceed US$1 million per year today.[12]

From the start, the cluster imported mostly capital goods and intermediate technology-intensive goods such as machinery, farming equipment, and genetic materials (eggs). Since the mid-1990s there has been some degree of import substitution through the development of equipment and machinery in Chile and imitations of foreign models adapted to local conditions, as well as the arrival of an important number of international suppliers offering specialized technical support in the region. As for egg production, the increased seasonally adjusted national production capacity[13] is regulated by the Fishing Ministry, which, since the end of 2000, has restricted imports. As a result, imports dropped from 113 million in 2000 to around 32 million in 2001, while national production was approximately 350 million units.

---

[12] This includes promotion in fairs, promotion focused on markets and segments (such as hotels and restaurants), tasting sessions, organization of gastronomical events, advertising support at points of sale, and generic advertising in specialized publications.

[13] Through the management of photo- and thermal periods.

Collective Efficiency in the Cluster Development Phases

In addition to the external factors described above that acted as catalysts for the formation of the cluster, a series of collective initiatives and actions were undertaken more or less intentionally in the first two development stages of the cluster, between 1984 and 1993. The three most significant factors and actions that formed the base of collective efficiency in the cluster are collective organization capacity, technology training, and development of local supply of goods and services (Table 4.5). Collective organization capacity was demonstrated by the early creation of the Association of Salmon and Trout Producers,[14] an organization that led important collective actions. The association was responsible for convincing governing bodies to establish a minimal distance between coastal concessions for farming; the self-regulation of processing standards, later adopted by the sector authority (Sernapesca) to regulate quality standards in processing plants; and a promotional campaign, together with producers from Canada and Alaska, for salmon consumption in the United States. Today, the association represents its members before regulatory bodies concerning regulatory matters such as possible modifications to maritime concession regulations and defends members in situations such as accusations of dumping. Technology training is important at both local and national levels. There is a gradual development of local capacity to cover certain critical links in the value chain—such as the supply of fish eggs—by taking advantage of favorable conditions in nearby areas, public investment in the development of certain capabilities, and the ability of national businesses to attract foreign expertise, particularly by bringing in experts during the learning phase, and later by organizing periodic technical missions abroad by local enterprises with support from the public sector.[15] Moreover, there is an effort at the

---

[14] APSTCH, formed in 1986 and recently renamed SalmónChile, in order to include cluster suppliers.

[15] Support in the organization of these missions has come from cofinancing and cooperation through public agencies such as Corfo and ProChile.

Table 4.5. Collective Actions in the Chilean Salmon Cluster

Stage	Collective action and actors involved	Cause/incentive	Financing	Results
Initial learning	National producers: Salmoexport training.	Valued in target markets through a quality seal for exported products.	Private (90%). Contributions from firms, direct support from Fundación Chile (US$150 million/year).	*Satisfactory:* ends after 4–5 years, once Chile is positioned as global supplier.
Initial learning/ maturing	APSTCH: cooperation with regulatory authorities to establish a minimum distinction between harvest concessions and processing standards.	To aid sustainability of the activity and avoid erosion of comparative advantages.	Private (100%). Contributions from association member firms.	*Adequate:* industry meets norms.
Maturity	APSTCH and ProChile: promotional campaigns for salmon consumption in the United States together with Alaskan and Canadian producers. Also present in other markets.	Market development.	Public/private (50%/50%). ProChile and support from firms, channeled through the association (US$600 million).	*Optimal:* consumption rates increased in United States over 20% per year. Campaigns were ended in 1997.
Maturity	APSTCH: creation of the Salmon Technology Institute (INTESAL) (1994).	Development of local capacity for development and technology transfer.	Public/private (70%/30%). Corfo-Fontec channels support from firms to the association (US$1 billion for start-up and initial operations).	*Average:* despite important public support, firms favor developments that support their own needs. INTESAL has functioned as a job training body.

(continued on next page)

Table 4.5. Collective Actions in the Chilean Salmon Cluster (continued)

Stage	Collective action and actors involved	Cause/incentive	Financing	Results
Maturity, globalization	Five national producers: training and operations. Salmofood (feed producer).	Backward linkage by a group of producing firms.	Public/private (20%/80%). Concerned firms with start-up support from Corfo-Fontec for R&D.	*Important:* Salmofood has become the sole national supplier of salmon feed. Today a single firm is principal shareholder.
Globalization	APSTCH: collective defense against dumping claims.	To defend market position.	Private (100%). The whole industry. Government cooperates with support management (US$400 million).	*Satisfactory:* proper defense managed to keep fines at low levels.
Globalization	INTESAL, various firms, Universidad Austral: permanent water-monitoring program.	Agreement between Universidad Austral (located in Puerto Montt), INTESAL, and a group of firms to perform preventive monitoring for toxic agents in farming areas.	Public/private (50%/50%). Supported by Fondef-Conicyt, which supplies instruments (US$150 million/year).	*Too recent to evaluate:* large number of businesses actively supporting the initiative.
Globalization	Fundación Chinquihue, INTESAL, various firms, regional universities: development of the Chile Califica program to obtain public financing.	Presentation related to the government program Chile Califica, to grant and certify the professional skills of workers and technicians in an industry.	Public/private (70%/30%). Program for labor skills accreditation (US$100 million/year).	*In its initial stage:* selection of applications.
Globalization	SalmónChile, universities, government: signing of voluntary environmental agreement.	To contribute to the sustainability of the activity and avoid erosion of comparative advantages.	Public/private (30%/70%) (US$50 million/year).	*In its initial stage.*

national level to develop a capacity for training of specialized professionals (biochemists, ichthyopathologists, fish farming technicians, administrators specializing in fish farming, etc.) by universities and professional training institutes, located primarily in the region (Austral University, University of Los Lagos, Fundación Chinquihue, INTESAL, and other private educational institutions). A third source of collective efficiency in the cluster is development of local supply of goods and services, such as feeds, vaccines, floating pens, maritime transport, and nets, with an important presence of entrepreneurs from other areas of the country with industrial traditions such as Valparaíso, Bío Bío, and Santiago.

Support Institutions

Three types of institutional action can be identified in the cluster: regulatory activity, promotion and technological development, and education and training of human resources. The regulatory function performs a key role in the expansion of salmon farming production.[16] The importance of this function has been acknowledged by public and private actors since the 1980s, at the early stages of production expansion for commercial purposes. One recent example is the signing of the Collective Agreement on Clean Production (Acuerdo Colectivo de Producción Limpia) by the members of the cluster, SalmónChile, the regulating government authority (Conama), and the Chilean Economic Development Agency (Corfo), shortly after the implementation of the Environmental Regulations for Fish Farming (RAMA), which set environmental regulations for the water areas where activities are carried out. While the adaptation of regulatory institutions and functions to the industry has not been consistent with the industry's

[16] The regulation instruments include concessions and farming authorizations, quarantine and sanitary control for import of eggs and biological species, illness control and prevention, authorization for the introduction of exotic species, maximum sized for fisheries, distance between farms, environmental impact studies for fish farms, and environmental regulations for fish farming (RAMA). Health controls in processing plants are overseen by Sernapesca and the provincial health authorities.

growth, there is a consensus that they have not been major obstacles for development. In the performance of regulatory and control services, the ability of firms to cooperate has been crucial, because firms were aware of the harmful environmental effects that could result from poor control of sanitary aspects and of the possible impact of environmental harm on the industry as a whole.

Although interaction with regulatory bodies is not perceived as a significant problem today, the vast growth of production activities has outpaced all regulatory mechanisms and resources, and so the industry has had to adopt self-regulatory agreements and voluntary initiatives on several occasions. Some important advances in regulatory issues in the last decade include (1) Supreme Decree 604 of 1994, which improved conditions for the granting of coastal concessions and fish farming licenses and discouraged corruption on authorizations; (2) modification of the protocol for the import of salmon eggs in December 2000, establishing restrictions aimed at lowering the risk of introducing exotic diseases; and (3) the entry into force in December 2001 of RAMA, which established controls and mandatory practices to maintain the environmental quality of waters and has unquestionably improved the sector's ability to evaluate and anticipate environmental risks, establishing the conditions for the future evolution of the industry.

Opinion is divided within the cluster concerning the magnitude of the impact of promotional institutions on the evolution and performance of the industry. Nevertheless, it cannot be denied that such institutions played a fundamental role in the industry's start-up[17] and that today their role is reflected in the numerous cluster businesses that have participated in projects financed with public grants, often in association with some of these institutions. These funds were even cited by North American producers to support their dumping accusations against Chilean exporters in 1997.

---

[17] In particular, Fundación Chile, with the operation of Salmones Antártica; and IFOP, which established fish farming in Coihayque.

There has been some evolution in the emphasis of institutional promotion of the salmon cluster over the various phases of the cluster's development.

In the initial learning phase, pioneering institutional investment in promotion through Fundación Chile, IFOP, and international cooperation agencies emphasized the creation of public goods, such as diffusion of knowledge and basic infrastructure.

In the maturation phase subsidies from the Corporación de Fomento de la Producción (Corfo)[18] and ProChile were used to generate capacity (such as the cases of INTESAL and Salmonfood), and to explore new markets.

Promotion in the globalization phase was characterized by increased diffusion of funds available through grants and managed by Corfo and Conicyt (the National Commission for Science and Technology) for projects presented by individuals and by companies. Emphasis was on innovation, technological development, and environmental sustainability of the activity. Today, grant funds mobilize an annual amount of nearly US$10 million through no less than 30 projects geared toward fish farming in the country. Of that amount, around US$7.5 million is public funds, while the remaining US$2.5 million comes from private enterprises. Of these resources, nearly half are devoted to projects focused on areas of interest to the salmon cluster.[19] This level of spending has been stable since 1997, today representing 1 percent of the value of industry exports, which is considered low.

There are no sector evaluations of the results or impact of these support mechanisms for the industry, except sample multisector evaluations for each fund or instrument, which overall have shown a positive financial return. It is possible that the development of vaccines for specific diseases

[18] Chilean Economic Development Agency, under the Ministry of Commerce, with an extensive operating capacity.

[19] It includes the Fishing Research Fund (FIP) of the Vice Ministry of Fishing; the Promotion and Development Fund (Fndef) of Conicyt; Fontec, and FDI of Corfo; and the National Fund for Regional Development (FNDR), administered by regional governments. It does not include the Fund for Basic Research in Universities (Fondecyt), administered by Conicyt.

present in the region, once commercialized, will generate income several times above the total public R&D investment in the industry.

Perhaps one of the characteristics unique to the rapid export rate of the industry is its weak relationship with ProChile, the Chilean public agency for the promotion of exports, in comparison to other high-volume export products such as wine and agricultural goods. The breeding industry argues that the support ProChile can offer to fulfill its foreign promotional and marketing needs is so modest that it prefers to bypass ProChile altogether. Some businesses that process niche products, such as smoked goods, have generated sporadic intervention. In contrast, ProChile constantly keeps salmon as one of its high-profile products in its country image campaigns in several international markets. The problem salmon growers see is that these are generic campaigns for both products and markets, and they would prefer an action that is focused exclusively on salmon promotion.

With regard to educational and training institutions, as labor has become more diversified in each area, there has been a broader supply of technical and professional specialization. Similarly, labor related to different phases of production has seen improved qualifications as a result of accumulated experience and training, which is reflected in the increase in work productivity in the industry. These increases in productivity have not kept up with salary increases as a result of the reduction in the businesses' operational margins.

In recent years, extensive training for the regions' firms has emerged. With regard to professional training, some regional universities have offered educational opportunities with a specialized focus (biochemists, ichthyopathologists, fish farming technicians, fish farming administrators, etc.) since the early 1990s. Most of the new professionals, in contrast to the *pioneering* generation, come from the region's universities and professional institutions. As for the availability of qualified labor, it is believed to be a scarce resource, so that, when hiring new labor, firms tend to prefer youths who have graduated from local polytechnic schools and who will receive additional training and education once employed.

Dominant Governance Patterns

The predominant *governance*[20] pattern during the initial learning phase was a cooperation network among actors with low individual power and a significant common challenge: to develop a level of supply that would give them access to external markets that were used to receiving offers from a select group of developed nations.

As the cluster developed through different stages, these patterns changed. After the initial learning phase and the creation of positive externalities, some cluster actors chose to follow their own evolutionary paths. During the maturation stage, the priority became the acquisition of production capacity to maintain competitiveness in an industry whose operating margins were becoming increasingly narrow. Collective initiatives such as the creation of INTESAL, whose performance has met only in part the high expectations set on its design and creation, date from this period.

The internal governance of the cluster, which had been strong from the start, slowly lost its strength when moving from the maturation to the globalization stage. As a result of the sustained increase in the average size of the firms and their incorporation into the value chain, the progressive arrival of global actors, as well as the emergence of a supply of goods and services and intermediate goods from local small and medium-sized enterprises, interbusiness relations have increasingly adopted a quasi-hierarchical governance pattern, driven initially by the larger and financially stronger businesses in the cluster (i.e., food suppliers and producers). At the same time, the changes had an increasing influence on the end markets (final demand) in those areas where the national supply was no longer marginal. The case study does not represent a pure model of cooperative governance or strict hierarchy, however; the rules of the global game imposed more

---

[20] According to Humphrey and Schmitz (2002), the notion, within the concept of value chain, refers to interbusiness relations as well as the institutional mechanisms and arrangements through which the coordination of non-market-related actions takes place. See also Pietrobelli and Rabellotti, Chapter 1 in this volume.

demanding conditions of collective efficiency. Economies of scale in critical areas, such as R&D and technology upgrading in foodstuffs and feeding cycles, vaccines, and other components, have facilitated the entry of global actors into the cluster in recent years and forced local businesses that remained in the industry to grow. At the same time, this imposed more hierarchical relations with local small and medium-sized suppliers.

Upgrading in the Cluster

The main achievement of this cluster is that it introduced foreign species of fish into the region and reached a large-scale, competitive level of industrial production, demonstrating that it is possible to develop new production systems around natural resources that generate virtuous forward and backward linkages in the absence of a tradition of production in the field. The cluster began by introducing the species, as well as most of the machinery and technology, later developing local adaptation and production capacities.

In fattening and processing the fish, buying and adapting technology have dominated the three phases of the cluster. In hatchery, technology has been acquired initially through transfer, then through local development based on licensing. And in the final phase, with direct incorporation of transnational affiliates. In food production, adaptation and R&D were crucial to staying in the market. In "hard" technologies, purchase and some import substitution, particularly for equipment such as lighting equipment, structures, biotechnology supplies, and "soft" technology such as processing software and others, have dominated.

Two fundamental needs can be identified in the introduction of improvements and innovations of production processes along the production chain. The first need is to minimize the biological risks inherent in the industry, including the quality of the genetic material, control of illnesses, and water safety. The second need is to expand operating margins through improved performance of diets, safety of farming facilities, better management of the harvest period, and reduction of losses due to mortality during transportation. Improvements in the processing plants have been made as a result of quality assurance programs.

In short, the upgrading of processes and products and the incorporation of new related functions and sectors have been made possible and assisted by a variety of factors that, depending on the cluster stages, include collective efficiency and favorable governance, as well as individual actions (Table 4.6).

Table 4.6. Innovation and Upgrading in the Chilean Salmon Cluster

Upgrade	Practices	Leadership/action	Impact/results
Process upgrading			
Hatcheries	Acquiring national eggs	IFOP, Fundación Chile, universities: collective action	Reduced external dependency
Farming	Photo- and thermal-period management	University-supported business and subsidies for R&D	Improved management of harvest seasons
Fattening nurseries	Introducing automatic feeders	Individual firms	Increased yield (feeding/ final product)
Processing plants	HACCP Certification, ISO9000	Firms with institutional support	Product quality assurance; market placement
Product upgrading			
Hatcheries	Selection of eggs and breeders Increased value added of products	Institutional and private R&D with subsidies from firms	Improvement of standards
Processing plants	R&D in feeds	Individual, individual with public subsidies for R&D (both)	Increased operational margins; increased yield
Direct providers	Vaccine development		Reduced losses due to fish mortaiity

(continued on next page)

Table 4.6. Innovation and Upgrading in the Chilean Salmon Cluster
(continued)

Upgrade	Practices	Leadership/action	Impact/results
Functional upgrading			
Along the chain	Integration of various production phases	Larger farming enterprises	Economies of scale in logistics; maintains specialization and separation of functions
Toward commer-cialization	Alliances between firms and commercialization channels	Individual actions, strategies of each enterprise	Better use of market niches; optimization of mix of products to be marketed
Intersectoral upgrading			
Biotechnology industry	Development of national solutions (vaccines, diagnostics kit, laboratories, analysis)	Private and university R&D supported with public subsidies; collective action	Solving problems that affect only the Chilean cluster; ability to intro-duce new improvements
Fish-farming facilities industry	Products: floating cages, premises, storerooms	Private R&D supported with public funds	Development of solutions tailored to national industry

Source: Author's elaboration and Maggi, Montero, and Parra (2000).

Conclusions and Considerations for the Design of Development Policies

The product around which the salmon cluster in southern Chile was created set special conditions for industrial organization. First, the area offers a production factor that is unique and cannot be reproduced elsewhere. Furthermore, the large-scale production of a perishable product intended for foreign markets also imposes logistical and service requirements that did not previously exist for the industries of the region. Finally, one specific complex condition is that the production process involved both fresh and salt water phases.

These conditions required the introduction, adaptation, and finally diffusion of knowledge and skills to a wider population capable of acquiring and using such knowledge and skills. The result was a gradual regional specialization that incorporated, at the regional level, all the phases of the production cycle and also the principal suppliers of materials and services. In the words of an industrialist interviewed: "We thought we were growing salmon, but they are the ones who made us grow."

We are facing what Rullani (2000) called an evolutionary learning process based on a special interaction between the territory, the production actors located in it, and the global market. This process has been strengthened by a dynamic demand that drives the rapid expansion of a supply restricted by the availability of only a few production sites worldwide. In the case of the Chilean cluster, this learning process is more obvious because of the massive expansion of production in an area that is far from the main centers of industrial activity and services. Within this general framework, one of the first challenges for the local small and medium-sized enterprises operating in the cluster is to search for mutually beneficial relationships with the production businesses at the core of the value chain. However, this requires certain conditions, explained in detail in what follows. *There is a trade-off between size and specialization.* Thus medium-sized enterprises will be sustained only as long as they develop specialization advantages related to a specific phase of the project (e.g., eggs, vaccines, services, niche-produced products). The remaining enterprises must grow to reach a minimum size to face the dynamics of the market and the required upgrading.

However, specialization limits the volume of the operations so the level of R&D required for specialization is difficult to achieve. For this reason, collective forms of R&D should be encouraged. The possibility of subsidizing transaction costs, which would lead to formation of associations between firms and R&D centers, should be explored (e.g., research hours, use of teams, analysis, technological antenna).

In order to favor a more advantageous inclusion of the cluster's suppliers and strengthen future competitiveness, it would be advisable to increase both the "sticks" and "carrots" in the keeping of standards and environmental regulations related to the provision of these services. With that objective, several instruments may be promoted simultaneously: (1) programs for improving SMEs' management, (2) development programs for suppliers with the participation of the contracting businesses geared toward meeting standards, and (3) increased demand for and control of compliance with service standards, clearly defining the penalties for violations.

The three main requirements for the development of Chilean fish farming are increased water concessions, increased research and development, and increased road and port infrastructure. In order to address these requirements, public–private sector relationships should be reinforced.

The regulatory framework has just recently begun to be updated in areas such as granting of new concessions and environmental control of the farming phases. The systems for zone concessions and environmental impact evaluation must be updated in order to avoid bottlenecks. Despite the recently achieved advances in water control regulation, the needs to properly measure and transfer prevention practices and to control environmental damage still exist. In order to fulfill both these needs, institutional programs for technology transfer might be essential for the region.

Similarly, in the area of R&D, it is imperative to strengthen research teams that can support systematic research in areas such as control and prevention of illnesses specific to the national species, diet innovation and control of fattening processes, and improvement of genetic material. It is important to promote alliances among R&D centers, as well as between these centers and firms, when developing the procedures for allocating available resources.

With regard to the requirements for investment in road and port infrastructure in the area, joint public and private investment seems the only viable alternative in the medium term, considering government budgetary constraints and the high cost of these works in relation to the size of the population that would directly benefit from them. The ability of the regional industry itself to propose solutions is crucial to facilitating the allocation of public resources.

References

Aguilar, Alvaro. 2002. Estudio de valorización de la piscicultura de IFOP en Cohiayque. Instituto de Fomento Pesquero, Valparaíso. Unpublished.

Fundación Chile. 1994–2002. *Compendio de la acuicultura en Chile.* Santiago: Fundación Chile.

Humphrey, J., and H. Schmitz. 2002. *Developing Country Firms in the World Economy: Governance and Upgrading in Global Value Chains.* Report No. 61, INEF, Duisburg.

Infante, R. 2002. *Acuicultura y biotecnología.* Santiago, Chile: SalmónChile AG.

Maggi, C., C. Montero, and C. Parra. 2000. La industria del salmón en la Décima Región: un cluster globalizado. Project report, ECLAC/GTZ Project "Natural Resources Cluster Development Strategies," Santiago, Chile.

Pietrobelli, C. 1998. *Industry, Competitiveness and Technological Capabilities in Chile: A New Tiger from Latin America?* London: Macmillan.

Pietrobelli, C., and R. Rabellotti. 2002a. How Can SMEs in Clusters and Value Chains Make the Best of Globalization? Paper presented at IDB-MIF Workshop, Inter-American Development Bank, Washington, D.C., September 19.

———. 2002b. What Can Be Done to Assist SMEs to Participate Gainfully in Global Markets? Paper presented at IDB-MIF Workshop, Inter-American Development Bank, Washington, D.C., September 19.

ProChile. 2000. *Análisis regional de las exportaciones chilenas.* Boletín No. 77, Universidad Católica del Maule, Santiago, Chile.

Rullani, E. 2000. Sistemi locali e produzione di conoscenza. Paper presented at OECD meeting "Enhancing the Competitiveness of SMEs in the Global Economy," Bologna, June 14–15.

Vidal, L. 2002. Oportunidades de inversión para la acuicultura en la región de Aysén. Final report, ILPES/ECLAC, Santiago, Chile.

PART II

Upgrading in Clusters and Value Chains in Furniture, Metalworking, and Software Sectors

Chapter 5

The Segusino Cluster: Boom and Bust in Furniture Exports

Eduardo Zepeda Miramontes

During the 1990s, Mexican rustic furniture unexpectedly began to penetrate competitive U.S. and European markets. These markets quickly expanded, and the value and volume of exports multiplied. A large part of this expansion took place during the process of forming a kind of industrial district in Chipilo, a small town located in the state of Puebla, about 12 miles from the state capital city of Puebla. Chipilo had traditionally been a dairy village with a population of 5,000. Cows were removed from the stables and the stables became craft shops for manufacturing rustic furniture for export. Organized around a growing "leader" company, numerous craft shops began producing according to a pattern that emulated several of the factors that characterize the successful operation of so-called industrial districts. This phenomenon extended to regions close to Chipilo, where artisan workshops were also opened. The creation of jobs benefited the region, and workers were coming in from neighboring regions such as Teziutlán and Atlixco and some neighborhoods in the city of Puebla. With this notable increase in employment, wages also went up, earnings increased, and urban infrastructure and landscape improved, particularly in Chipilo. But despite several initiatives implemented to improve the region's productive capabilities, by the end of this same decade the boom

I would like to thank Rogelio Grados for his valuable research assistance.

evaporated, numerous shops closed, factories were having financial problems, and the region fell into a crisis.

This chapter discusses the main factors that boosted rustic furniture exports in Puebla and describes the formation of traditional furniture manufacturing clusters in the region. We then discuss improvements in production and cooperation as key elements for success in a value chain. The next section examines possible causes for the decline in rustic furniture exports in Puebla. The final section attempts to draw some lessons from this case with regard to formulating public policies.

This discussion is based on approaches emphasizing several possible sources of competitiveness, such as collective efficiency, the interactions between firms and the institutional environment, and the strategic importance of the relationships formed within the value chain for the sustainability of their success in the global economy. Background information is derived from open-ended interviews with two companies and a survey questionnaire completed by 24 businesses. These 26 businesses represent a rather varied sample that provides a balanced overview of regional rustic furniture production.[1] Prior studies were also used, primarily Domínguez (2001) and Morán (1999), in addition to secondary statistical information from population censuses and economic censuses, foreign trade statistics, macroeconomic indicators, and data compiled by *Expansión* magazine.

Furniture Exports from Mexico

Mexico's furniture industry had its great export boom during the 1990s. Between 1992 and 1999, the value of exports tripled, growing from US$148

---

[1] These 26 include Segusino and five other large companies; of the latter, three agreed to be interviewed. The remaining 22 interviews were conducted at small workshops with a maximum of 40 employees and maximum sales of US$135,000 per week. These shops can be divided into three groups according to their respective modes of operation. The first group, comprised of 15 businesses, includes businesses working on a 100 percent subcontracting basis, generally through exclusive subcontracting arrangements. Of these, 13 work for Segusino, so this sample is practically a census. A second group of four workshops includes businesses that are currently exporting. The third group, made up of five businesses, involves enterprises that are working independently for the domestic or foreign market and also resort to manufacturing under subcontracting.

Table 5.1. Mexico's Exports of Wooden Furniture (Maquiladoras and Non-maquiladoras), 1991–2001

	Wooden furniture exports[a]		Maquiladoras		Non-maquiladoras	
	US$ millions	%	US$ millions	%	US$ millions	%
1991	23.88	100	n.a.	n.a.	n.a.	n.a.
1992	148.18	100	n.a.	n.a.	n.a.	n.a.
1993	152.76	100	n.a.	n.a.	n.a.	n.a.
1994	170.81	100	145.23	85.03	25.58	14.97
1995	197.53	100	154.68	78.31	42.85	21.69
1996	289.61	100	187.42	64.71	102.19	35.29
1997	387.56	100	187.13	48.28	200.43	51.72
1998	449.08	100	222.86	49.63	226.22	50.37
1999	452.90	100	239.44	52.87	213.47	47.13
2000	487.65	100	250.62	51.39	237.03	48.61
2001	397.97	100	205.04	51.52	192.93	48.48

Source: INEGI, *Anuario Estadístico de Comercio Exterior*, 1991–1999.
[a] 94.03 in trade statistics.

million to US$453 million. Mexican furniture exports are derived from two types of industries: maquiladoras, which are characterized by assembly-type businesses, and actual manufacturing plants, which differ in their organizational structure, technology, and performance in foreign markets.[2] On the one hand, exports from the maquiladora industry grew at a relatively steady rate between 1994 and 1999, and because their main destination was the United States, they started to slow down only in 2001, with the onset of the U.S. recession. On the other hand, exports from manufacturing establishments have been more variable over time. They experienced rapid growth from 1994 to 1997, but very moderate growth in 1998 and negative growth in 1999 (Table 5.1).

In Puebla, rustic furniture exports played a leading role in the increase of sales abroad. Considering exports from non-maquiladora companies

[2] Maquiladoras, or assembly plants, tend to locate in northern Mexico, preferably in Tijuana, Baja California. However, there are also exports made by manufacturing plants in different parts of Mexico that have smaller plant sizes and pay lower wages. See Martínez (1994).

alone, Puebla represented only 20 percent of the domestic total in the first years of the decade, but in 1999, it accounted for close to 70 percent. Its growth was spectacular, as from 1993 to 1996 its value rose from US$4 million to US$147 million, which is equivalent to doubling the export values every year. However, growth in rustic furniture exports remained typically an uneven process with ups and downs. Exports to the United States more than doubled between 1994 and 1995 and maintained an average growth rate of around 80 percent in subsequent years. Exports to Canada multiplied threefold in 1996 and fivefold in 1997, but in other years there were both large and small increases, as well as decreases. Exports to countries outside North America, mainly to Europe, grew at increasingly higher rates until 1996, the year in which they had their greatest increase, and grew at slowing rates afterwards. Overall, Mexican furniture and rustic furniture exports from Puebla tended to slow toward the end of the 1990s.

While this slowdown might be attributed to the international recession, the U.S. market, the main export market for Mexican furniture and for furniture overall, continued growing between 1998 and 2000, though at varied rates. Thus, it is unlikely that the slow growth of Mexican exports at the end of the decade could be explained by a downturn in international markets. The onset of the Mexican furniture export crisis was most likely a product of the industry's own shortcomings, and the situation was worsened by the international recession. The drop in the rate of Mexican exports can be explained only by resorting to a set of micro and macro, domestic and international, factors. First, the decade of the 1990s was characterized by significant changes in the export structure: the spectacular progress made by China, Canada, and Indonesia in the U.S. market was matched by the decline of Taiwan, Denmark, and Mexico (Table 5.2). Thus, Mexico simply lost ground compared to exports by other countries, whether for reasons of price, quality, reliability, or design.[3]

Various signs indicate that a good part of the market loss was due to price issues. According to interviews, domestic and international competi-

---

[3] Amighini (Chapter 8 in this volume) finds similar trends in international markets.

Table 5.2. Origin of U.S. Imports of Wooden Furniture: Top 10 Exporting Countries, 1992–2001

		1992		2001		1992–2001 change in exports	
Country	Ranking	Exports to the U.S. (US$ millions)	% share	Exports to the U.S. (US$ millions)	% share	(US$ millions)	(%)
1 China	8	69	3.8	1,898	29.9	1,828	26
2 Canada	2	222	12.3	1,307	20.6	1,084	8
3 Italy	4	128	7.1	454	7.1	326	0
4 Indonesia	9	48	2.7	377	5.9	329	3
5 Mexico	3	142	7.9	372	5.9	230	−2
6 Malaysia	7	80	4.4	364	5.7	284	1
7 Taiwan	1	572	31.7	281	4.4	−291	−27
8 Thailand	5	94	5.2	227	3.6	133	−2
9 Brazil	11	24	1.3	126	2.0	102	1
10 Philippines	12	24	1.3	110	1.7	86	0
Subtotal	—	1,480	82.0	5,514	86.8	4,111	5
Others	—	324	18.0	841	13.2	516	−5
Total	—	1,805	100.0	6,355	100.0	4,550	—

Source: U.S. Department of Labor, Bureau of Labor Statistics (www.bls.gov/mxp/home.htm).

tion forced international furniture prices relevant for Mexican exports to drop about 25 percent between 1997 and 2002. Similarly, in Puebla the preshipment value of rustic furniture exports continued to drop between 1993 and 1999.[4] Although with a different order of magnitude, the import price index for the wooden furniture classification in the United States dropped 6 percent between 1995 and 2001.[5] Moreover, the boom-and-bust cycle tends to reflect variations in the real exchange rate. The influence of the exchange rate can also be seen in the performance of rustic furniture exports to countries outside North America.

[4] Source: SECOFI (the Ministry of Commerce and Industrial Development).

[5] According to opinions expressed in the press and in interviews, the main source of downward pressure on prices was Asian competition. Prices for furniture of Asian origin were 33–40 percent lower than prices set by producers in Puebla. Source: Author's interview and published interview with María del Carmen Rodríguez and Germán Sánchez Daza, *La Jornada de Puebla,* January 6, 2003.

Rustic Furniture Exports from Puebla

Much of the rustic furniture export boom began in the state of Puebla. However, figures for the state's manufacturing situation suggest that this state's strength clearly does not lie in furniture production. In fact, Puebla's manufacturing structure is dominated by large automotive plants which account for half of the production value, value added, gross capital formation and manufacturing employment within the state.[6] Following these are different kinds of businesses such as textiles and clothing that are represented mostly by small establishments with low pay, low value added, and low per-worker capital investment. The wooden furniture industry comes in at a modest sixth place in terms of share of gross production value; it is mainly comprised of small enterprises and represents 5 percent of the state's businesses and 3 percent of its manufacturing employment. The pay is relatively low, half the average rate paid in the beverage industry and one-eighth of what is paid in the automotive industry, and very similar to what is being paid in the clothing industry. Its productivity and capacity utilization are also very low, similar again to those in the clothing industry (Table 5.3). Based on these indicators, no prediction could have been made of the leading role it would play in exports.

Puebla's rustic furniture export boom did not involve the entire state. Firms targeting international markets were actually concentrated in Chipilo, in many ways different from the typical context in Puebla. Unlike the state, which has a high poverty rate, Chipilo is classified within the low-poverty range. Only 1.5 percent of its population is illiterate, only 0.4 percent of the households lack gutters, only 2.9 percent lack plumbing, only 1.6 percent do not have electricity, and only 0.2 percent have dirt floors. The town has good urban infrastructure and a good educational and technical base because it hosts the National Professional and Technical Education School (Conalep) and because of its proximity to the city

[6] The remainder of manufacturing is spread out among other, smaller sectors, including alcoholic beverages and the cement industry.

Table 5.3. Basic Statistics on Manufacturing Industry, Puebla, 1999

	Number of firms	Employment	Employment per firm	Value added per firm	Value added per employee	Wages per employee	Value added/ production
Total manufacturing	29,459	225,188	7.64	817.89	107.00	36.91	0.27
Automotive[a]	83	23,888	287.81	104,619.78	363.51	132.02	0.21
Clothing[b]	602	26,400	43.85	2,657.82	60.61	36.01	0.28
Beverages[c]	2,583	61,723	23.90	776.56	32.50	18.94	0.46
Textiles[d]	179	5,657	31.60	10,031.41	317.42	51.10	0.48
Cement[e]	1,800	6,434	3.57	675.93	189.10	24.32	0.43
Wooden furniture[f]	1,413	7,383	5.23	240.13	45.96	17.00	0.34

Source: Author's processing of INEGI (1999) Economic Census data.
[a] ISIC code 3841. [b] ISIC code 3220. [c] ISIC code 3130. [d] ISIC code 3212. [e] ISIC code 3691. [f] ISIC code 3220.

of Puebla, with its higher-education institutions, and to Cholula, where the University of the Americas is located. Chipilo also enjoys a high level of ethnic integration and a tradition of hard work which translates into a strong potential for joint effort.[7] However, a static approach would fail in its predictions of Chipilo's industrial vocation, because until the early 1990s Chipilo was a dairy town.

The Chipilo boom required a radical change in the population's economic activity; it started with and revolved around one company: Segusino. Founded in 1987 by Antonio Zaraín, one of the company's main activities is exporting rustic furniture, for which it adopted the model of Italian industrial districts and made use of a stockholding structure that reflected the social structure of Chipilo. By naming the company Segusino, a reference to the town in Veneto, Italy, from which many immigrants came, Zaraín was establishing a symbolism that would reward him with trust and commitment from local residents, while at the same time allowing

[7] Thirty-eight families from Segusino in the Italian region of Veneto arrived in Chipilo in 1882.

him to draw on the image of progress in the furniture industrial districts of northern Italy.[8]

With 20 employees and a 1,600-square-foot plant, Segusino started producing furniture items that were sold in the domestic market and abroad in equal proportions. Not long thereafter, Segusino opened a shop in California to sell its furniture directly and began selling to the European market through a French distributor contacted at the High Point Furniture Fair in North Carolina. Segusino's initial client base was highly specialized, mainly galleries and collectors, but the market quickly broadened, and exports multiplied in a short time. In 1989, the first steps were consciously taken toward building an industrial district type of production system. Instead of increasing the size of the factory, it addressed the increase in outside demand by creating three independent shops that were closely tied to Segusino. Later, the number of partner shops increased, and the company itself expanded to an area of 32,000 square feet with 86 employees (Domínguez, 2001).

Thus, by following the experience of the Italian industrial districts, Segusino organized its production through the integration of small workshops that were relatively independent, but closely related through cooperative practices. By blending work, kinship, residential, and friendship linkages with ethnic issues, this company encouraged the creation of the shops with which it was partnering. In exchange for an exclusive contract for its production, Segusino would provide the shop with financing, training, and assistance. The first workshop exemplifies the types of linkages that were being established. At Zaraín's initiative, the head upholsterer at his old company opened the first workshop, operating under an exclusive subcontracting system with Segusino and supported by credit from Segusino. To become a partner, Segusino demanded compliance with standards addressing experience, quality, working conditions, machinery, and training, locating the shop in Chipilo with a covered area of at least

[8] Although Zaraín is not a Chipilo native, he married a woman from Chipilo after becoming widowed. See Domínguez (2001).

5,250 square feet, and an exclusive contract with Segusino. Most of the owners of these shops are Chipilo residents of Italian origin, invited to quit their former occupations, which mostly involved cattle raising, and open up a shop, and supported in doing so.[9]

The growth of the Chipilo cluster lead by Segusino was spectacular. By 1995, this company was already among the 500 largest companies in Mexico listed by *Expansión*, and in 1996, it won the national export prize. By 1998 its total sales had surpassed US$33 million, of which 96 percent was being exported to 58 countries. The products of this company and its partner shops came to represent over half of Mexico's non-maquiladora rustic furniture exports. While it had started out exporting mainly to the United States, by 1999 only one-fourth of exports were still going to the U.S. market. Foreign markets were handled through exclusive contracts between Segusino and its distributors—which sometimes became partnerships—and through its own stores and distribution companies. Although only 5 percent of the cluster's annual sales were being made domestically, this was enough to ensure its leadership in the domestic market through its 27 furniture outlets (Morán, 1999). Its impact on employment was also significant. In its best year, there were 145 shops in operation employing some 3,000 workers, mostly in production.[10] Segusino directly employed 2,400 people at its 30 industrial facilities and offices, including workers and technical and management-level employees.

But the bust was equally surprising. The year 1999 saw the start of declining sales and exports. In 2000, exports had dropped to US$20 million. In 2002, its sales abroad were only US$7 million: only 14 work-

---

[9] In a random sample of 33 Segusino workshops operating in 1999, it was found that 70 percent of the owners were previously active in the livestock business. Interviews conducted as part of the author's own fieldwork found that 70 percent of the owners of Segusino subcontracting shops in late 2002 used to be active in the livestock business.

[10] This figure of 3,000 employees was reached by supposing that each shop provided employment to 20 people. Segusino's total employment, both direct and indirect, was 5,400 workers, a figure that is close to the 6,000 reported by Morán in 1999, but that is lower than other estimates (given in interviews) that reported a figure of 8,000.

shops were still active, and Segusino had cut its payroll to 200 workers.[11] In the first days of 2003, Segusino closed down and began a process of liquidation.

The Segusino cluster's success in foreign markets spurred a process of imitation, and new furniture producers emerged in the same town and in other parts of the state of Puebla. Employment in the rustic furniture industry grew rapidly, and the number of companies multiplied. The number of companies exporting rustic furniture reported in Puebla rose from 15 to 60 between 1993 and 1998.[12]

As a reflection of this process, the number of establishments in the entire wooden furniture industry in Puebla rose from 203 to 319 between 1995 and 1999, and its employment grew from 1,915 to 5,357. A small number of medium-sized plants emerged following the success of the Segusino cluster, and five to eight established themselves as successful regional clusters by subcontracting small workshops. Numerous independent shops were also set up, filling orders for foreign clients buying furniture on a wholesale basis, or satisfying fluctuating demand from larger companies. Altogether, according to figures from the IMSS (Mexican Social Security Institute), two medium-sized establishments were registered in 1995 with between 101 and 250 workers; this number rose to eight in 1999 (Domínguez, 2001, Table 10), which together with Segusino, represented one-half of the jobs in the entire industry for that year. The other half was represented by small and micro-sized establishments, which increased in number from 200 to 338 between 1995 and 1999 and generated an increase in employment from 1,400 to 2,600.

The fall of the rustic furniture export industry in the state of Puebla was also very sharp. Although in November 1998 the IMSS had recorded

---

[11] Information from personal interviews and from several issues of *Expansión*.

[12] Sources: Puebla office of the Ministry of Commerce and Industrial Development, and Domínguez (2001), Table 13. Because of a problem with records, these figures include only countries other than Canada and the United States. However, we can assume that the number of exporting companies would be very similar if exports to these countries were included.

Table 5.4. Puebla Employees in Wooden Furniture Manufacturing and Repairs Registered with Social Security, 1996–2002

Date	Number of employees	Yearly change	
		Number	Percentage
1996	3,294	—	—
1997	4,596	1,302	39.53
1998	5,281	685	14.90
1999	5,255	–26	–0.49
2000	4,294	–961	–18.29
2001	3,309	–985	–22.94
2002	3,041	–268	–8.10

Source: Instituto Mexicano del Seguro Social (IMSS) (www.imss.gob.mx), March 2003.

5,281 employees in the entire industry in Puebla, by August 2002 employment had dropped to 3,041 workers (Table 5.4). Nevertheless, this decline was not as dramatic as in the case of Segusino, because none of the medium-sized companies visited was in a difficult situation, and a couple of them were still expanding.

The Segusino Export Cluster

As mentioned earlier, the main activities in rustic furniture exports revolved around the Segusino cluster. In this section we review the cluster's development and structure. In its functional and production aspects, the Segusino cluster's value chain is essentially hierarchical. In our interviews with workshops associated with Segusino, we noted that decisions and initiatives were typically made by this company; a certain acknowledgment of hierarchy was clear. While this indicates strong leadership, it could also be a sign of a lack of initiative and creative commitment by the workshops, of their relative inexperience, and of a decision-making structure hampering innovative action by the shops.[13]

[13] Based on data from Domínguez (2001:221), it may be said that over half the shops surveyed did not feel that decisions were being made in a participative manner.

However, in spite of the hierarchy, Segusino maintained a relationship of support and cooperation with its shops.[14] Segusino provided support in several areas and encouraged improvements in quality and innovation. For example, it created an annual award for quality that was presented at a special ceremony. It organized a point system for rewarding production and quality improvements. It provided support through advisory assistance and financial resources to workshops that were looking to modernize. According to our interviews, Segusino often provided financial support to its partner shops for buying machinery (10 out of the 13 shops reported this). Along these same lines, Domínguez reports that 72 percent of the shops interviewed stated that their partnership with Segusino was beneficial, and 66 percent said they had received technical assistance from Segusino (Domínguez, 2001:221). These measures were deliberately intended to achieve process upgrading through the creation of a trained labor force (Schmitz, 1995; Pietrobelli and Rabellotti, Chapter 1 in this volume).

Moreover, factors such as friendship and kinship played important roles. According to data from Domínguez (2001), half the shop owners interviewed in 1999 had gone into business because of Segusino's initiative. Many of them were in some way relatives of Zaraín. A glimpse of the list of shops that Segusino has had through the years underlines the importance of the ethnic factor: approximately 80 percent of owners' surnames are of Italian origin.

Production is planned entirely by Segusino, based on existing orders, marketing strategies, and a demand forecast. Products and orders are variable because of the artisan nature of the business. By late 2002, organization of production was such that Segusino was responsible for supplying nails, glue, and wood to partner shops. The wood utilized is domestic and is imported in times of scarcity.[15] Because the quality and condition of

---

[14] See *La Jornada de Oriente,* January 3, 2003, for an opposing view.

[15] Domestic wood becomes scarce during the rainy season because most Mexican wood comes from natural forests located in places where there are seldom proper roads (see Domínguez, 2001).

wood are extremely important in furniture manufacture, Segusino built several facilities for kiln drying and sealing the wood to ensure that the wood's properties met the requirements and hatcheries to give the wood an accelerated woodworm effect, which gave furniture its antique appearance. In this area upgrading was also possible through the vertical integration of productive processes.[16] For their part, partner shops were expected to manufacture the furniture in accordance with specifications and deliver it without final finishing; Segusino would make payments for the deliveries on a weekly basis.[17]

The international dimension of the rustic furniture market became crucial to ensuring that all furniture items reached a minimum quality level. A quality supervision system was organized to this end and directed by Segusino, which would go to each shop and intervene at various times during the production process, including a final inspection once the items were completed and before sending them off to its own facilities. Some international distributors would send quality assurance supervisors to Segusino facilities during periods of high volume. This system allowed a low defect margin to be achieved. According to our interviews, almost 90 percent of the shops in the Segusino cluster reported a reject rate of less than 1 percent, and these rejects were repaired at the same shop in 80 percent of these cases.

Furniture finishing was carried out at Segusino facilities in order to prevent damage during transportation from the shops and to ensure better quality control. Hardware, latches, and forged pieces were installed at this stage; they were produced at iron working and forging shops belonging to Segusino and also at a small number of partner shops. Finally, packing and shipping were carried out at Segusino facilities.

---

[16] See Schmitz (1995) and Pietrobelli and Rabellotti (Chapter 1 in this volume) for a discussion of actions of this kind and their impact on competitiveness.

[17] This procedure was changed because of the difficulties that Segusino was going through at the time of this fieldwork. Persons interviewed stated that it was becoming more common for furniture not to be paid for until Segusino had received payment for the shipment and that shops had to purchase the wood from Segusino before manufacturing the furniture.

Many changes and improvements were achieved during the cluster's development. The creation of forging shops, woodworm hatcheries, and kilns for drying wood are transformations indicating vertical integration and upgrading in the industry. Better organization within the shops and in their production systems and investments in urban infrastructure are also examples of improvements that undoubtedly favored upgrading.

Significant efforts were also made for workforce training in the Segusino cluster. This was especially necessary as the Mexican workforce is not among the best-trained workforces in the world: a national survey during the mid-1990s found that 25 percent of Mexican workers had received some training at some point in their lives, while the same figure for Taiwan amounted also to 25 percent—but *every year* (Zepeda, Alarcón, and Félix, 1997).

The cluster was making full use of the government programs during the boom years and was cofinancing these programs. Of these activities, those carried out through the Compite, Como, and Crece programs are particularly noteworthy. Additionally, according to our interviews, Segusino had a mandatory two-week training program that was held twice a year, and 12 of the 13 plants interviewed reported that they had been trained in previous years. The topics mentioned were furniture quality, woodcutting, use of machinery, glues, finishing, ISO 9000, and competitiveness.

Having learned from his own experience the importance of distribution in the furniture business, Zaraín made repeated efforts to ensure that Segusino would participate in this lucrative and strategic part of the value chain (Kaplinsky, 2000; Schmitz, 1995). Right from the start, he opened a furniture store in California (Domínguez, 2001:198). Participation at international fairs is a must for all incipient exporters, and Zaraín made the most of his participation. Attendance at the High Point fair meant entry into the European market, through collaboration with a French distributor. Partner shops were not involved in these activities.

The firm followed a consistent strategy based on its relationship with distributors in order to create a Segusino brand image of authentic, quality rustic furniture with creative and functional designs. Within a few years of operation, Segusino had created partnerships with three distributors in the United States to control 65 percent of the rustic furniture market (Domínguez, 2001:192). In other countries, Segusino opted for the franchise system, which meant that all Mexican rustic furniture sold or distributed by these franchises had to be made exclusively by the Segusino cluster. This same channel was used for organizing distribution in Mexico. In 2002, Segusino had 35 stores in Mexico, 3 of which were owned by the company itself, and the remaining 32 of which operated under franchises.[18] These actions taken directly by Segusino prevented vertical organizational structures from being set up by distributors abroad, which could have inhibited the functional upgrading of local producers. On this issue, Segusino's experience presents an interesting variation to what has been reported in other studies showing that a quasi-hierarchical organizational structure may inhibit functional upgrading (Pietrobelli, Rabellotti, and Giuliani, Chapter 9 in this volume).

Despite these efforts, part of the problems that finally led Segusino into bankruptcy originated in the area of distribution. In 1999, Casa Rústica, a distribution company in the United States, went bankrupt and failed to pay Segusino a US$1.3 million debt. This was a hard hit that created problems for the operation of the company in subsequent years and came along with the closing of other stores in Germany and Denmark.[19] It was not long before this took its toll on the cluster. Between 1998 and 2000, Segusino's leverage indicator rose from 0.730 to 4.863, and its liability ratio dropped from 2.365 to 1.206 (Table 5.5). Twenty shops located in Chipilo also went bankrupt. Later in 2002, Segusino's financial problems became more serious when the English distribution company Pueblo Nativo decided to get its furniture supply from other producers as a result of rumors that were already predicting Segusino's demise.[20]

---

[18] See www.franquicias.com.

[19] *La Jornada de Oriente,* January 3, 2003, and author's own interviews in 2002.

[20] *La Jornada de Oriente,* January 7, 2003, p. 5, and January 3, 2003, p. 3.

Table 5.5. Basic Balance Sheet Information on Segusino, 1995–2000 *(US$ millions)*

	Total assets	Total liabilities	Equity	Sales	Exports	Exports/ sales	Leverage (liabilities/ equity)	Liability ratio (assets/ liabilities)
1995	4.75	1.67	3.08	11.74	—	—	0.542	2.844
1996	9.60	2.67	6.92	17.47	17.13	.9801	0.386	3.596
1997	11.88	4.47	7.40	24.66	24.27	.9839	0.604	2.658
1998	16.93	7.16	9.77	33.32	31.99	.9600	0.730	2.365
2000	13.72	11.38	2.34	21.92	20.01	.9132	4.863	1.206

Source: Author's processing of information published in *Revista Expansión*, various issues.
Note: Data for 1999 are unavailable.

One of the key phases of any value chain involves product design. In fact, production and export of rustic furniture requires a considerable amount of initiative, power, and vision on the part of the supplier. In principle, one could consider close collaboration between the producer and the buyer to be a necessity. However, in the case of traditional Mexican furniture, the definition of the product cannot come exclusively from the buyer, at least not in the early stages. Unlike in other sectors, such as the garment industry, in the furniture industry we do not have a product that has been created and developed in international markets and that thereby requires a close knowledge of these markets. The commercial success of traditional wooden furniture lies in its "exotic" nature, that is, its character as something foreign, and a buyer residing in the country where the market is cannot completely do without the designer in the developing country.

According to interviews, Segusino was in charge of furniture design, and its distributors followed. Design was entrusted to a department created specifically for this purpose. In this way, Segusino started building a catalog that eventually contained some 1,000 furniture items. Notwithstanding an annual design contest for its workshops, design functions were still concentrated at the Segusino company. This proved not to be the best strategy. According to our interviews, furniture designs rarely, if ever, originated from shops belonging to Segusino. The manifest desire to cooperate in design never became a reality, and this proved to be a strategic weakness. While Segusino was designing on paper, in its design contest, the shops were being asked to present their proposals in wood, that is, as a real piece of furniture. This procedure actually complicated the relationship between Segusino and its shops. The need to present these furniture items in wood involved costs for the shops without much benefit forthcoming. After all, Segusino already had a catalog of 1,000 furniture items, and the shops felt there was not much left to be done. In addition, Segusino's innovative designs were presented on paper apparently without ever having been built as prototypes in wood. Thus it was up to the shops to build the designed furniture in wood, with all the costs involved, and to suggest changes to the paper designs. These suggestions were hardly taken into consideration, and the shops had to keep on struggling with their adaptations. Here, the negative consequences of a quasi-hierarchical organizational structure became clear, because it limited the cluster's potential to achieve effectively an upgrading of its products (see Schmitz, 1995; Pietrobelli, Rabellotti, and Giuliani, Chapter 9 in this volume, for other examples).

Furniture Exports beyond the Segusino Cluster

Among the numerous shops that emerged during the rustic furniture export boom in Puebla, some were able to grow until they reached considerable size. They gained ground in the export market and also started organizing their own clusters, though in a more elementary fashion than Segusino. These companies have not reached Segusino's scale, but they have succeeded and not only maintained operations of considerable magnitude into 2003, but were also making plans for expansion. These companies include Muebles Rústicos Chipilo, Rústicos Santa Fe, Kopal Muebles Rústicos Mexicanos, Rústicos Tonalí, and Rústicos San Rafael.

Most of these companies were created during the export boom years by following the Segusino organizational model, but with some differences.[21] Some of the owners of these companies had learned from Segusino, either as company employees or as owners of partner workshops. The major difference is that most of these companies tend to be more vertically integrated, with less subcontracting. For example, one of these companies handles most of its furniture production in its own shops and only subcontracts a small portion of its production to its partner shops. Another of these companies works as an independent shop but on a large scale. Under normal conditions, production is carried out at its three facilities, but it resorts to subcontracting with shops when necessary, and at times the company itself also accepts orders for producing under subcontract.

The importance of training has also been recognized by these companies, either in-service at the factory or by taking courses offered by the Banco de Comercio Exterior and Compite.[22] Unlike Segusino, these companies did not participate very often in other government program support, such as Femex and Altex, because they felt the programs were not useful and access to them was too complicated. At two of the three companies visited we observed a continuous and intense process of innovation in the production process, both in its organization and in the incorporation and adaptation of machinery and technical improvements in procedures.[23] But unlike Segusino, design did not receive the same attention. Their catalogs were either based on Segusino's or made by imitating antique furniture designs with some adaptations often provided by distributors. This last factor represented one of the most widespread concerns among the largest

---

[21] In interviews carried out in late 2002, we were able to obtain detailed information from only one company and general data from two more, plus some indirect information regarding the way two other companies were operating.

[22] In his 1999 survey, Domínguez (2001) found that among the large companies in his sample of exporters, the most frequent issues were improvements to the production process, safety and health, quality, and the use of computing, which we assume to be in management areas.

[23] Domínguez (2001) found that in 1999, the large companies had often incorporated machinery, and that machinery had reduced employment by up to 50 percent because one machine could replace up to four functions.

companies, given the clients' lack of knowledge of international markets.[24] Finally, these companies normally sold their products to specific stores or distributors abroad and did not identify any plans to advance along this section of the value chain.

Another section of the rustic furniture industry in Puebla includes small, independent workshops, which are set up as artisan-type businesses in order to fill small furniture orders. Their production is sold in both the domestic and the export market, through direct contracts with distributors or end clients or through manufacturing subcontracts. Distribution does not fall within their concerns. Furniture design is also copied and adapted from other catalogs or provided by clients. Use of machinery and imported materials is less frequent at these shops than at the large factories. Although the export business requires training, here it is provided more sporadically (for examples, see Zepeda, Alarcón, and Félix, 1997; Garro and Llamas, 2003).

Overall, we can conclude that rustic furniture production and exporting in Puebla beyond Segusino has achieved more elementary cluster-type forms of organization, hierarchically related to global productions.

The Industrial Cluster of Chipilo

Even when Puebla rustic furniture export was confined to a small geographic area, we cannot properly speak of just *one* district or *one* regional cluster. More than a regionally integrated value chain, what was created was a combination of clusters, but with little interaction among them. This was essentially a set of quasi-hierarchical systems of relatively independent businesses that were led by one principal company that defined the rules of the chain. However, there was no further coordination among these systems. Thus, the hierarchical and quasi-hierarchical systems were not successful at forging joint actions to develop a real network of producers and boost

[24]According to data collected by Domínguez (2001), 30 percent of a sample of exporting companies stated in 1999 that their weakness in product design was an obstacle to exporting.

their collective efficiency. Among these quasi-hierarchical systems, the largest cluster was headed by Segusino, with associated workshops producing exclusively for this firm. A second group was formed by the clusters led by the five to eight medium-sized enterprises that grew during this period, in addition to the workshops these enterprises subcontracted. In addition, there were also small and microworkshops producing independently. Some kind of cooperation existed among these groups, but it was generally limited. Likewise, collective efficiency was also limited, with vertical cooperation between the head company and its associated workshops, but not with the other clusters. Only the independent workshops, not bound by an exclusivity agreement, at times cooperated "horizontally" by sharing subcontracting projects. In sum, in Chipilo we do not observe an integrated industrial district, but rather, early attempts aimed at increasing competitiveness through occasional but incomplete collective actions.

Actions that achieved greater collective efficiency included the various forms of cooperation that involved large and small businesses and that were targeting the expansion of the production scale, the deepening of the division of labor, and the vertical integration of the industry by integrating areas such as kiln wood drying or the woodworm effect or expanding design. Under the leadership of Segusino, public sector action was triggered. The company was a key factor in developing training courses, in improving urban infrastructure in Chipilo, and in driving the attempt—failed—to create a furniture institute (see below). These institutional factors and productive scaling led to increased capacity and competitiveness, as they integrated many of the elements that form collective efficiency (Pietrobelli and Rabellotti, Chapter 1 in this volume).

The spillover from the economic boom brought benefits for the population. Export earnings, payment of local taxes, and wage increases led to improved levels of well-being. However, wage increases could not be sustained over time, and the extraordinary pressure the export boom placed on the labor force did not lead to increased productivity. With this generalized export furniture crisis, many of these jobs were lost, and most work was carried out though informal market-type contracting. But even in the midst of this boom, to a large extent because of how quickly it had occurred, pressure on the labor supply sparked a rise not only in wage levels, but also in labor turnover. In one of the shops subcontracted to Segusino, most of the workers had not been there longer than 12 months (Morán, 1999). In less than a year's time, a worker could easily work in several different shops and go from being a machine operator's assistant to a skilled operator and master workman. Thus, competition among shops for the most highly skilled workers ended up raising labor turnover and, more importantly, wages. If wages increase "excessively," profits melt away and jobs disappear, especially in microbusinesses. If turnover goes out of control, ongoing training and intracompany labor mobility are called into question. According to information taken from the Domínguez survey (2001), labor turnover was perceived as a real problem only in small companies. According to that same survey and our interviews, large companies did not see turnover as a major stumbling block.

But beyond the opinions expressed in these interviews, the increase in turnover does not seem to have brought any great consequences. In the furniture industry, the transfer of a worker from one shop to another meant that certain companies were gaining a skilled employee and that the worker was receiving higher pay. It also assured that innovations were distributed throughout the industry. It was not, then, the situation of the northern Mexico assembly plants (maquiladora) industry, in which pressures on the labor market, whether large or small, are prevented from prompting wage hikes by the discipline and coordination among manufacturing operations that prevent competition for labor via offers of higher pay.[25]

In our interviews with shops partnering with Segusino, we observed that communication among them was good, because they know each other well, due to how small and integrated the community of Chipilo is. In the best of times, the exchange of information among shops included technical details such as the milling, assembly, and sanding of furniture,

[25] Labor rotation in the maquiladora industry has been studied extensively; see, for example, Contreras (2000).

administrative issues, and the lending of materials such as nails and glue (but not wood). Ethnic and social capital played a very important role in the formation of this network of workshops. Nevertheless, with the onset of the crisis, cooperation and exchange of information decreased. Jealousies and distrust arose regarding the method of distribution of production quotas. With or without good reason, there was a perception that certain shops were being unjustly favored. The climate became adverse to cooperation as a result of the boom itself, and the scarcity of relatively skilled labor, the "pirating" of workers, only increased the level of distrust among the various workshops.

The very limited participation, then and now, of furniture makers in business associations is a clear reflection of the scanty horizontal cooperation that exists among them. For example, the National Manufacturing Industry Chamber of Puebla (CANACINTRA-PUE), the main organization that brings together small and medium-sized entrepreneurs at national and state levels, had only 23 members from the furniture industry. A manifestation of this lack of cooperation is that no specific furniture industry chamber was ever formed, despite the value and growth of these exports.

Independent of CANACINTRA-PUE, the formation of an association of furniture makers—mainly rustic furniture makers—was promoted during the export boom years. This was an attempt to avoid a drop in prices due to competition among the different producers in the region and in anticipation of competition from Asia. The organization was called the Puebla Association of Furniture Manufacturers (AFAMPUE). The fact that this group was promoted by Zaraín conditioned its scope and limited its success. Producers in the region interpreted the initiative as a move to protect the interests of Segusino above the interests of the furniture makers as a whole. A lack of commitment dictated that, over the course of time, the group no longer addressed issues of real importance to the furniture industry.

Another instance of cooperation came with the development of the ITA (Integración de Talleres Asociados). This organization was set up in March 2000 by Segusino-subcontracted shops as a means of coordinating production activities and providing legal assistance. By the time the ITA was formed, the climate was highly strained, and only two factors induced shops to belong to the organization: first, to solve their problems with the IMSS and the Ministry of Finance as simply as possible (reducing paperwork and wasted time), and second, in the hope of achieving an increase in furniture prices. Initially, the ITA had a membership of 70 establishments but did not include the two factories from Chipilo or their subcontracted shops. As the crisis worsened and shops closed, the number of ITA members also dropped. By the end of 2002, the group had only 12 active members left.

The low membership levels of general business associations can be explained, in part, by a lack of awareness about the services they offer. CANACINTRA-PUE provided services to industrialists in the lumber business that included intermediation in negotiations with Semarnat for the application of environmental standards in the industry, cooperation in facilitating the visit of a supplier from Argentina's lumber industry, and other, more general services. However, 18 out of 24 establishments reported that they were unaware of the services and benefits CANACINTRA-PUE offered. Six interviewees reported that they had never received any benefit whatsoever from CANACINTRA-PUE. This response reveals a clear lack of confidence in the organization. For its part, CANACINTRA-PUE has mainly acted as a mediator between affiliated companies and federal and state government agencies.

ITA provides support services in the negotiation of legal matters related to taxation, labor regulations, and environmental standards. The level of knowledge of benefits and services is relatively high among members. Moreover, we could detect scattered evidence that some of the shops were interested in joining because this gave them an opportunity to discuss with Segusino the pricing of furniture. The organization's leadership and the course it took made it clear, however, that there would be no opportunity to negotiate prices within that forum.

In 1999, Segusino headed up an initiative to create the Furniture Technology Center (CETEDEM), which represented what was, perhaps, the greatest effort ever to foster productive competitiveness in the handcrafted furniture business.[26] Unfortunately, the initiative never really worked. CETEDEM was proposed by Segusino and 30 other companies, including the most important firms in Chipilo. The project was already backed by sufficient investment commitments and the participation of a broad range of organizations, whose efforts were oriented toward emulating the experiences of similar centers in other countries in the promotion of cooperation and productive technological and organizational development for the furniture industry. Although the fact that the initiative came from Segusino meant that it seemed more likely to be successful—thanks to Segusino's commitment and experience at an international scale—this actually worked against the initiative. Segusino's leading role was ultimately a drawback because many producers viewed the project with a jealous eye and responded apathetically to the call to participate. But the most important reason that the CETEDEM project never got off the ground was the decline in furniture exports and the crisis into which the Puebla industry was plunged, creating a perverse effect that further aggravated jealousies and increased the level of distrust.

The Export Decline Led by Segusino

A combination of factors explains the fall of Segusino and the decline in the rustic furniture industry. The structure of the regional value chain suffered from weak horizontal cooperation and a high degree of segmentation which jeopardized its productive and organizational strength. In addition, Segusino was experiencing financial setbacks that seriously affected its operations.

One of the well-known causes of the fall of Segusino is the excessive increase in costs caused by an inflated payroll. In a public interview, Zaraín acknowledged that there were 246 employees on the payroll performing

---

[26] The closest Mexican example is the Instituto del Mueble A.C., promoted by the furniture sector of CANACINTRA.

activities that could have been covered by 50.[27] This same topic of excess staff came up repeatedly at an interview we conducted in 2002. According to figures compiled by *Expansión*, the 70 percent increase in total sales between 1995 and 1996 was accompanied by a 365 percent rise in total employment. Consequently, the amount of sales per worker fell nearly two-thirds, from $35,000 to $13,000 per worker. In 1997, when total sales grew nearly 30 percent, the rate of sales per worker dropped another 14 percent.

Secondly, Segusino was trapped in a bind that would eventually squeeze earnings as a consequence of the drop in the furniture export price: the international price of furniture before transportation costs fell an average of 25 percent between 1997 and 2000, that is, from $100 to $75 (author's interviews). Four other possible factors influenced this price reduction: (1) downward pressure due to competition from other national rustic furniture producers, (2) the market entry of "Mexican rustic" furniture manufactured in other countries (including Asian and Eastern European countries) that was being offered at much lower prices, because these manufacturers could reduce costs by not complying with rustic furniture density and manufacturing specifications,[28] (3) a dwindling demand for this type of furniture, due to a progressive wearing out of the market niche, and (4) a plunge in the international wooden furniture market in developed countries.

The fall in international prices was compounded by the increase in international production costs. Two essential aspects must be noted here. First, the increase in labor costs, wood, and other inputs priced in pesos. As mentioned earlier, the pressure to supply a growing furniture demand led to a hike in wages, without a comparable increase in productivity. To a certain extent, this is a problem of a shortage of skills. Secondly, the actual exchange rate faced by the rustic furniture industry, and by the manufactur-

[27] *La Jornada de Oriente*, January 9, 2003, p. 3.

[28] According to data provided in our interviews, a typical piece of rustic furniture can be offered at a price 25 percent lower than Mexico's.

ing industry in general, appreciated. The failure to maintain a stable real exchange rate placed intense pressure on furniture production in Mexico in the presence of foreign competitors. Between 1996 and 2001 the cost of labor, wood, glue, and energy at least doubled, while at the same time, the exchange rate rose, which meant a decrease in the sales price in domestic currency. Earnings thus vanished, worsening the situation of Segusino and harming other manufacturers.

The exchange rate is important for exports, especially in developing countries, where exports are usually labor intensive. In this period, in Mexican official circles it was argued that the exchange rate was "neutral" as Mexican manufacturing exports grew rapidly. Between 1996 and 2001 the real exchange rate, according to official estimates, appreciated 16 percent. But the producer price index for exports increased 43 percent, which points to a problem in competitiveness. The experience of rustic furniture manufacturers is not far from what could have happened in other exports with a high domestic content, such as shoes. Thus it is not surprising that many manufacturers face serious difficulties in competing in international markets when the currency is "strong."

Policy Lessons

The export of rustic furniture in Puebla experienced a boom-and-bust cycle over one decade that began in the early 1990s and peaked in 1999. Starting out with only a production plant and limited industrial experience in the region, within just a few years a budding export base was formed by clusters of businesses with networks of subcontracted workshops, with an organizational framework similar to that of an industrial district. Public policies also played a role, with several state and federal programs supporting training and the creation of an urban infrastructure. However, the experiment was halted in the early years of the 2000 decade, when global exports fell and employment collapsed.

The dynamic axis of the export success was built around the cluster we have called Segusino, from the name of the leading company. Under this firm's leadership, a quasi-hierarchical cluster was formed, in which the lead firm kept control of product design and deeply influenced its distribution. In the area of production, conscious efforts were made to establish cooperative practices in labor training and product innovation. At Segusino, advances were made in vertical integration through the incorporation of processes that ensured wood supply and treatment at the times and in the amounts and quality required. Segusino was responsible for all of these actions, and the associated workshops had little say in important decisions such as what to produce, how to produce it, and above all, at what price. It was a collective action clearly directed from above. Although it is not clear to what extent collective efficiency was limited by the extremely hierarchical nature of the production structure, it is clear that the cluster as such grew more vulnerable by making the fate of the workshops dependent on what was happening at the lead firm. Segusino's bankruptcy, which became apparent in the early years of the 2000 decade and was attributable to the inadequate handling of liabilities and an excessive increase in payroll, led the whole production cluster out of the market. The cluster's workshops were perfectly capable of continuing to manufacture but were unable to drive the process on their own.

In addition to Segusino, other clusters and businesses with export production capabilities emerged in the area. Concentrating in manufacturing and leaving distribution to other players, these firms established a production capacity that survived the boom-and-bust cycle of the Segusino cluster. Some of these firms were even undergoing an expansion process at the time of the present fieldwork. Apparently, then, focusing on production strengthened their position in the market, even when it kept them from what is usually the most dynamic and profitable part of the value chain, distribution. We may argue that these firms were implicitly benefiting from the actions of the Segusino cluster by imitating its successful initiatives, learning from its tests, and benefiting from a labor force that was trained, directly or indirectly, in the Segusino cluster. In any event, the improvement in collective efficiency of the Chipilo-Puebla region was constrained by the lack of cooperation among the different production clusters.

Industrial and development policies played an important role in the development and export of rustic furniture in Puebla. Since the late 1980s, industrial policy has been redefined in Mexico, focusing on the promotion of small and medium-sized enterprises, including support for their insertion in international markets as suppliers or direct exporters (Alarcón and Zepeda, 1998; Clavijo and Casar, 1994; Sánchez, 2002; Sánchez, Fernández, and Pérez, 1994; Zepeda and Middlebrook, 2004). Segusino attracted public support in several different ways, and especially in government-supported training programs, export support, and participation in fairs and international events. There was also an attempt to create an institute to promote technological development in the wooden furniture industry, sponsored by Segusino together with public institutions and unions. This firm, with its network of workshops and the support of corresponding local governments, invested in urban infrastructure for the town of Chipilo.

However, a review of the experience of Puebla and the extensive use of public programs suggests that the industrial policies available were not sufficient. A crucial issue is how to reach a diffusion and quality of training similar to that of the Asian market, with 25 percent of its workforce trained every year. In the international furniture market Mexico competes with countries whose labor capabilities greatly surpass its own, such as Italy and Canada, and with countries whose workforce is cheaper, such as China and Indonesia. The only way to compete under these circumstances is through the overall strengthening of the population's educational capacity. The effectiveness of two one-week training courses per year for workers who have barely completed a low-quality primary education is inevitably limited.

Public policies should be geared toward building the necessary social network so that productive efforts are translated into sustainable advances in international markets, with growing participation in high-value-added segments of the value chain. The high level of distrust toward government programs, although justifiable in many cases, must be overcome. Cooperation among producers is highly precarious and is hampered by an institutional weakness inherited from decades of corporatism. The overall simplification of regulations, including those in regard to social security, taxation, and promotion, and their transparent implementation deserve urgent action.

A fundamental issue in the formulation of public policies involves technological development and promotion of the use of advanced skills, in order to promote value chains capable of fostering the attainment of higher income levels in developing countries. Efforts to establish CETEDEM were aimed in this direction. However, this was an initiative that was not given enough time to take form, and those factors that have hindered cooperation, such as the lack of transparency in initiatives and of open invitation from the outset for all proposals, were not addressed in a timely fashion.

This review of the experience of rustic furniture export in Puebla highlights the importance of advancing and building on actions that strengthen collective efficiency: first, by granting local cooperation the importance it deserves; secondly, by placing the appropriate importance on the establishment of methods of production and collective decisions that facilitate process and product upgrading; and lastly, by fostering in all possible ways the nonsubordinate inclusion of local SMEs in the value chains. A key element in this process is the careful reconsideration of the relationship between public and private sector actions to address upgrading and competitiveness, such as the low educational levels of Mexican workers.

REFERENCES

Alarcón, D., and E. Zepeda. 1998. Liberalization, Structural Adjustment and Labor Market Performance in Mexico. In *Innovation, Productivity and Competitiveness in North America,* ed. C. Murray et al. Montreal, Quebec: McGill-Queen's University Press.

Clavijo, F., and J. I. Casar. 1994. Las restricciones al crecimiento de la economía mexicana y la necesidad de una política industrial para el fomento de la competitividad. In *La industria mexicana en el mercado mundial: elementos para una política industrial* (Serie El Trimestre Económico No. 80), ed. F. Clavijo and J. I. Casar. Mexico City: Fondo de Cultura Económica.

———, eds. 1994. *La industria mexicana en el mercado mundial: elementos para una política industrial.* Serie El Trimestre Económico No. 80. Mexico City: Fondo de Cultura Económica.

Contreras, Óscar F. 2000. *Empresas globales, actores locales: producción flexible y aprendizaje industrial en las maquiladoras.* Mexico City: Centro de Estudios Sociológicos, El Colegio de México.

Domínguez, M. 2001. Cooperación interempresarial: el caso de Puebla. Doctoral dissertation, School of Political Science, Universidad Nacional Autónoma de México (UNAM), Mexico City.

Garro, J., and M. Llamas. 2003. El premio a la capacitación en México. In *La situación del trabajo en 2003,* ed. E. de la Garza and C. Salas. Mexico City: Editorial Plaza y Valdes.

Kaplinsky, R. 2000. Spreading the Gains from Globalization: What Can Be Learned from Value Chain Analysis? Institute for Development Studies, University of Sussex, Sussex, U.K. Unpublished.

Martínez, María Eugenia de la O. 1994. *Innovación tecnológica y clase obrera: estudio de caso de la industria maquiladora electrónica R.C.A. Ciudad Juárez, Chihuahua.* Mexico City: Miguel Ángel Porrúa Editores and Universidad Autónoma Metropolitana Unidad Iztapalapa.

Morán, R. 1999. Ganaderos que fabrican muebles. *Revista Expansión* [Mexico].

Sánchez, F., M. Fernández, and E. Pérez. 1994. *La política industrial ante la apertura*. Mexico City: Fondo de Cultura Económica.

Sánchez, G. 2002. La manufactura en Puebla. Unpublished.

Schmitz, H. 1995. Collective Efficiency: Growth Path for Small-Scale Industry. *Journal of Development Studies* 31(4):529–566.

Zepeda, E., D. Alarcón, and G. Félix. 1997. Empleo, competitividad y apertura económica: la pequeña y mediana empresa en la manufactura mexicana. In *Reestructuración económica y empleo en México*, ed. E. Zepeda and D. Castro. Mexico City: Fundación Friedrich Ebert.

Zepeda, E., and K. Middlebrook. 2004. Ensamble y manufactura en la industria maquiladora: ¿corriendo para permanecer en el mismo lugar? In *Desarrollo económico y la industria maquiladora de México,* ed. K. Middlebrook and E. Zepeda. Mexico City: Universidad Autónoma de México.

CHAPTER 6

Local Production and Innovation Systems in Brazil: The Metalworking Cluster in Espírito Santo

Arlindo Villaschi Filho, José Eduardo Cassiolato, and Helena Lastres

This chapter addresses an interesting experiment of institutional and industrial capability building in Espírito Santo, which until the early 1970s was among the three poorest states in Brazil. The focus is on the *capixaba*[1] metalworking local production and innovation system.[2] By local production and innovation system we mean a system comprising different agents (not necessarily or exclusively enterprises), participating in a process of collective learning, that may have a significant impact both on enterprise competitiveness and on social capabilities improvement. This approach to the analysis of industrial systems incorporates features of both the literature on clusters and collective efficiency and that on technological capabilities (Caniëls and Romijn, 2004).

The analysis concentrates on the interactions between a group of large enterprises, competitively inserted in the global market, and a cluster of SMEs that supply them with metalworking parts and services. Therefore, although the supplier firms sell their production to the domestic market, they are in fact connected to the international market through

[1] This is a Tupiniquin Indian word, nowadays used to indicate anybody and anything from Espírito Santo in the southeast of Brazil.

[2] This case was previously investigated by the authors within the framework of a larger study involving 26 cases analyzed since 1997 by a Brazilian research network, RedeSist. The general aim of this network was to investigate local production and innovation systems, in Portuguese defined as *arranjo* (see http://www.redesist.ie.ufrj.br).

their customers, the large exporting enterprises.[3] Our particular focus is on how cooperation between large exporters and their local suppliers of parts and services has rapidly and significantly enhanced the suppliers' industrial capabilities.

The leaders of the local production system are producers of low-value-added commodities (steel, iron ore pellets, paper pulp) facing fierce competition in the international market, which is characterized by excess production capacity, relatively weak technical barriers to entry, and a stagnant demand. This market situation has compelled producers worldwide to search for new strategies to increase productivity and cut costs. For the large *capixaba* enterprises, one of the novel strategies pursued has been the upgrading of the industrial capabilities of their local suppliers of parts and services, achieved as a consequence of the establishment of cooperative relationships. These relations—mostly but not exclusively informal—have been based on a vision of local SME suppliers as a collective entity, and relations have been mediated by CDMEC (the Center for the Development of the Capixaba Metalworking Industry). This is an organization which was put in place in the late 1980s in order to strengthen the competitiveness of small and medium-sized metalworking enterprises. The center gained momentum during the 1990s as new opportunities arose from an increasing demand on the part of large companies and other local customers. Besides fostering cooperation schemes within the local production cluster, CDMEC has also been very active in lobbying for winning more contracts for its associates.

The empirical evidence presented is based on fieldwork carried out in two different stages. In a first round (between January and October 2000), a questionnaire survey was undertaken on a sample of 35 SMEs, six large customers, and several supporting organizations (Villaschi and Lima, 2003). From October 2002 to February 2003, some SMEs, large customers, and supporting organizations were again contacted for open interviews. In the first survey, the goal was to investigate the process of institutional

[3] In the terminology proposed by Sverrisson (2004), the local SMEs are part of an auxiliary chain of a global commodity chain.

building that occurred during the 1990s, enabling SMEs to build the capabilities required to supply local large customers. In the second round of fieldwork, we focused on the most recent changes that contributed to increasing the local innovation capabilities of SMEs.

The following section presents a general overview of the local system, after which we focus on the learning and innovation processes taking place in the system. The final section addresses some policy issues, with particular attention to innovation.

The Main Characteristics of the Local Metalworking Cluster

The main agents that comprise the *capixaba* metalworking production system are (1) SMEs, to a large extent suppliers of large companies; (2) large enterprises producing low-value-added commodities for export; (3) an institution, CDMEC, aimed at supporting SMEs in improving their competitiveness; and (4) other local organizations.

The SMEs of the Metalworking Cluster

The core of the system is comprised of some 50 SMEs, which manufacture made-to-order machine parts and components and provide maintenance and assembly services. In 2002, 10 percent of the cluster firms had average sales of about US$15 million; 60 percent of them had average annual sales of US$3.5 million; and the remaining 30 percent had annual sales of about US$1 million. In terms of employment the average size is 30 employees.

In general, firms do not specialize in just one product but try to diversify as part of a strategy for coping with changes in the demand pattern. Prevailing activities are grinding and boiler works and, in a few cases, foundry work. For such activities, on average 70 percent of the SMEs' production is subcontracted to the large leading firms, demanding parts and accessories for maintenance and assembly lines. As concerns other services such as engineering and project design, they have been traditionally supplied by firms located outside the local system. Nevertheless, their relationships with the local cluster have recently increased, with some of them joining CDMEC and increasingly taking part in joint activities with the local firms.

In most cases, firms started out producing for just one major customer. More recently, many of them, although maintaining some specialization, have begun to supply several large companies. Geographical proximity to one customer was crucial at the beginning but is now of decreasing importance as a competitive advantage. It is also worth mentioning that CDMEC's activities, such as meetings, field trips, and seminars, have had an important role in promoting better acquaintance between SMEs and all their large customers.

The Large Anchor Firms

The largest firms in the *capixaba* metalworking cluster, acting as "anchors" of the system in the sense proposed by Markusen (1996), are Companhia Vale do Rio Doce (CVRD; iron ore pellets), Companhia Siderúrgica de Tubarão (CST; steel), Aracruz Celulose S.A. (paper pulp), and Samarco Mineração S.A. (iron ore pellets). It is important to stress that all the firms mentioned have traditionally been linked with public industrial development projects. This confirms Sverrisson's (2004:23) idea that "government initiatives . . . may often be the best or even the only way for Third World exporters to enter global commodity chains, and they may also be important in promoting upgrading activities in the chain." Below are short descriptions of each of the four anchor companies.

CVRD (state-owned until the late 1990s and then privatized) was established in the 1940s and specializes in iron ore extraction. Since the beginning its strategy has been to build up a modern and integrated mine–railway–harbor system. In the 1960s, as a strategy to overcome location advantages of its Australian competitors in the emerging Japanese market, it built iron ore pellet plants that could supply the increasing demand for concentrated iron ore fines. Subsequently, other plants were built in collaboration with some of its main customers in world markets (e.g.,

Japan, Italy, Spain, and South Korea). In Espírito Santo CVRD produces 32 million tons of iron pellets, most of which is exported.

CST was first conceived as a joint venture with Italy's Italsider, Japan's Kawasaky Steel, and Brazil's SOE Siderbras as part of the second national development plan (II PND, from 1974 to 1979) strategy to substitute the country's imports of intermediary goods and diversify its export base. Its location in the Grand Vitoria metropolitan area was mainly for geographical reasons: proximity to an important input source of iron ore and modern harbor facilities built by CVRD in the previous decade. Moreover, this large investment was also considered important for modernizing the local economy, which was until the 1960s highly dependent on low-quality coffee exports. Its production capacity in the 1980s was 3 million tons of steel slabs mainly for export. CST today produces 4.7 million tons of continuous casting steel plates, most of them sold in the international market. Moreover, in 2002 CST began in-plant production of hot strip steel plates with a nominal capacity of 2 million tons per year, mainly for the domestic market. At the beginning of the 1990s, the company was privatized and sold to banks and pension funds. Since then, its shareholder composition has been changing along with what has been taking place in the world steel industry, and today its main shareholders are France's Usinor (38 percent), CVRD (22 percent), and some Japanese partners (8 percent).

Aracruz Celulose was also established within the framework of the II PND's strategy of import substitution and export diversification. It started as a reforestation project in the latter part of the 1960s that now comprises more than 170,000 hectares of eucalyptus plantations, about half of them in the northern part of Espírito Santo and the rest in the southern part of the Bahia state. Then in the 1980s, with strong financial support of BNDES (the Brazilian national development bank), Aracruz started producing 400,000 tons of paper pulp per year; in the 1990s it expanded its production capacity to 800,000 tons per year. In 2002, a new plant brought its capacity to two million tons of paper pulp per year, which places Aracruz as the world leader of paper pulp produced from eucalyptus. Most of its production is exported to Europe (37 percent), North America (37 percent), and Asia (23 percent).

Samarco started its activities in the 1970s as a joint venture between Samitri (owner of iron ore mines in Minas Gerais) and Marcona, producing 3.3 million tons of iron ore pellets. Nowadays it produces over 8 million tons of these products, sold mainly in the international market. Since 2000, it has been part of the CVRD conglomerate.

Altogether with their manufacturing operations in Espírito Santo, these companies generate revenue of about US$6 billion per year. Although their importance in employment generation has been decreasing in the past 10 years (as a result of increasing downsizing and outsourcing), they employ 6,000 people locally, representing a very important source of employment in the local economy. Besides these four anchors, a few other local producers play an important role in the process of industrial capabilities building of local SMEs: ESCELSA (Espírito Santo Centrais Elétricas S.A.; energy); Companhia Espírito Santense de Saneamento (CESAN; water and sewage supply); Carboderivados S.A. and Carboindustrial S.A. (carbo chemical); FLEXIBRÁS Tubos Flexíveis Ltda (flexible industrial tubes); Companhia Siderúrgica Belgo-Mineira (steel); Telemar Telecomunicações (telecommunications); and Chocolates Garoto S.A. (a local chocolate factory among the three with largest market share in the country, recently acquired by Nestlé).

Institutional Setting: CDMEC

The major coordination role in the system's institutional setting is played by CDMEC. It was set up in 1988 with strong support from the Development Bank of the State of Espírito Santo (BANDES), an important contribution from some leading firms, particularly Aracruz Celulose, CST, and CVRD, and active participation of a few local SMEs. BANDES especially has played a key role, first in the 1980s in the identification of the main needs of the local system, and secondly in the design of policies to satisfy needs, of which CDMEC was the most important outcome. Then BANDES kept sustaining

CDMEC activities, for instance, by providing financial support for studies to identify potential local suppliers to the large anchor firms. At the beginning only 18 local SMEs joined the center; now the number of SMEs has increased to more than 60. In addition to SMEs, members include some of the anchor firms, training and consulting firms, and representatives of supporting organizations such as the university, SEBRAE, and others.

The main aim of CDMEC has been to increase the percentage of purchases made by anchor customers in the local market. This program has been sustained by the state government, which conditioned the issue of environmental licenses on an increase of local provision to the anchor companies. As a result, in Aracruz for instance, local SMEs have increased their participation from 1 percent of total purchases in 1991 to 35 percent in 2002.

Additional aims of CDMEC are the strengthening of local technological and industrial capabilities and the improvement of the collaboration between SMEs and their large customers. CDMEC has played a major role in fostering exchange of information and cooperation agreements among its members and between them and other national and international firms. Local SMEs choose to become members of CDMEC because it is a way to get closer (through regular meetings and field trips organized by the center) to their main customers and at the same time to get easier access to information.

Since its inception, CDMEC has focused on improving the capabilities of local suppliers by enhancing their opportunities to become suppliers of the large leading firms. More recently, the center has also started to support local metalworking SMEs in diversifying their market toward other large firms in other states in Brazil and other Latin American countries, as well as toward those companies that have shown interest in the exploration of natural gas and petroleum in Espírito Santo state and off its coast.

The networking function performed by CDMEC among its members includes promotion of consortia combining different specializations of local SMEs. An example is the CONVIX consortium, which involves five local electromechanical SMEs. Through the consortium, the SMEs can participate in several important projects involving some of the main leading firms of the state. In addition, a number of informal agreements among local SMEs, motivated by the needs of their large customers, are fostered by CDMEC. Because individual SMEs might have problems of reliability in the delivery of goods and services, cooperation among them for producing specific orders is seen as a proper response to the anchor's management needs and its target of reducing transaction costs.

CDMEC has also organized international trips to visit some of the world's main metalworking enterprises. For example, a 1997 trip to Europe, the Hot Strip Mill (HSM) Mission to Europe, aimed at putting local SMEs in contact with some European firms qualified to become suppliers of CST's project of production of hot strip steel. The mission had the political backing of the state government and was used as a way to foster negotiations between small local players and some international suppliers. As a result of this mission, some of the participating firms were subcontracted by CST.

The most recent focus of CDMEC's activity has been in the field of training and improvement of human resources. Among the services supplied are training courses for top managers and certification courses for shop floor workers. In addition, CDMEC is engaged in intense activity to increase the awareness of the large leading firms about the potentials of and progress made by the local SMEs.

Other Institutions Supporting SMEs

In addition to CDMEC, another important organization aimed at strengthening the local industrial capabilities of SMEs is PRODFOR (Program for the Development and Qualification of Local Suppliers). The program's main inspiration and initial support came from Aracruz Celulose and Samarco Mineração to raise managerial and organizational capabilities of SMEs. The experiment has been so successful that its focus has been expanded to providing certification services to any enterprise that requires it, not only in the metalworking industry.

In the field of education and research, the two main institutions are the Federal University at Espírito Santo State (UFES) and the Federal Center for Technical Education (CEFETES). Until very recently in key areas such as engineering, UFES was the only institution in the region providing university degrees at the undergraduate[4] and graduate level.

Although there is quite a strong relationship between the large anchor firms and UFES, this is not the case with their smaller local suppliers. From interviews with university researchers and SME entrepreneurs, it was clear that there is a communication gap between them. On the one hand, most of the research activities that are developed at the university's technological center are not regarded as relevant by most SMEs; on the other hand, the university's lecturers and researchers indicate that, although there are potential areas for cooperation with SMEs, such cooperation hardly ever occurs.

As for CEFETES, it offers basic and technological courses in several engineering areas such as electro-technic, metalworking, and metallurgy. CEFETES also offers short-term courses in issues like work safety, transport, and the environment. Furthermore, it hosts a program—CEQUAL (Certification of Labor for Mechanic and Electric Activities)—which is heavily used by firms needing certification for their labor force. This project was set up under the sponsorship of some anchor firms and is technically supported by ABRAMAN (the Brazilian Maintenance Association) and by SENAI (the System of Industry Labor Training run by the Confederation of Industrial Employers). Currently CEFETES leads four research projects which are directly linked to the activities in the cluster: an engineering teaching network under the sponsorship of FINEP (the National Agency for Financial Support of R&D and Innovation Activities); a project to develop new techniques for fast process manufacturing in cooperation with UNICAMP (University of Campinas, São Paulo State); and two other projects, one on continuous casting of thin slab,

[4] In the past two years, some private universities have started offering undergraduate engineering courses.

in direct cooperation with CST, and another on operational aspects of tube transportation.

The perception one gets from people both at SMEs and at anchor companies is that interaction with CEFETES is easier than with the university. As a matter of fact, many SMEs employ some of CEFETES' graduates and host some students for on-the-job training. The existence of direct contacts definitely helps bridge the gap between educational organizations and SMEs (Lundvall, 2002).[5] Unlike the university, where the incentives for professors to interact with firms are reduced because their career depends on other traditional performance indicators like number of publications, in CEFETES frequent interactions with the local economic community are highly valued in the evaluation system by the Ministry of Education to become eligible for extra funds. In confirmation of this, both SMEs and anchor companies declared that they are quite satisfied with the ability of CEFETES to fulfill their demand for qualified labor.

In general, the quality and availability of local labor is considered to be a very important competitive advantage by most of the SMEs interviewed. Part of this availability is definitely due to the training provided by CEFETES and, to a lesser degree, by UFES. It is also worth mentioning that some of the qualified workers in the SMEs have come from large anchor companies, after their internal restructuring process implemented throughout the 1990s.

Learning and Innovative Capabilities in the Local System

Little explicit cooperation on innovation among SMEs and other institutions has been recorded in earlier studies (Villaschi and Lima, 2003). When cooperation occurs it is mostly limited to exchange of information, and the most important partners of local SMEs are CDMEC (for 62.5 percent

[5] According to data from CDMEC, about 80 percent of the labor force of its associates are qualified workers (many of them graduated from CEFETES), whereas only 10 percent have graduated from college.

of sample firms), equipment suppliers (51.6 percent), customers (48.9 percent), and other competing SMEs (45.5 percent). There is also some cooperation with customers (30 percent of sample firms) and a little with the university (13 percent) in order to test new products.

Local innovation is primarily fostered by processes of learning-by-doing and learning-by-using taking place in the SMEs, often directed to fulfill some request coming from the anchor companies. According to the findings of our survey, most innovations in the SMEs are the result of in-house learning and of informal relations with their customers. The main source of technology transfer is the purchase of new machinery and equipment. In most cases these are supplied by firms from São Paulo, Rio de Janeiro, and Minas Gerais, and most SMEs rely on direct technical assistance from their suppliers and on information collected in technological fairs and from the specialized literature.

CDMEC also plays an important role as a source of information, especially with respect to procurement of contracts and markets. Moreover, CDMEC organizes meetings and workshops where information is exchanged among SMEs and large companies. It is important to stress that the exchange of information with large customer companies is restricted to contacts with their procurement and supply departments. Generally, SMEs do not have relationships with R&D or engineering departments. Thus, interactive learning aimed at a more systematic innovation process is very limited among SMEs, and in the few cases it happens, it involves mainly CDMEC associates and is geared toward minor incremental process innovations. On the side of large anchor firms, SMEs' technical expertise is not usually considered a relevant source of knowledge; what really counts are cost, quality, and delivery reliability. Nevertheless, some changes in attitude have recently been detected, as for example in the case of local suppliers of Aracruz's third plant.

In sum, the importance of Marshallian externalities is highly recognized by most enterprises in the cluster. Thus, their geographic proximity to large customers is regarded by both SMEs and their anchor customers as a very important competitive edge. Local labor quality and its availability are also highly valued. Part of this is due to training provided by local institutions such as CEFETES. In conclusion, there is evidence that there has been a steady upgrading among local SMEs and that this is in part the result of cooperation among them and the large anchor firms, importantly fostered by local institutions.

Concluding Remarks

This chapter has explored the experience of an industrial cluster developed under very specific conditions. First, it is located in a state whose economic structure has radically changed during the past 40 years, transforming itself from a mainly rural economy based on coffee into a dynamic manufacturing system. Secondly, its emergence is explained by the increasing role played by a group of competitive SMEs, producers of metalworking parts and services, that have managed to become suppliers of some large enterprises, producing commodities and competing in the international market.

From this analysis, some policy considerations may be derived, with special attention to how to foster cooperation and learning and how to embed innovation capabilities in, and spread them among, SMEs.

The first consideration is that the creation of a common identity among SMEs in the cluster requires financial backing and a long-term perspective. SMEs' entrepreneurs usually operate within tight time and budget constraints, and they seldom have a broader vision about the potential and challenges of their industry. Secondly, the existence of a "network broker" (an *articulador*) is key in this process of building up a common identity and increasing SMEs' awareness of the need to invest in upgrading their capabilities. Thirdly, it is important to emphasize the need to foster processes and activities that lead to and improve interaction and cooperation among the different actors within the cluster; examples are joint training programs, joint purchase and sales activities, and consultancy and R&D projects.

A fourth consideration addresses how to involve large firms in the cluster. On this point, the initial incentive provided by the state and linked with the issuance of environmental licenses has played a key role. But apart from that, the establishment of various initiatives to increase the opportunities for direct contact between SMEs and their customers has also been crucial for the process of upgrading. An example is the initiative of Aracruz taking a group of SMEs abroad to visit some of the paper pulp industry's leading international companies.

Finally, embedding and diffusion of innovation capabilities requires much more than having R&D facilities and research capabilities in place. As shown in this chapter, interactions among existing organizations that imply some form of cooperation and learning require orchestrated efforts and the clear identification of common goals. An illustration of this is the lack of interactions between the local federal university and the SMEs. Thus, it is not simply a matter of competence on the supply side. There must be mechanisms in place that can build the bridge between the supply and SMEs' demand, which often is not very sophisticated, with many entrepreneurs who do not really know what they need. In the particular case analyzed in this chapter, there would be room for joint actions between CDMEC and the anchor companies in order to build bridges between the university research apparatus and the SMEs' needs.

What these observations illustrate is that agglomeration of SMEs should not be left alone in the process of upgrading. The evidence presented shows that the anchor companies have been important for opening opportunities to their local suppliers, but nevertheless there have been very limited (if any) "new opportunities for international knowledge diffusion that lower-tier network suppliers should strive to exploit" (Ernst and Kim, 2001). This diffusion, when it occurs, takes place mainly through technology embodied in machinery and equipment and does not add much to the firms' dynamic competitive advantage.

Knowledge transfer is not an automatic process and requires a significant level of absorptive capacity on the part of local suppliers, together with a complex process to internalize and disseminate knowledge. Bearing this in mind, and on the basis of the present evidence, it seems that a more explicit and continuous innovation policy must be sought. Such a policy must involve the creation of awareness, the search for partners, the building of trust and sharing of knowledge, and the organization of networks. Even if this is not a complete checklist for designing policies for networking and targeting the promotion of innovation capabilities, it suggests the complexity of such a task.[6]

[6] Finland's experience offers interesting lessons in this regard. See, for example, Schienstock and Häamäläinen (2001).

REFERENCES

Caniëls, M., and H. Romijn. 2004. Conceptualizing Technological Capability Building in SME Clusters in Developing Countries. In *Linking Local and Global Economies: The Ties That Bind*, ed. C. Pietrobelli and Á. Sverrisson. New York: Routledge.

Cassiolato, J. E., H. M. M. Lastres, and M. L. Maciel, eds. 2003. *Systems of Innovation and Development*. Cheltenham, U.K.: Elgar.

Ernst, D., and L. Kim. 2001. Global Production Networks, Knowledge Diffusion, and Local Capability Formation. Paper presented at the Nelson and Winter DRUID Summer Conference, Aalborg, Denmark, June 12–15.

Lundvall, B. 2002. *The University in the Learning Economy.* Working Paper No. 02-06, Danish Research Unit for Industrial Dynamics (DRUID), Copenhagen Business School/Aalborg University.

Markusen, A. 1996. Sticky Places in Slippery Space: A Typology of Industrial Districts. *Economic Geography* 72:293–313.

Pietrobelli, C., and Á. Sverrisson, eds. 2004. *Linking Local and Global Economies: The Ties That Bind.* New York: Routledge.

Schienstock, G., and T. Häamäläinen. 2001. *Transformation of the Finnish Innovation System.* Helsinki: Sitra.

Sverrisson, Á. 2004. Local and Global Commodity Chains. In *Linking Local and Global Economies: The Ties That Bind*, ed. C. Pietrobelli and Á. Sverrisson. New York: Routledge.

Villaschi, A., and E. Lima. 2003. The Metalworking Production System in Espírito Santo: Commodity Exports and Local Industrial Capabilities. In *Systems of Innovation and Development*, ed. J. Cassiolato, H. Lastres, and M. Maciel. Cheltenham, U.K.: Elgar.

CHAPTER 7

Value Chains and Software Clusters in Mexico

Clemente Ruiz Durán

In the recent literature, regional economists and geographers have presented a variety of arguments for the development of high-tech clusters, based on examples including Silicon Valley in California (Saxenian, 1983), Silicon Glen in Scotland (Haug, 1986), Silicon Fen near Cambridge, England (Keeble and Kelly, 1986; Keeble, 1988); and the cluster around Route 128 near Boston (Dorfman, 1983). It has been noted that, in all of these cases, the grouping of certain capabilities creates a favorable environment for the development of the software industry. These include the presence of educational institutions offering a large supply of engineers, scientists, and technicians, combined with the regional promotion of key industries through subsidies or tax reductions; favorable living conditions, particularly in university towns; availability of venture capital; and creation of forward and backward linkages. This type of analysis has spread to developing countries. Balasubramanyam and Balasubramanyam (2000) note that the development of the software industry in Bangalore, India, has benefited from the presence of educational centers, such as the University of Bangalore, offering 14 degree programs in engineering, as well as from the strong presence of large companies demanding software and the government's support for the development of the industry. The main difference between these clusters has been their production strategy. In industrial countries, the focus has been on software development for the domestic market, whereas in India and other developing countries, the emphasis has been on export.

The development of high-tech clusters is now taking place in other developing countries, most notably in Mexico where, as part of its industrial modernization process, regional software clusters aimed at the domestic market have been created. This chapter examines the productive linkages taking place within the software industry and looks at how these linkages have given rise to the formation of clusters in Mexico. The premise is that, in the software industry, there is not just one value chain, but chains distributed throughout the country, thereby generating agglomerations of knowledge.

The software value chain cannot be understood following the typical logic of industrial chains, because software development has changed significantly in recent decades from a process vertically integrated with hardware, in which the value chain was mainly linked to computer (mainframe) manufacturing, to a decentralized system based on object-oriented programming and distributed programming. This shift has made it possible to divide production into small segments to be subcontracted remotely, using the Internet. This process is the result of the emergence of clusters of knowledge, which are fueled by production processes carried out thousands of miles away. Such is the case of Silicon Valley, which synergistically interacts with clusters in Bangalore and in Taiwan (Saxenian and Hsu, 2001), or the cluster on Route 128 in Massachusetts, which has a synergistic interaction with the Irish cluster in Dublin and the Israeli cluster.

One key question that arises from this discussion is: if production processes can be integrated internationally, do national agglomerations of producers serve a purpose? The software production process requires a concentration of knowledge institutions, in which both formal and informal relationships exist. In all cases, educational institutions are crucial to the development of a skilled workforce, together with the concentration of software production; as programmers communicate with each other, exchanges of ideas are critical to the production process. As Castells and Hall (1994) mention in their book *Technopoles of the World*, the synergy generated in situations of face-to-face interaction is key to the development of the software industry. This interaction cannot take place in isolation, simply by receiving messages over the Internet. It is by firmly grasping this concept that the most successful software developers create nodes of knowledge, as in the case of the "three Is": India, Ireland, and Israel.

The software production process involves a highly complex effort, as the fundamental idea is to generate a product for a specific purpose, which can vary from a PC application to developing embedded software. The key to this process is researching and developing the solution to the problem. Later, "patterns," that is, standardized ways to solve a problem that may be repeated, are created and, in some cases, packaged software is produced and trademarked. Pattern creation is equivalent to "production" in this sector. While each phase involves a distinct effort, the first stage requires the greatest effort. The cost of the production process initially rises, when research and development is conducted and has the highest cost; then, after the pattern is created, the cost declines, and producing the package has a relatively low cost.

The development of each of these stages can be described as follows (Figure 7.1):

1. *Research and development.* This stage requires the largest investment.
2. *Creation of patterns.* Once an idea has been conceived and a solution has been found, developers construct patterns that allow for the process to be repeated. At this stage, costs decrease considerably because the basic knowledge required for the specific solution has already been acquired. The challenge is to create a process that may be repeated through the use of patterns.
3. *Registration of trademarks and patents.* The registration of trademarks and patents may be the final step in the software development process. In this stage, the developing firm seeks to protect the copyrights of the product by registering it with the patent office, and then perform a mass distribution of the product.

Figure 7.1. Software Production Value Chain

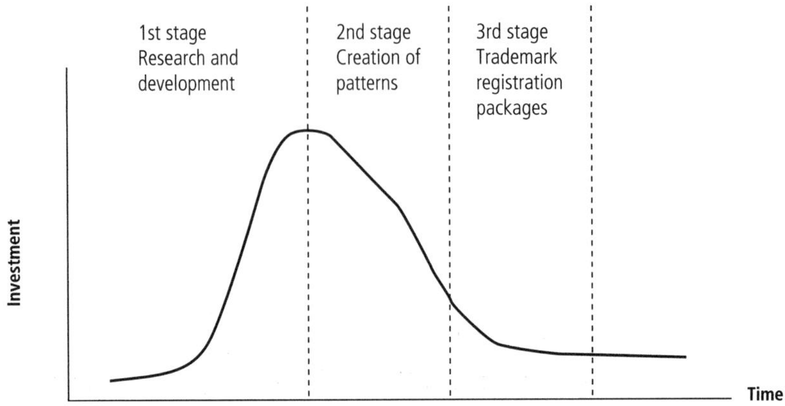

These stages can be carried out in an integrated fashion at one production center, or they can be divided, and some tasks assigned to centers with lower wage costs, which is what has led to the creation of remote development centers such as those in India. Once a region has engaged in this sector, it must also define its specialization within the sector. Thus products can be grouped into five main categories, according to the level of value added: the lower-value-added level would include data processing, database creation and consulting; the second level would consist of outsourcing (offshore or near shore); the third would include customized products; the fourth package development; and the fifth and most profitable group would include trademark registration. These categories involve a progressive learning process in which various groups of skilled workers are paid on the basis of the product they are developing (see Figure 7.2).

From this perspective, the (local) value chain can be integrated with the global value chain or simply be part of a national or even local chain. Local clusters can exist independently of global value chains by addressing domestic software needs. If the process is guided by a global value chain, production will most likely be associated with what has been termed outsourcing, either offshore or near shore, while local value chains are

Figure 7.2. Value Chain in the Software Industry

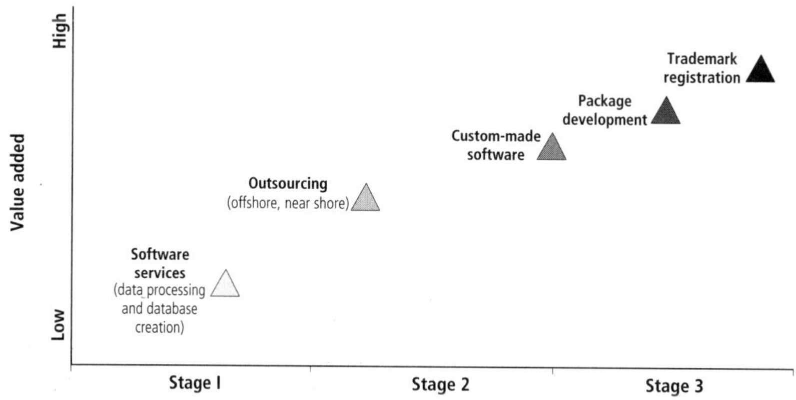

generally associated with customized software. Nevertheless, the various forms of organization that can emerge in these cases vary considerably. We will now examine the case of Mexico to demonstrate the nature of these processes.

The Software Industry in Mexico

The software industry has undergone a period of considerable expansion worldwide. According to *World Planet*, it sustained an average annual growth rate of 13 percent in the 1993–2001 period, reaching US$196 million in 2001. The United States has the largest market share with 50 percent of the total. Germany, the United Kingdom, Japan, France, Canada, and Italy together account for 30 percent of the market, and the remaining 20 percent is distributed among other countries. Mexico's market share is 0.31 percent, for a total of US$597 million. The growth of the software market in Mexico, at 9 percent annually in 1993–2001, has been lower than the growth observed worldwide in the same period. However, this slow growth process, compared to that recorded for the rest of the world, has been sustained by the participation of multinational companies (Microsoft, IBM, Oracle, SAP) and supported by a large microenterprise development. The 1999

Industrial and Services Census reported that there are 2,095 information technology businesses in the country: 92 percent of them are microenterprises, 7 percent are small businesses, 0.88 percent are medium-sized businesses, and large companies account for only 0.20 percent. Of these firms, 238 engage in software publishing and development. It is estimated that this sector employs around 22,000 people.

In Mexico, the development of the software industry has been localized in certain regions (Secretaría de Economía, 2002). Over the past decade, the most prosperous regions were those that had set up infrastructure for the development of new technologies early on; they were also able to develop their management capabilities and attract foreign investment. In contrast, those regions that failed to invest in infrastructure and labor early on were unable to synchronize their development with the rest of the country, which has led to increasing regional inequality. As a result, the software industry has been concentrated where major synergies have arisen among three different actors: local government, entrepreneurs, and institutions of higher education. Together, four regions—Mexico City, Monterrey, Guadalajara, and Aguascalientes—have helped create a large base for the development of the software industry in the country. In addition, small software clusters are developing elsewhere in the country, such as those in Morelos, Guanajuato, Baja California, and Yucatán that have grown over time (Ruiz Durán, 2003; Ruiz Durán and Dussel, 2002).

This dynamic business growth has been developing over the past 20 years, due in large part to the change in the organizational structure of major hardware companies. When personal computers were introduced, these companies were forced to change their strategy, which opened the door for engineers formerly employed at large companies, such as IBM, to start their own businesses and offer services including redesign, remodeling, and maintenance to the clients of the same multinational firms. At the same time, other software developers emerged, including developers of customized and single-platform, registered trademark and packaged software. In the following sections we will briefly analyze the software clusters emerging in these regions.

The Software Cluster in Mexico City

The software cluster in Mexico City began developing more than two decades ago with the opening of the IBM plant in the Legaria region. Later, with the diffusion of the personal computer, more software companies specializing in specific (primarily administrative) applications began to emerge. In this case, the demand for software came about in two different ways. One demand arose directly from the developers themselves, and the other resulted from the hiring of systems engineers for in-house work. The latter occurred more frequently in the public sector, which became the largest consumer of software in the country. This is how the first software cluster was created by the city-based federal public sector. In the mid-1980s, the federal government, through INFOTEC (Information and Services Technologies), generated a basic nucleus centralizing requests for customized software from all government entities.

In this case, a value chain was created linking government-run companies, government ministries, and INFOTEC. At first, public entities contracted systems engineers, and software development was carried out at the public entity (in-house). Later, the chain-based model of organization was made available to public sector agencies and started generating more demand from private companies. Thus, the public software sector served as a model for collective learning that developed into a software market. Nevertheless, since this gradual opening, the private sector has announced it would like the federal government to find a way to promote the privatization of the software development of the government ministries and INFOTEC, so that these entities will turn to the market to develop new customized software.

During the 1990s, the private sector, faced with the need to increase its competitiveness, started to perceive a need for new administration models and generated specific demands. This gave rise to the creation of more diverse businesses to supply different types of software: administration and management, Internet applications, production, technical services, banking and stock market applications, telecommunication applications, and health and education applications. At first, private businesses followed the example of the public sector and started contracting engineers to develop in-house software. However, the need to cut costs quickly led to out-of-company purchases, creating a progressive demand that could not be met by large multinational software companies, either because of their cost or because their software packaging was not appropriate for Mexican accounting practices and legislation. This led to the creation of a cluster of software businesses specialized in the administrative field, and a software community began to form. This community maintains indirect communication and engages in informal conversations to exchange viewpoints regarding the evolution of the market.[1]

The software cluster in Mexico City specialized mainly in accounting and administrative tasks and in products for competitiveness analysis. Activities kicked off with a group of microenterprises that began developing accounting packages and custom-made solutions, which allowed them to grow into medium-sized businesses; a number of these even developed into consortia, some with up to 500 employees.[2] These firms maintain interaction with large transnational software companies, because the goal of the transnational companies is to have all developers use their platform. According to the 1999 census, the software publishing and development cluster in Mexico City is made up of 130 businesses, employing around 2,500 people, with an average productivity of US$23,000, of which wages account for about a third.

The software cluster in Mexico City can be viewed as a typical case of external economies in which the presence of an extensive cluster of

---

[1] The need for these conversations, according to Rafael Bernal, Software Commissioner of the Mexican Association for Information Technologies (AMITI), is that they provide insight on the market pulse and more accurately define the market niche to be served. AMITI is the largest association of software developers in the country and aims to serve as a spokesperson before the various groups in Mexican society and also to expedite the use of information technologies within society (AMITI, 2002).

[2] Such is the case of Hildebrando, a company based in Mexico City with nearly 500 employees working in software development, primarily administrative.

institutions of higher education was critical to the development of the cluster and created favorable conditions for collective actions that would help facilitate the development of economies of scale, thereby placing local firms in a competitive position both nationally and internationally.

The Cluster of Monterrey, Nuevo León

The city of Monterrey, located in the state of Nuevo León, is the country's third-largest economy with 7 percent of the GDP and is one of the most industrialized cities in the country and home to some of Mexico's largest companies. Here, the software industry emerged as a result of the needs of large companies, the impetus coming from the consortium made up of FEMSA (formerly Cervecería Moctezuma), the Alfa group, the Cementos Mexicanos group, the Vitro group, Banorte, Serfin, and others. The development of software companies came about as a result of systems engineers working with companies belonging to the Monterrey group, as was the case of the founder of Softtek, the leading software factory in the cluster, and of spin-offs from other companies, as was the case of Neoris, which emerged from the Cemex group. Softtek managed to partner with General Electric on an outsourcing plan. Initially, Softtek was formed as an administrative solutions development firm focusing on the financial system, and it has since grown considerably to become the largest software development company in Mexico. When it began diversifying its supply and markets, it sought to form alliances with transnational firms looking to outsource and develop in Mexico, taking advantage of the low cost of labor. Currently, Softtek employs about 2,000 people and is the largest software factory in Mexico.

The Monterrey Technological Institute of Advanced Studies and the University of Nuevo León played a key role in the industry's development, as most of the systems engineers responsible for creating the industry are graduates of these institutions. A strong link exists between these institutions and local firms: training programs are offered for students at companies, and this generates ongoing interaction.

As a result of this interaction among the various firms, the government of the state of Nuevo León has developed an ambitious software industry development program for the 2002–2010 period. In this program the state government proposes strengthening the industry by focusing on provision of programs aimed at the U.S. market, based on the concept of outsourcing and taking advantage of Mexico's geographical proximity to the United States (near shore). In this case, the goals are ambitious, seeking to raise the number of businesses 10-fold. This implies that some firms will be CMM-3 (Capability Maturity Model Level 3) certified and others will be CMM-5 (Level 5) certified, which are high standards for the industry. This certification is very important in the industry, serving the purpose of assessing software development companies and ensuring that their development processes have met international standards and can be documented and reproduced. This is an international quality standard aimed at systematically improving the software development process. The certification model assesses the maturity of software processes and identifies the key practices required in order to increase their maturity. The CMM certification levels are as follows (the short-term goal of the enterprises is to obtain Level 3 certification):

Level 1—Initial: The software process is characterized as ad hoc and is sometimes chaotic. Few processes are defined, and success depends on individual efforts.

Level 2—Repeatable: Project management is established to track cost, schedule, and functionality. The necessary process discipline is in place in order to repeat previous successes on projects with similar applications.

Level 3—Defined: The software process for both management and engineering activities is duly documented, standardized, and integrated into a standard software process for the organization. All projects are approved and designed according to the organization's standard software process for developing and maintaining software.

Level 4—Managed: Detailed measures of the software process and product quality are collected. Both the software process and products are quantitatively understood and controlled.

Level 5—Optimizing: Continuous process improvement is enabled through quantitative feedback from the process and the piloting of innovative ideas and technologies.

This evolutionary evaluation process is based on the idea that predictability, effectiveness, and control of the organization's software process will improve as the organization progresses toward the final level of certification.

The Jalisco Cluster

During the 1990s, the state of Jalisco became a major producer of personal computers and printers, driven by IBM and Hewlett-Packard, which then attracted a large number of suppliers and some original equipment manufacturers (OEMs) from different parts of the world to the region. Because of this agglomeration of specialized businesses, the region has come to be known as the Mexican Silicon Valley.

As a result of the business expansion in the Jalisco region, the 13 universities in the metropolitan area designed new programs in related fields, which brought about a large growth in the labor supply. The flow of engineering professionals working in information-technology-related fields gradually increased. This highly skilled workforce was in great demand in the computer industry. Instead of seeking employment, many of them took the initiative to start their own software businesses to complement the hardware companies. This situation was reinforced in the mid-1990s by IBM's setting up a software factory at its Salto, Jalisco, plant, which employed 500 software developers and engineers. In addition, 151 microenterprises and SMEs were designing different types of software. It is important to note that only 60 have a storefront and offer mainly traditional computer services, including systems integration, programming, training, systems administration and maintenance, computer equipment rental and leasing, and Web hosting. Data processing, network services and electronic information services are still in their infancy. Unlike what has happened in other clusters in the country, Guadalajara's supply profile is geared toward small and medium-sized business, rather than large companies. Therefore, the value chain tends to be more dispersed.

The software industry value chain in Jalisco is linked to a local and national process aimed at supplying regional businesses. One of the most noteworthy examples is Computación en Acción's management solution software. Some of these small producers have managed to consolidate their position and have moved into international markets, opening field offices in the United States. The interaction between local producers and the IBM software factory can be attributed to two basic phenomena: first, many of the entrepreneurs who now have their own businesses had been trained at the IBM factory, thus reducing the cost of education; and secondly, the presence of IBM has pushed the developers to promote the use of open-source software, which has become a key component in the government's software development program.

Through the Council of Science and Technology, the government has implemented a program to further develop the software industry, identifying market niches, particularly in the area of packaged software and traditional computer services. The program includes an ambitious training program designed for 12,000 individuals working in the areas of firmware and semiconductor design, software testing, and multimedia development, as well as Internet and software design. Additionally, the Jalisco state government has decided to create a 22-hectare Technopole in the Guadalajara metropolitan area in order to accommodate the new software companies.

The Software Cluster in Aguascalientes: Methods and Procedures for the Formation of Clusters

In the above cases, the software cluster formation process derived from an existing market, followed by public sector action aimed at reinforcing the task initiated by the producers. This case differs from the others in that the Aguascalientes state government actively participated in the design of an explicit plan to create clusters. Until the late 1970s, the local economy was fueled by agricultural growth, complemented by wine production and the garment industry. This situation changed radically, however, in the 1980s, when a process to promote foreign direct investment (FDI) was initiated, successfully attracting companies from the automotive sector (Nissan) and the electronics sector (Texas Instruments, Xerox, and others) and generating substantial growth in the local economy. The question then is: what produced this extraordinary growth? In order to provide insight into the evolution of this process, the three main phases of the state's development are described.

Phase 1 was the transition from an agriculture-based economic structure to a manufacturing-based structure. In 1974, the newly elected governor decided to promote a radically different development strategy during his term of office (1974–1980), shifting the emphasis of government action from agriculture to manufacturing. This process was carried out after consultations with the proprietors of companies active in the strongest production industries: agriculture, wine, textiles, clothing, railroad repair, and some from the metallurgy sector. Similarly, the new government established contact with trade unions in order to gain insight on the primary concerns of workers. Also, in 1973, Nacional Financiera (NAFIN) decided to promote the development of medium-sized cities in 23 states as part of the National Decentralization Program. This program included the creation of industrial parks that provided the physical infrastructure, as well as business development services and a wide array of support mechanisms such as tax incentives and project evaluation assistance. The state government utilized the program effectively, creating a trust for the construction of the Aguascalientes Industrial Park and donating 200 hectares, 40 of which would be urbanized with the assistance of NAFIN. The effort to quickly strengthen the necessary infrastructure and services led to new investment in the state and an expansion of the local manufacturing base. Three national engineering firms and the first car parts dealers were among the key businesses set up in the late 1970s.

Phase 2 involved attracting investment. As a result of the success of the first industrial park built to attract new investors, the decision was made to promote three additional parks. These years of industrial development, the first half of the 1980s, were highly successful in at least three areas. First, the creation of necessary infrastructure components laid the base for new investments. Second, the establishment of institutional networks such as chambers of commerce created an environment in which common problems could be addressed, favoring the formation of a single common approach to resolving them. And lastly, a change was made in the state's image, from that of an agricultural state to that of an emerging industrial economy. The availability of a critical mass of suppliers and buyers made the state an attractive alternative for companies looking for a suitable location for their plants. The first international company to take advantage of these opportunities was Texas Instruments (TI), which began exploring options for a manufacturing plant in 1979. In this specific case, TI was able to modify elements of the import substitution policies related to restrictions on property held by foreigners, which required the direct approval of the president of the republic. When TI decided to set up operations in Aguascalientes, Xerox and Nissan soon followed. Once this environment was created, the state government reinforced these tendencies through institutional reforms aimed at improving the business environment, promoting public–private agreements on resolving specific problems of the businesses and establishing efficient local economic development agencies. All of this contributed to advancing the growth of the economy in Aguascalientes.

Phase 3 focused on formation of alliances between local and foreign companies. As a result of the strong growth in foreign investment, the government of Aguascalientes began to look for ways to forge links with national providers. In some cases foreign companies, such as Nissan, arranged for their Asian suppliers to relocate to the area, thus creating a cluster of top-rate suppliers. On the basis of this idea the Aguascalientes government decided to promote sectoral clusters in order to strengthen the value chains in the state's provinces. The government took actions to ensure that this process would in fact be implemented and developed a method for the creation of clusters. The first step was to create a civil association to coordinate the efforts of each industrial cluster. This practice was first implemented in the automotive industry and later spread to sectors dominated by foreign investment, as well as to more traditional sectors such as the clothing and furniture industries.

As a result of these processes, Aguascalientes was transformed from an agriculture-based economy to an economy with a strong manufacturing industry. Numerous lessons on policy were learned through this process, including the formation of clusters for the purpose of exploiting competitive advantages, a policy which involved the participation of the business sector in the decision-making process of the state.

Origin of the Software Cluster in the City of Aguascalientes

It is within this framework that the software industry began to develop as an integrated part of the production processes (embedded software) in the automotive and electronics industries, the latter with Xerox and Texas Instruments. These companies contracted local systems engineers to adapt software to the specific needs of the plants in Mexico. As a result, a number of these engineers received basic training in programming, which many of them later drew on to start their own software businesses in the 1990s. In this setting, software firms began to multiply, and in 2000, the government of Aguascalientes decided to promote the development of a high-tech cluster through the Ministry of Economic Development (SEDEC). The initiative to create this cluster arose from consultations that the government promoted within the business sector, in order to ensure that the elements were in place to carry out actions that would truly have an impact on the most dynamic and productive sectors of the state economy. Thus, the formation of the information technology business cluster in Aguascalientes is a public–private cooperation initiative, also involving some educational institutions that have played a key role in ensuring that cluster businesses implement training programs and quality assurance courses. The legal entity proposed for this cluster was the same as that used for other clusters, a civil association known as INNOVATIA.

This proposal presented in meetings organized by the government was the result of the efforts of a large group of local entrepreneurs who, attempting to increase their competitiveness in the market, decided to join efforts and channel their collective energy toward a common goal, which could also bring them individual benefits. Prior to this effort, IT firms in Aguascalientes operated independently, as there had been no way to coordinate efforts, nor were there any chambers or associations to perform this role.

Currently, there are approximately 250 information-technology-related businesses operating in the state, of which 50 are engaged primarily in software development and 34 form part of the cluster. This group includes large companies such as Demesys (a General Electric subsidiary), PC Market, and Telecomunicaciones Modernas.

The cluster enterprises are in the process of establishing themselves in the local and regional market. Only one company, with 100 percent Mexican capital, exports its psychometric packaged software; the remaining businesses sell within the region, and very few market their products nationwide. In turn, the structure of the production chains in these types of businesses is generally vertical, which is the result of limited interaction among entrepreneurs prior to the formation of the cluster. Still, some enterprises have a process that incorporates other production processes and therefore, these production chains involve outsourcing. It is important to note that one of the first tasks of the cluster was to integrate the member enterprises' software production processes, for which it sought the support of the Universidad Autónoma de Aguascalientes (UAA), the primary source for training and quality assurance courses.

Governance Structure of the Aguascalientes Cluster

The Aguascalientes cluster shows an interesting governance structure in which various actors from the main sectors of society are active members of the board of directors. Board members include representatives from UAA, the Universidad Tecnológica Regional, the State Ministry of Economic Development, and the National Institute of Statistics and Geography (INEGI). The board elects a cluster president from among the entrepreneurs, who carries out duties with the support of a treasurer and a vice president; additionally, a director oversees the area of operations and is assisted by an advisor, who submits results to the cluster president.

The implementation of this system of government could be reproduced in other entities in the country, while preserving its particular characteristics.

Characteristics of Software Development Enterprises That Form the INNOVATIA Cluster in the City of Aguascalientes

The cluster enterprises specialize mainly in management, production management, and support for higher education institutions. In this regard, the Aguascalientes cluster entrepreneurs affirmed the need to conduct, as one of their initial activities, an assessment of the situation of the local industry in order to ensure the availability of the elements needed to formulate a plan of action.

The study prepared by Deloitte and Touche (2003) noted that of the total member enterprises, a third of businesses' income comes from customized software development (32 percent), followed by technical support (31 percent) and infrastructure (29 percent). Additionally, 90 percent of the enterprises are classified as micro and, considering software development personnel alone, none of these enterprises has more than 15 staff members. Sixty-two percent of the businesses have a low staff turnover rate. In the previous two years, 20 percent the businesses had reduced staff in percentages ranging from 53 to 83 percent as a result of low national economic growth. Nevertheless, all of the enterprises expected to grow in terms of jobs over the subsequent two years, provided the national economy recovered. The study revealed that while the level of education of staff employed by cluster businesses was acceptable, 63 percent of total personnel had not mastered a second language, which was identified as a major area of weakness. Of the businesses surveyed, only 14 percent of employees had advanced English skills, while 18 percent had an intermediate level of English, followed by lower percentages for other languages. The study mentioned that for the most part, cluster enterprises believed that the educational offerings were inadequate in terms of quality and quantity. This perception differed from that of local educational institutions and therefore, efforts needed to be made to bridge the gap and achieve a greater convergence of views between these two groups. The study also revealed that most of the enterprises did not have formal staff training programs in place, but rather tended to offer training in response to market demands. Furthermore, there were no policies in place regarding the percentage of income to be allocated to this area.

Based on these findings, the most urgent programs were implemented by the cluster, including training, international standard certification (Capability Maturity Model) for the businesses, and the creation of a product catalog to be used as part of the marketing strategy of cluster enterprises. The catalog involved the participation of 13 enterprises and offered a total of 60 products, ranging from customized software development and medical software to the marketing of customized solutions. These initiatives received strong support from SEDEC and from institutions of higher education involved in the development of the cluster (UAA). The lines of action proposed by the cluster for its medium-term development are as follows:

- *Marketing:* Considerable efforts have been made to improve marketing skills. For example, with support from universities and the state government, enterprises have received training and quality assurance courses aimed at increasing the competitive advantages of the cluster. This was even among the main arguments that contributed to the formation of the cluster.

- *Linkage:* The linking of the agents that could participate in the development of information technology has also been one of the pillars of the cluster. Currently, the linkage with institutions of higher education aimed at exploiting resources appears to have been successful. For example, a quality assurance course on the CMM is offered by UAA.
- *Training:* Training has also been identified as a priority in the cluster and therefore, links are being formed in this area.
- *Image:* The image of the cluster is strongly tied to the marketing of its products, and thus marketing strategies have been implemented.
- *Development:* The development of new business opportunities among member enterprises is critical to the survival of the cluster. Entrepreneurs are well aware of this.
- *Quality:* The quality of the developments will depend on the efforts made with regard to linkage. Accordingly, the cluster is collaborating with UAA on the creation of an institute to offer the IT businesses training in processes subject to quality certification based on international standards (for example, the CMM).

The initiatives aimed at quality and training are the actions that have maintained unity within the cluster thus far, largely because these are the enterprises' main areas of deficiency. The deficiency is due to a variety of factors, including the small size of the enterprises (an average of 5–10 employees), which has limited the investment in staff training and in the development of new skills. This type of support is important because the majority of cluster businesses did not allocate resources for staff training, which led to a slowdown and insufficient upgrading.

One of the keys to the continued development of the cluster has been the training courses offered to employees of cluster enterprises, promoted by cluster management board and SEDEC and offered by UAA. Enterprises pay only 20 percent of the cost of this training, and the rest is covered by SEDEC. Together, the cluster enterprises have initiated a CMM certification process that would allow them to standardize, register, and improve their software production processes with an aim to achieving better practices, which would increase their competitiveness in the market. Hence, they have sought the support of SEDEC and UAA to enable the university to adapt the certification guidelines and procedures to the particular characteristics of the cluster enterprises.

Many of the cluster enterprises find that the creation of business networks successfully generates business prospects among cluster members; this sometimes takes the form of outsourcing schemes. In fact, prior to the formation of the cluster, many enterprises subcontracted third parties at noncompetitive rates and with limited or no information about the other businesses. Now this process is carried out more efficiently, and with a higher level of assurance, because cluster members have access to a business network that provides information on other enterprises. Many enterprises are awarded development projects based on recommendations from other cluster members. Another factor that has been identified as a problem area for the cluster enterprises that needs to be addressed in the medium term is that most of the enterprises do not have a market for their products other than the national market. Only a few enterprises, with assistance from SEDEC, have secured funding to develop a business plan targeting the export (primarily Latin American) market. Additionally, meetings among the cluster enterprises have been held to develop joint projects and begin marketing abroad. According to the 2003 SELECT report, 80 percent of technological developments are not put on the market because they are developed in government agencies or offices of the government. Thus, marketing remains an area of strategic importance.

The Role of Policy and Institutional Networks

Following the plans proposed for the development of the industrial groupings in the state, a civil association, INNOVATIA, was created.

This association groups the enterprises of the software cluster and now includes 34 enterprises, with sales averaging around US$4.3 million. In this context, the entrepreneurs sought to secure institutional support for the project from the local government, specifically the State Ministry of Economic Development. Their efforts played a key role in speeding up the government's actions.

As a result, the local government decided to create CEDITI (Information Technology Development Center), a technical support institution to support the development of information technologies, in cooperation with CONCYTEA, the local counterpart of the National Science and Technology Council (CONACYT). The purpose of this institution is to coordinate activities and policies for the development of the local information technology industry. CEDITI seeks to create work programs consistent with the strategic guidelines of the IT cluster, which would ensure interaction between the cluster and member enterprises. CEDITI promotes five strategic programs: development of human capital, incubation of information technology businesses, promotion of competitiveness, research and development of new technologies, and infrastructure development planning.

The initial amount of investment required for the creation of this center is approximately US$679,000, which will go toward funding the first two strategic programs. The Science and Technology Council, together with the State Ministry of Economic Development, in cooperation with the cluster management board, is the local government organization that will promote the development of the center and its linkage with state-run academic institutions at a national level. In order to strengthen this process, a manual containing practices to be followed by all cluster enterprises has been prepared. Furthermore, the federal and state governments have decided to create a Technopole to provide a common space for software innovation. This space will house, in addition to software enterprises, an institution of higher education (Monterrey Technological Institute of Advanced Studies) to serve as a base for human resource development for the cluster. This reveals how the state of Aguascalientes is currently the first Mexican experience targeting the development of *formal* clusters.

The Technology Council of the State of Aguascalientes has been working closely with the cluster management board on the construction of CEDITI. In the initial phase of the project, its primary role is to secure funding for the construction of the building through support funds earmarked for infrastructure. This demonstrates the state government's formal commitment to the IT industry, which is in line with the software industry development program.

Similarly, the support that cluster entrepreneurs have received from the local government through the State Ministry of Economic Development is contributing greatly to the success of the cluster. Of the activities carried out, the training and quality management courses (already mentioned), financed mainly by SEDEC, are among the most noteworthy. Furthermore, the local government has purchased land in order to group the cluster enterprises together in one location. Moreover, SEDEC is responsible for defraying the majority of the administrative expenses generated by the cluster, which total US$1,800 per month. In 2001, the cluster budget was US$136,000, and by 2002, this amount had risen to approximately US$364,000. A large portion of these resources is allocated to training.

In addition to the formal funding support, the development of the cluster is closely linked to the development of institutions of higher education which, in Aguascalientes, include UAA, the Technological University of Aguascalientes, Bonaterra University, and the Monterrey Technological Institute of Advanced Studies at Aguascalientes. These institutions have supported the development of the cluster with a critical mass of 18,000 engineers and technologists and several additional synergies. The participation of the Technological University of Aguascalientes includes the generation of a large number of graduates in the area of systems and computing. These graduates have found an important source of employment in many of the businesses belonging to the Aguascalientes cluster. Furthermore, the Technological University has participated in professional internship programs in which students in their final semester of study perform unpaid internships at local businesses. UAA has crucially helped the operation of one of the key programs of the cluster: training developers in the implementation of new production processes (languages). The university also plays a central role in the system for certifying businesses in the cluster in accordance with international standards for the improvement of production and software development processes (CMM), because it is the university that will attempt to adapt the guidelines of this system to each individual enterprise. A representative of the university also sits on the Board of Directors of the cluster.

Bonaterra University, a partner institution of Universidad Latinoamericana based in Mexico City, has managed to incubate a successful firm that has maintained its ties with the university. Its experience may be usefully reproduced in other state universities.

There is great interest within the cluster in establishing these types of linkages. With regard to quality, for example, the cluster in conjunction with the UAA has launched a series of courses to present the international quality criteria for software development to the entrepreneurs, and thus to help them become eligible for CMM certification.

Establishing links between the software development cluster and educational institutions involves a collective effort with the end goal of certifying the cluster. This has been led by the cluster director, supported by the state government through the Ministry of Economic Development and UAA, which together have been informed of the procedures that must be followed for a business to become CMM certified. The goal is that, in the end, the university and the Center for the Development of the Software Industry will be the organizations providing the necessary advisory services to the cluster enterprises, so that each individual enterprise will be prepared to become CMM certified. Nevertheless, collective certification is a response to the particular characteristics of the businesses belonging to the cluster.

The Production Chains That Fuel the Cluster

The performance of the value chain in Aguascalientes is based on the demand of local and regional businesses and, in some cases, of firms located abroad. Only Demesys, an affiliate of General Electric, uses an outsourcing scheme. For its part, human capital inputs are supplied by the state institutions of higher education, and a reduced number of businesses have hired staff from other entities in the country. Furthermore, the establishment of informal networks among software developers is one of the components that businesses have been working with in recent years. Formalizing these networks is one of the factors that gave rise to the creation of the cluster of software businesses, in which formal networks would contribute to the consolidation of the member businesses. A characteristic of this group of software development businesses is that because it is a more integrated cluster than groups in the rest of the country, demands are centered primarily on cluster businesses. Dispersion is reduced, and the demand of the grouped businesses increases, which creates a virtuous cycle of expansion that encourages new businesses to join the group. This is also a result of the influence this cluster has on local industry (70 percent of local businesses are part of the cluster).

Contribution of Aguascalientes to the Discussion on Information Technology Clusters

The evolution of INNOVATIA brings new elements to the discussion on the creation and development of clusters, because it systemizes the process of establishing an information technology cluster. It was created very recently so figures on its performance are scarce, but employment is already at 230, with 121 software developers (14 percent of them speak English). The cluster has a budget of US$364,000 (in 2001) and the state government is supporting it with only US$21,600.

The government's main contribution has been the establishment of a successful cluster formation formula: the setting up of a civil association financed by the state government and run by the producers. Also, the state government's interest in increasing activity in the cluster led to the creation of a technological development institute, which allows the government to drive changes to the processes. In addition to the state effort, there is the linkage between universities and entrepreneurs that has been extremely difficult to achieve in other regions. Representatives of the universities are part of the cluster's board of directors, as are representatives of the National Science and Technology Council, which is able to provide funding, if necessary, through mixed funds for the development of national industry. However, the role that universities will be asked to perform in the development of new technologies and the creation of more formal networks with member businesses has yet to be determined. These institutions should play a more active role in order to ensure, above all, that the critical human capital is available for the expansion of the cluster.

Mexico's Lessons on Policies for Cluster Formation

The information technology cluster formation process in Mexico has opened up a new area of discussion on the formation of clusters, as high-tech clusters require a small amount of capital and a high concentration of skilled labor. In addition, the main input is the formation of human capital through the direct linkages with educational institutions, which allows for business growth. The territorial dimension of this type of cluster development is linked to the existence of centers of higher education and their efforts to help the cluster enterprises obtain certification.

In Mexico, formation processes of information technology clusters have followed diverse paths, but it is clear that the business demand for software has driven the industry's development. In Mexico City, the government had its own software company and then began privatizing some development projects in order to create more opportunities for the private sector. This type of action should increase in the public sector, federal as well as local, in order to further boost the industry.

Transnational corporations have also played a central role in the development of software clusters. One way is by promoting the use of their platforms so that new software developments would be built on them, launching promotional programs in various regions of the country, as

Microsoft has done. Moreover, some transnational companies have created global value chains using Mexican companies. The most noteworthy case is Softtek in Monterrey, the country's leading software provider, whose developments can be compared to those taking place in Bangalore, India.

The main driving force of software development in Mexico has been the administrative revolution, and therefore, the majority of solutions and packages are aimed at this market. In most cases, the software cluster formation process has been market-driven, while the strength of the business sector has been the driving force behind the need to involve local governments and even the federal government. The only case in which the cluster formation process was carried out jointly by the private and the public sector was in Aguascalientes, which is the most integrated in terms of interbusiness cooperation. State governments have been innovative in their participation and have managed to create an environment of healthy competition, in some cases developing market niches (Jalisco), while in others providing strategies for growth and for supplying the U.S. market (Nuevo León). In other cases, commitments have been made to certify the cluster as a whole, and in all cases, state governments are firmly committed to the development of Technopoles, where entrepreneurs are brought together in a single location for the purpose of generating interaction and exchanges among producers. Interaction among producers is essential in developing these types of clusters because it generates competition as well as incentives for cooperation. This chapter demonstrates that there is plenty of room to support a development policy for this type of cluster, targeting the promotion of international competitiveness, and above all, relying on the most valuable resource any economy has: human capital.

References

Asociación Mexicana de la Industria de Tecnologías de Información, A. C. (AMITI). 2002. Propuesta para el uso y aprovechamiento de las tecnologías de la información y las comunicaciones. AMITI, Mexico City. Unpublished.

Balasubramanyam, V. N., and A. Balasubramanyam. 2000. The Software Cluster in Bangalore. In *Regions, Globalization, and Knowledge-Based Economy,* ed. J. H. Dunning. New York: Oxford University Press.

Castells, Manuel, and Peter Hall. 1994. *Technopoles of the World: The Making of Twenty-First-Century Industrial Complexes.* London: Routledge.

Deloitte and Touche. 2003. *Estudio de competitividad sectorial.* Mexico: Deloitte and Touche.

Dorfman, N. 1983. Route 128: The Development of a Regional High Technology Economy. *Research Policy* 12(6):299–316.

Haug, P. 1986. U.S. High Technology Multinationals and the Silicon Glen. *Regional Studies* 20(6):103–106.

Keeble, D. 1988. High Technology Industry and Regional Development in Britain: The Case of the Cambridge Phenomenon. *Environment and Planning C* 7:153–172.

Keeble, D., and T. Kelly. 1986. New Firms and High Technology Industry in the United Kingdom. In *New Firms and Regional Development in Europe,* ed. D. Keeble and E. Weaver. London: Croom Helm.

Ruiz Durán, Clemente. 2003. Mexico: The Management Revolution and the Emergence of the Software Industry. In *Industrial Agglomeration: Facts and Lessons for Developing Countries*, ed. M. Kagami and M. Tsuji. Tokyo: Institute of Developing Economies, Japan External Trade Organization.

Ruiz Durán, Clemente, and E. Dussel. 2002. North American Integration and Development: The Computer Industry. Facultad de Economía, Universidad Nacional Autónoma de México (UNAM). Unpublished.

Saxenian, A. 1983. The Genesis of Silicon Valley. *Built Environment* 9:7–17.

Saxenian, A., and J. Y. Hsu. 2001. The Silicon Valley–Hsinchu Connection: Technical Communities and Industrial Upgrading. *Industrial and Corporate Change* 10(4):893–920.

Secretaría de Economía. 2002. *Programa para el desarrollo de la industria del software.* Mexico City: Secretaría de Economía.

Part III

Upgrading in Clusters and Value Chains: Methodological Approaches in Measurement and Policy Support

CHAPTER 8

Upgrading in International Trade: Methods and Evidence from Selected Sectors in Latin America

Alessia Amighini

From a development perspective, developing countries' participation in global markets has often raised concerns regarding their gains from integration in world trade. The size and scope of developing countries' integration in world markets has substantially increased in the last 50 years as many developing countries have shifted out of primary production and entered international markets with products at different levels of industrial processing. But still the question of *how* developing countries might gain from export-oriented activities is as high as ever on the development agenda.

In the 1950s, participation of developing countries in world trade was mainly through exports of unprocessed primary products versus imports of manufactured goods. This pattern of specialization often resulted in "immiserizing growth," growth that expands a country's exports and worsens the terms of trade sufficiently that the country's real income falls (Bhagwati, 1958). This occurred because the terms of trade of these primary products—the prices they got compared to the prices they paid to import manufactures—systematically declined, mainly due to global oversupply combined with low elasticity of international demand for unprocessed primary commodities. At that time, the major option economists

The views expressed in this chapter reflect the opinions of the author and do not necessarily reflect those of UNCTAD.

and development agencies could envisage to avoid a falling terms-of-trade effect was a shift out of primary production and a move into production of manufactures.[1] Since then, many developing countries—mainly in Asia and partly in Latin America—have succeeded in emancipating themselves from primary exports and specializing in manufacturing. But many other countries, especially among the least developed, are often still dependent on primary production and trade. For them, dependence on primary commodities is still a major reason for their inability to increase living standards.

Since the 1990s, the globalization of production processes has expanded and altered the pattern of participation of developing countries in world trade. Nowadays many developing countries can take advantage of global product markets that are disintegrated on a world scale due to fragmentation of production across countries and regions. Many of them are specializing in manufacturing at different levels of industrial processing. However, this new pattern of specialization is posing similar problems to those of unprocessed primary commodities. Low barriers to entry, global oversupply and declining terms of trade are affecting many manufacturing sectors, so that some segments of these markets are actually being commodified. Therefore, many agents are locked into lower-value segments of trade and start suffering from the same immiserizing pattern of specialization as countries specialized in primary commodities.

The development challenge now is therefore to move out of commodity segments of the market, defined as both primary and manufactured products that are subject to falling terms of trade (Kaplinsky and Readman, 2000). This may be called upgrading in the global economy (see Pietrobelli and Rabellotti, Chapter 1 in this volume). Upgrading can be attained in two ways. First, upgrading can be attained by shifting to

---

[1] Much less attention was instead given to another way toward industrial upgrading, that is, upgrading through primary processing. The belief that there would be scope for other developing countries to follow Asia down the road to export-oriented manufacturing inspired the whole wave of trade regime reforms that were central to the structural adjustment programs promoted by international development organizations and developed country governments in many developing countries (Owens and Wood, 1997).

other noncommodified segments within the same market. This shift can be called vertical process integration, if higher-value-added activities are performed which were previously carried out by other firms, sectors, or countries, or vertical process disintegration, if low-value-added activities are outsourced to other firms, sectors, or countries.[2] In the primary sector, this type of upgrading refers to vertically integrating into intermediate and final processing activities, which are usually among the highest-value-added stages of production. In manufacturing, this type of upgrading refers to the shift from lower- to higher-value-added activities, which do not necessarily correspond to higher degrees of industrial processing (e.g., design and marketing often capture higher margins than industrial processing in the case of many manufactures).

Secondly, upgrading can be attained by decommodifying the products in which a country is specialized. For products to be decommodified, firms and countries should be able to create or increase barriers to entry in the same segment of the market, that is, to increase product differentiation. The latter can be attained through diversification of existing products with respect to their characteristics (horizontal product differentiation), so as to expand the variety of the same product type, or through diversification with respect to their quality (vertical product differentiation), so as to expand the quality ladder. In primary products, vertical product differentiation allows capture of higher export margins, because saturated global primary commodity markets allow for increasing quality premia.[3] Horizontal product differentiation involves the production of new varieties (as opposed to varieties of higher quality) of the same unprocessed commodities. New varieties allow a shift out of products facing deflationary price pressures only to the extent that they create entry barriers and have

[2] In the literature on global commodity chains (see below), this type of upgrading is referred to as "functional upgrading," defined as a change in the mix of activities from lower- to higher-value-added ones.

[3] This is, for example, the case of coffee. The Arabica/Robusta coffee price spread has been increasing, from 5–20 percent of the Arabica price during the 1970s–1980s to 17–58 percent in the 1990s (World Bank, 1999:68).

substantial learning or technological requirements. In both cases, the possibility of increasing export margins depends on the level of entry barriers in differentiated production, which affects long-term expected returns. Similar reasoning applies to manufactured products, which are becoming increasingly diversified in terms both of variety and of quality, because of capital- and skill-abundant industrially advanced countries trying to escape direct competition from labor-abundant developing economies.[4] Also in the manufacturing sector, successful diversification requires a relatively high level of entry barriers; otherwise, the increasing degree of competition due to an increasing number of producers would lead to declining unit prices, that is, to new products' being commodified.

Assessing upgrading from a development perspective has been so far the primary focus of a growing empirical literature on global commodity chains or global value chains. GVC analysis has mainly been concerned with manufacturing production, and in particular, with textiles and garments, with a regional focus on Asia (Gereffi, 1999a, 1999b), and to a lesser extent, with primary commodities from sub-Saharan Africa, in particular, fish (Gibbon, 2001), fresh fruits and vegetables (Dolan, Humphrey, and Harris-Pascal, 1999), and cotton (Gibbon, 2001).The major aim of GVC analysis is to examine power relations in global value chains and to explore the possibilities for upgrading through a shift from lower- to higher-value-added productive activities. Although the capacity of countries to shift to higher-value-added production is an important aspect of upgrading, yet another major aspect of upgrading is the capacity of countries to compete on international markets for the same products. According to some recent empirical evidence, one of the most interesting trends in global competition among developing and developed countries is competition through differentiation of products in terms of quality (vertical product differentiation). There is some evidence that rich and poor countries do

---

[4] This is most evident in the case of fibers and textiles, where industrialized countries create new high-quality market niches with a high intensity of skill and capital, whereas developing economies specialize in labor- and resource-intensive production.

produce and specialize in different levels of quality in the same markets, and therefore that the within-product unit value dispersion is increasing over time (Schott, 2001). That is, richer countries strive hard and succeed in expanding the quality ladder and gain higher quality premia. These unit value premia are positively and significantly correlated with per capita income of exporting countries. This trend suggests another perspective from which to look at upgrading in the global economy. A country upgrades in a given sector when two conditions are fulfilled: it produces a higher-value product *and* it competes in international markets, by supplying a higher-value product than its competitors' without losing market share. Strictly speaking, any increase in export earnings that results solely from a rise in market share without an increase in unit value should not be considered product upgrading. It is not upgrading first because it is not related to any innovation and improvement in market segment and second because it could lead to an immiserizing type of growth if increasing exports create downward pressures on prices.

This chapter provides evidence on some upgrading experiences in Latin America during the 1990s and complements the field studies presented in previous chapters. We focus on a particular type of upgrading: vertical product differentiation in the traded sector. We use international trade statistics disaggregated at product level from two major sources: FAOSTAT and UN Comtrade databases. We propose a method for analyzing export performance at product level that takes into account the evolution of world demand for a given product, the evolution of market shares for major world exporters of the same product, and the trend in export unit value. This method allows assessment of the different dimensions of the competitive position of a country on a given market with respect to its major world competitors.

We discuss some cases that are especially relevant for the development history of the countries considered. Among primary products, the fishing sector in Chile was at the origin of an export boom in the 1980s, and table fish has become one of the country's most competitive export sectors; the fresh fruit sector in Brazil is becoming more and more competitive in international (especially European) markets for quality fruit; the dairy sector is becoming an important sector in Nicaragua, mainly because of some direct investment which expanded productive and export capacity. Among manufactured products, Brazil is the world largest iron ore exporter, and the wooden furniture sector in Mexico, which is presently a case of declining international competitiveness, might shed light on the potential for export-oriented industrialization in labor-intensive manufacturing sectors.

The chapter is organized as follows. The second section proposes a method to measure product upgrading with international trade data, and specifically product upgrading through vertical or horizontal differentiation.[5] The third section provides some empirical evidence from Latin America. The fourth section discusses a case of downgrading in the labor-intensive manufacturing sector: wooden furniture in Mexico. The final section concludes the chapter with some remarks on the potential for industrialization through primary processing versus manufacturing, inspired by recent empirical literature on Latin America's comparative advantage.

Measuring Product Upgrading through International Trade Data

In this section we propose a method for analyzing product upgrading in international trade. Research on product upgrading is not new in international trade literature. Since the well-known contribution by Flam and Helpman (1987), the concept of product upgrading emerged in a number of studies, both theoretical and empirical, concerning vertical product differentiation; product upgrading is defined as an increase in the quality of a product, usually proxied by its unit value.[6]

---

[5] For other forms of upgrading at the firm level, or moving to a new value chain, see Pietrobelli and Rabellotti (Chapter 1 in this volume).

[6] The methodology to assess such upgrading is through indices of vertical intra-industry trade (VIIT) (see among others Fontagné and Freudenberg, 1997, and Fontagné, Freudenberg, and Péridy, 1998).

The method proposed here broadens the concept traditionally adopted in international trade studies by including other factors that determine the capacity of a product to upgrade in final markets (besides the increase in unit value), namely:

- a competitiveness factor (i.e., the ability to increase market share in product *i*);
- an external market factor (i.e., the evolution of world demand for imports of product *i*).

These factors should be considered complementary when exploring the capacity of a country to compete in a given market. If a country raises its export earnings in a given product, this might be due exclusively to an increase in its market share without any improvement in unit value of exports, or even with a reduction in unit value. In a development perspective, the same export performance might have very different implications for growth prospects in that sector. An improvement in export performance resulting exclusively from an increase in unit value of exports (with unchanged market share and world demand) suggests that the country is upgrading toward higher segments of the market and this is likely to have positive implications for growth prospects in that sector. On the contrary, an improvement in export performance resulting from a rise in market share, but with nonincreasing unit value, is likely to bring an immiserizing type of growth, that is, increasing export earnings due to a higher export volume selling at a lower unit value.

The method proposed here analyzes export performance of individual countries at product level.[7] The method evaluates the evolution of export value over a certain period of time by dividing market value into different components, which may be attributed to the following factors:

[7] This is the only level at which it is possible to compute unit values. At higher levels of aggregation, it is not possible to define unit value of exports. In this chapter, we refer to a six-digit disaggregation level.

1. changes in world demand for imports of a given product *i*;
2. changes in the export competitiveness of a country for a given product *i*;
3. changes in the quality of a country's exports of a given product *i*.

We first divide the evolution of country *A*'s export value of product *i* from time *t* to time *t* + *n* into two parts: one part is associated with the change in export volume of product *i*; the other part is associated with the change in the unit value of country *A*'s exports of product *i*. Formally, this may be expressed as

$$\begin{aligned} \Delta X_i &= X_{i,t+n} - X_{i,t} \\ &= V_{i,t+n} Q_{i,t+n} - V_{i,t} Q_{i,t} \\ &= V_{i,t+n} (Q_{i,t+n} - Q_{i,t}) + Q_{i,t} (V_{i,t+n} - V_{i,t}), \end{aligned} \tag{8.1}$$

where $X_{i,t}$ is country *A*'s export value of product *i* at time *t*, $Q_{i,t}$ is country *A*'s export volume of product *i* at time *t*, and $V_{i,t}$ is the unit value of country *A*'s exports of product *i* at time *t*.

Considering that the evolution in the export volume of product *i* by country *A* might depend on a change in world demand for product *i*, on a change in country *A*'s market share for product *i*, or both, (8.1) can be written as

$$\Delta X_i = V_{i,t+n} (M_{i,t} \, \Delta Q^{w}_{i} + \Delta M_i Q^{w}_{i,t} + \Delta M_i \, \Delta Q^{w}_{i}) + Q_{i,t} (\Delta V_i), \tag{8.2}$$

where $M_{i,t} = Q_{i,t}/Q^{w}_{i,t}$ is country *A*'s market share of product *i* at time *t* and $Q^{w}_{i,t}$ is the world export volume of product *i* at time *t*.

Equation (8.2) breaks down country *A*'s export performance of product *i* over a given period of time (from *t* to *t* + *n*) into three parts attributed to the following:

Table 8.1. Conditions for Defining Product Upgrading

Export value	External market conditions	Competitiveness	Unit value
ΔX_i	$\Delta Q^w{}_i$	ΔM_i	ΔV_i
>0	>0	≥0	>0
>0	><0	>0	>0

1. a change in external market conditions, that is, in world total imports of product *i* ($\Delta Q^w{}_i$);
2. a change in country *A*'s competitiveness, that is, in country *A*'s market share (ΔM_i);
3. a change in the unit value of product *i* exported by country *A* (ΔV_i).

Following the method above, we define *product upgrading* as a situation in which positive export performance of product *i* from country *A* is due to a rise in unit value of exports *together with* either increasing market share (regardless of the evolution of world demand) or a nondecreasing market share (provided that world demand has improved). Table 8.1 summarizes the possible cases: a case of increasing market share for higher-value products in either expanding or declining markets, and a case of shift to higher market niche in expanding markets.[8]

Before applying this method to some selected exports from Latin America, we compare it with another way of assessing the export performance of a product on international markets proposed by Kaplinsky and Readman (2000) in a study of the wooden furniture sector. Their intent is essentially methodological: to explore whether it is possible to capture the upgrading performance of particular productive sectors in different countries by focusing on international trade statistics. Among the four trajectories that firms and countries could adopt in pursuing the objective

[8] In all other possible cases, the outcome is ambiguous: it could suggest either downgrading or withdrawal from international markets.

of upgrading (i.e., improving process efficiency, introducing new products or improving existing products, changing the mix of activities, and moving to a new value chain),[9] Kaplinsky and Readman focus on a particular strategy for upgrading, "the extent to which final product prices reflect the capacity of firms (or a sector or an economy) to compete in final product markets" (2000:4). They propose a classification of upgrading and downgrading economies in a particular sector based on the performance of market shares and export unit values. They measure product upgrading by a relatively good price performance (in that unit values either grow more rapidly or fall less rapidly than those of competitors) and by a complementary improvement in (or stability of) market shares.

The difference between their method and the one proposed here lies, first of all, in the very definition of product upgrading and, consequently, in the range of possible outcomes emerging in the analysis of the export performance of a given product. In Kaplinsky and Readman (2000), four possible outcomes emerge: a country is upgrading in a particular sector over time if it has a nondecreasing market share together with increasing unit values relative to competitors. In contrast, if a country has a decreasing market share combined with decreasing unit values relative to its competitors, this is suggestive of collapse of international competitiveness and withdrawal from international markets. There are two other possible but more ambiguous cases; that is, when a country has a nondecreasing (decreasing) market share and decreasing (increasing) unit values, the position of the country depends on trajectory. The worst possible case is represented by an increasing market share combined with decreasing unit values, which is suggestive of an immiserizing growth path in that sector. The opposite case—decreasing market share together with increasing unit values—is more ambiguous, in that it can suggest a shift of the country to higher-quality products, which sell at higher prices, but to restricted

[9] For a comprehensive discussion of various types of upgrading, see Kaplinsky and Morris (2001).

market niches (this hypothesis, however, cannot be tested without other information on unit prices).

The method of analyzing upgrading that is proposed here, by including the impact of world market conditions on export performance, results in a more complex set of outcomes. As in Kaplinsky and Readman (2000), a country is upgrading in a given sector over time if it raises its market share together with unit value, regardless of the evolution of external market conditions over the same period. However, contrary to Kaplinsky and Readman (2000), a country is upgrading in a given sector if it has an increased unit value (with nondecreasing market share) only if export value has increased *and* market conditions have improved over time (i.e., if it is shifting to a higher market niche in expanding markets).

Selected Upgrading Experiences in Latin America in the 1990s

In this section we describe some examples of upgrading experiences in Latin America during the 1990s. For each of the markets considered, we provide an overview of world market trends, then assess the competitive position of the country with respect to other major exporting countries.

Chile: Competing on the World Salmon Market

The fishing sector has played an important role in the Chilean economy and in the country's export success (Schurman, 1996). The expansion of the fishing sector in Chile was part of a global response to the regulations on table fish introduced in response to cod overfishing in most North Atlantic littoral countries. Together with the rationalization of North Atlantic factory fishing fleet operations, and with the exploitation of new table fish species (such as tuna), two other trends emerged which affected Chile: the expansion of aquaculture (for prawn and salmon) and the expansion of fishing grounds that occurred mainly in the Southern Hemisphere, where new, relatively low-cost fleets were often started from scratch by local businessmen (Gibbon, 2001).

In this section we analyze the position of Chile in the global market for salmon, which is a major export item for the country and one of the most important table fish markets in the world. We assess the capacity of Chile to compete with other major world exporters on different segments of the same market, from the lowest to the highest level of primary processing, that is, from fresh or chilled salmon, to frozen salmon, up to smoked salmon. Global production of salmon from culture and capture expanded at a very fast pace during the last two decades. A large proportion of this increase was due to the rapid expansion of farmed salmon, of which Atlantic salmon is the main species. In South America, salmon is one of the major products with the best potential for expansion of production (together with trout, shrimp, tilapia, and *Gracilaria*) (FAO, 1997). Salmonid culture has developed almost exclusively in Chile, with a growth rate superior to any other culture activity in the region (the average growth rate in 1984–1989 was 88.2 percent; in 1990–1995, 37.7 percent; FAO, 1997). Salmonid cage farms are concentrated on the southern coast of the country, where the lakes for smolt production are also located (see also Maggi, Chapter 4 in this volume). The industry has benefited from numerous protected coastal areas, cheap fishmeal derived from the rich anchovy fishery, and alternate harvesting seasons with respect to European producers (FAO, 1997). According to FAO (1997), prospects for annual percentage growth rates exceed 20 percent in the short term, considering the advantages of the country for salmonid production and the fact that it is already an established industry.

Chile ranks among major world exporters of frozen salmon: it is the second-largest world exporter of frozen Pacific salmon after the United States, with almost 40 percent of world exports in 2000, and the second-largest world exporter of frozen Atlantic salmon (14.03 percent in 2000) after Norway (74.07 percent in 2000) (Table 8.2).

Chile's competitiveness in the international market for frozen Pacific salmon has hardly any rivals. With a 20 percent increase in its market

Table 8.2. Analysis of Export Performance of Chilean Salmon Relative to Major World Competitors, 1990–2000

	Export earnings[a]	Competitiveness	Unit value
(a) Salmon, fresh or chilled, whole—external market conditions:[a] 24%			
Chile	**0.96%**	**19.79%→2.44%**	**22.57%**
Norway	5.4%	n.a.→51.45%	–6.53%
Sweden	62.7%	0.16%→8.45%	–13.36%
Germany	71.2%	0.16%→7.60%	–13.73%
United Kingdom	61.0%	n.a.→7.48%	–8.80%
Canada	8.5%	51.19%→9.27%	35.07%
Denmark	4.1%	28.57%→4.83%	–6.11%
United States	7.7%	n.a.→4.71%	–1.96%
Ireland	3.4%	n.a.→2.13%	1.71%
(b) Salmon, Pacific, frozen, whole—external market conditions:[a] 11%			
Chile	**18.4%**	**20.79%→38.44%**	**17.48%**
Russian Federation	4.3%	6.71%→10.62%	–33.29%
United States	–4.0%	n.a.→42.55%	27.86%
Canada	–20.0%	65.26%→3.76%	–7.00%
Japan	13.0%	0.84%→0.98%	–3.38%
Denmark	2.7%	1.17%→0.51%	–25.58%
(c) Salmon, Atlantic or Danube, frozen, whole—external market conditions:[a] 26%			
Chile	**19.4%**	**22.51%→14.03%**	**14.61%**
Norway	8.7%	n.a.→74.07%	12.83%
Germany	30.0%	0.50%→1.05%	16.90%
Denmark	6.7%	66.23%→3.81%	–15.70%
Sweden	–4.0%	3.94%→0.87%	2.82%
United Kingdom	–15.0%	1.82%→0.55%	–29.57%
Canada	–0.3%	4.73%→0.21%	39.78%
(d) Salmon, smoked, including fillets—external market conditions:[a] 12%			
Chile	**24.2%**	**0.77%→2.23%**	**17.67%**
Germany	22.0%	4.56%→10.54%	–20.98%
Poland	75.0%	1.93%→6.14%	151.01%
Netherlands	6.6%	2.02%→2.22%	–8.63%
Denmark	3.0%	86.51%→40.96%	–6.48%
United Kingdom	1.0%	n.a.→13.34%	–0.62%
Norway	3.4%	n.a.→10.56%	–8.73%
France	–2.2%	n.a.→4.89%	14.14%

Source: Elaborated from UN Comtrade.

[a] Compound annual growth rate.

share over the 1990s and an increasing export unit value relative to its competitors, Chile is the only country in the world that experiences a clear upgrading. The third-largest exporter, the Russian Federation, also recorded a slight increase in its market share (from 6.71 percent to 10.62 percent over the decade), but it is capturing lower margins relative to competitors. The leading exporter in 2000 was the United States with a share of about 42 percent. Canada, which was the leading world exporter in 1990 with more than 65 percent of world exports, dropped down to a modest 3 percent in 2000, combined with a decreasing export unit value relative to competitors. Denmark also experienced both decreasing market share and export unit value.

The competitive position in the international market for frozen Atlantic salmon is less rosy. Chile registered increasing export unit value relative to competitors, but it was accompanied by a slightly decreasing market share. Its major competitor is Norway, which is leading world exports with a share over 74 percent and an increasing export unit value relative to other major exporters. Norway took Denmark's position as a world export leader: Denmark had over 66 percent of world exports at the beginning of the 1990s, but then experienced a sharp decrease in market share and unit value—as in all the other segments of the salmon market—which is suggestive of the country's withdrawal from international markets.

As regards international competition on smoked salmon, Chile is definitely not a leading world exporter by volume (only 2.23 percent of world exports in 2000). Major world exporters are Denmark (40.96 percent), the United Kingdom (13.34 percent), Norway (10.56 percent) and Germany (10.54 percent). Most traditional exporters of smoked salmon (except Germany), however, seem to be experiencing falling competitiveness on international markets with decreasing market shares and unit values. The most evident case here is again Denmark, which accounted for more than 86 percent of world exports at the beginning of the 1990s but halved its market share in the following decade. The only two countries showing an increase both in market share and in export unit value relative to competitors are Poland and Chile. Poland has a higher market share (6.14 percent) than Chile and fast increasing export unit values relative to competitors and is therefore Chile's major rival. Chile is nevertheless on an upgrading path and has succeeded in entering the highest level of processing and value added.

As regards fresh salmon, Chile has registered a sharp decrease in its market share (from around 20 percent to 2.44 percent during the 1990s), although this was accompanied by an increase in export unit value relative to competitors. Canada, the world's leading exporter at the beginning of the 1990s, faced a similar trend. Those countries that have increased their market shares (Norway, Sweden, Germany, and the United Kingdom) all suffered from decreasing export unit values relative to the average of all major exporters and seem therefore to have entered a downgrading path. From our perspective, the fact that Chile is withdrawing from the market of fresh salmon and at the same time upgrading in frozen and smoked salmon suggests that the country is successfully shifting from unprocessed to processed activities.

Brazil: A Promising Fresh Fruit Sector

After the Plan Real in 1994, Brazil became a major fruit producer. However, only after the currency devaluation did Brazilian fruit became competitive on international markets; Brazil has now become a new player in the international market for quality fruit.

Apples are among the primary products in which Brazil is becoming competitive. Chile, which used to be the main apple supplier in Latin America (after France, the leading world producer, and the United States), is now strongly affected by competition from Brazil. The competition of Brazilian products is mainly due to a horizontal differentiation consisting of new varieties of Royal Gala that are well colored and superior graded.[10]

---

[10] Unless otherwise indicated, this and the following pieces of information are taken from an interview by Fructidor with Denis Parisot, managing director of Partrade Ltda in Brazil (Parisot, 2001).

Moreover, competitiveness on international markets is improving due to seasonality factors (the apple harvest in February corresponds to the end of Royal Gala stocks in Europe) as well as to lower shipment costs to Europe from Brazil than from Chile. In the American market, competitiveness is also improving following trade liberalization through regional trade agreements, such as the North American Free Trade Agreement (NAFTA), which has expanded market access and provided strengthened mechanisms for combating nontariff trade barriers such as scientifically unfounded sanitary and phyto-sanitary (SPS) restrictions (Cook, 1999:2).

In the fresh fruit industry, most products are produced for domestic consumption,[11] in large part because of trade barriers and the technical difficulty and expense of long-distance shipping (Cook, 1999). In Brazil, out of an apple production of 967,000 tons in 2000, only 65,000 tons were exported. The 2001 harvest was poorer with 550,000 tons, which was mainly dedicated to the Brazilian market (only 30,000 tons were exported). This suggests that one of the major competitive strategies of South American producers is to invest in reliability and year-round stability of supply, as well as in preservation equipment to allow fruit conservation for 11 months, so as to be able to reduce imported fruit volumes.

For the reasons mentioned above, an analysis of the competitive position of Brazil in the international market for apples must look at both traded and domestic production and at net exports. Together with apples, we also focus on mangoes and melons, two other products in which Brazil is becoming competitive.

As regards apples, Brazil registered an impressive increase in exports from less than 10,000 million tons to almost 70,000 million tons during the 1990s. Brazil also improved its ability to serve the domestic market: imports have been declining over the second half of the decade, and net exports turned positive in 2000. The export unit value has been quite stable over the decade (Figure 8.1), but the potential for increasing margins is

---

[11] While a domestic production orientation usually prevails in the aggregate, a few countries, such as Chile and New Zealand, are totally export-driven (Cook, 1999:3).

Figure 8.1. Exports and Unit Value of Apples from Brazil

Source: Elaborated from UN Comtrade.

still to be captured following the introduction of new high-quality varieties for the export market.

As regards mangoes, Brazil registered a significant increase in exports in the last decade (from 4,633 million tons in 1990 to 67,172 million tons in 2000; Figure 8.2). This increase was not matched by expanded production, but by an increase in the share of production for exports (from less than 1 percent in 1990 to more than 12 percent in 2000).

As regards melons, Brazil was among the top 10 world exporters in 2000, but with a modest market share (0.87 percent). The export market is highly concentrated, with the top two world exporters—Spain and Mexico—accounting for 40 percent of total world exports (20.54 percent and 19.44 percent, respectively). Although at a lower scale, Brazil is improving its market position, with increasing exports and export earnings during the 1990s. With an increasing market share and slightly decreasing export unit values, the country's export earnings are not falling (Figure 8.3).

Figure 8.2. Exports of Mangoes from Brazil (Mt)

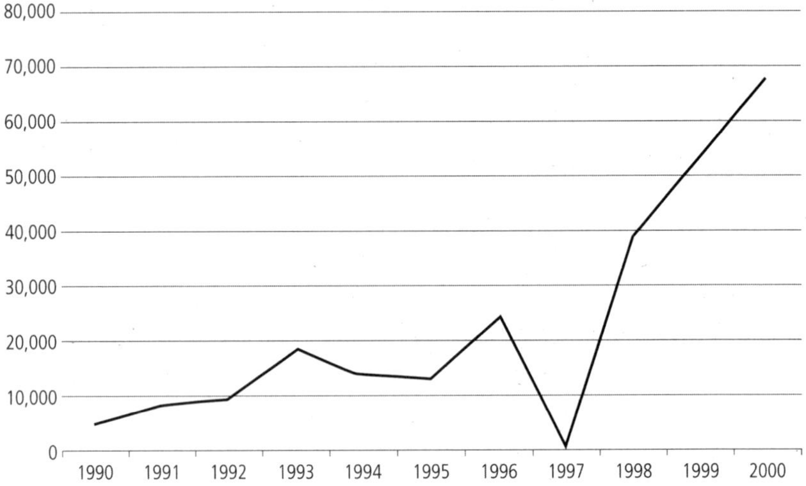

Source: Elaborated from FAOSTAT (http://apps.fao.org).

Figure 8.3. Exports, Export Value, and Unit Value of Melons from Brazil

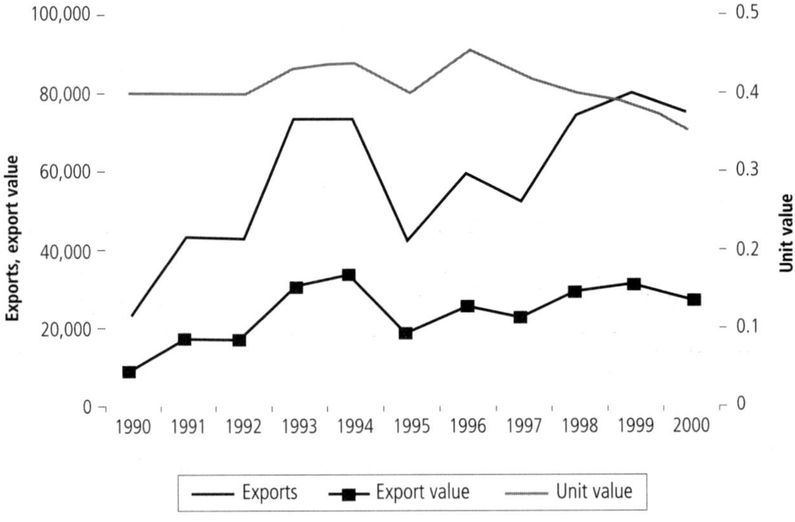

Source: Elaborated from UN Comtrade.

Nicaragua: Entering the International Market for Dairy Products

In this section, we analyze the position of Nicaragua in the global market for selected dairy products, which are serving an important share of the domestic market and also showing a good export potential. Because of the modest share of exported production, any assessment of the capacity of the country to compete with other major world exporters on different segments of the same market would not be appropriate. We therefore limit our comments to the evolution of export and import trends and explore the capacity of the sector to satisfy the domestic market and the expected export potential. The product categories considered are taken from the UN Comtrade classification of dairies.

As regards unprocessed fresh milk, Nicaragua has greatly improved its capacity to supply the domestic market with nonlight milk, as suggested by decreasing imports and by a net export balance in 2000 (compared to a trade deficit until 1999). In contrast, Nicaragua's position in low-fat fresh milk is worsening, with increasing imports leading to a worsening trade deficit (Figure 8.4).

As regards processed dairy products, Nicaragua shows an impressive increase in its exports, mainly of milk and cream (concentrated or sweetened), buttermilk, cream, yogurt, and cheese and curd (Figure 8.5). The highest-performing products in these categories are concentrated milk and cream (unsweetened), net exports of which have increased exponentially since 1993; yogurt, whose net exports also strongly increased in the last decade; and fresh and processed cheese, which are also showing increasing exports. Overall, the data suggest that, although the country is not among major world or regional exporters, its export potential seems to be quite significant. From an industrial development perspective, what perhaps matters most is the capacity of the country to supply and export processed products with a high potential to increase export earnings (see Artola and Parrilli, Chapter 2 in this volume).

Figure 8.4. Net Exports of Unprocessed Fresh Milk from Nicaragua (Mt)

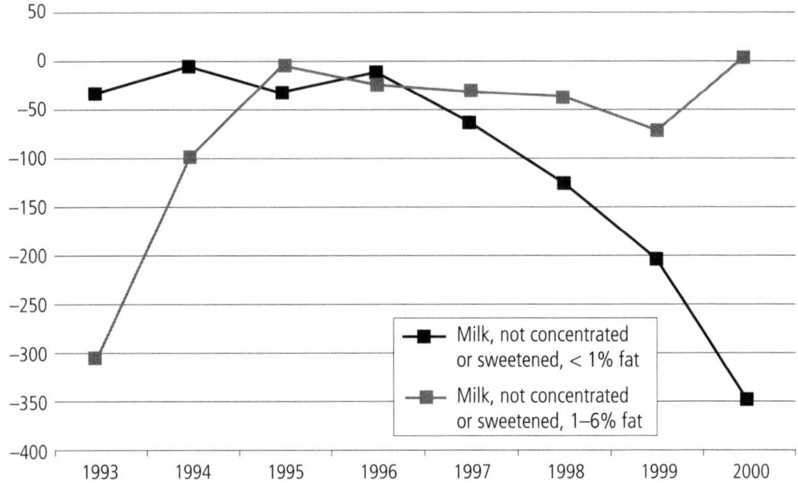

Source: Elaborated from UN Comtrade.

Figure 8.5. Export Trends for Selected Processed Dairy Products from Nicaragua (Mt)

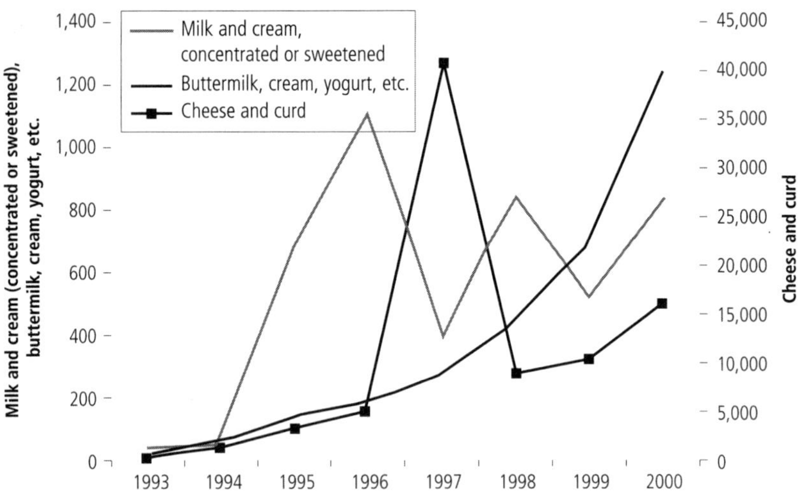

Source: Elaborated from UN Comtrade.

Brazil: A World-Leading Iron Ore Sector

Brazil is one of the world's largest iron ore producers,[12] the largest by value and the second largest by volume. Among the top 10 world exporters (together accounting for 97.09 percent of world exports in 2000), Brazil was responsible for a share of 38 percent, whereas the second-largest exporter by value, Australia, was responsible for 32 percent.

Among the main Brazilian companies in the sector, the Companhia Vale do Rio Doce (CVRD), operating in the state of Espírito Santo, is the world's largest iron ore exporter, as well as its largest producer (see Villaschi, Cassiolato, and Lastres, Chapter 6 in this volume). Other important Brazilian iron ore producers and exporters are Mineração Brasileiras Reunidas (MBR), Mineração da Trindade (Samitri), Sanmarco Mineração, and Ferteco Mineração. Brazilian iron ore production totaled 193.0 million tons in 1999, made up of 156.1 million tons of fines and lump ore and 36.9 million tons of pellets. In 1999, CVRD held 51.7 percent of the Brazilian market share for iron ore production in terms of volume and was responsible for 61 percent of total pellet production (BNDES, 2000; Table 8.3).

At the product level, the iron ore sector is strongly export-driven, with 72.6 percent of total production destined for export in 1999 (BNDES, 2000). The most export-oriented product in 1999 was pellets (93 percent of total production exported), followed by fines (64.1 percent) and lump ore (62.0 percent).

As regards the competitive position of Brazilian production, with respect to the country's status as the second major world exporter at the aggregate level, the analysis of market shares and export unit values in trade statistics suggests that Brazil is capturing higher export unit values on iron ore than Australia (probably because of Brazilian ore's higher iron

---

[12] Brazil's proven iron ore reserves total 19.7 billion tons, which ranks the country as having the sixth-largest reserves worldwide and compares to proven world iron ore reserves of 306.5 billion tons. However, taking into account the level of reserves in terms of the amount of iron contained in the ore, Brazil jumps to the number-one position worldwide. This is due to the high level of iron contained in hematite ore (60 percent), mainly found in the state of Pará, and in Itabirto ore (50 percent), mainly found in the state of Minas Gerais (BNDES, 2000).

Table 8.3. Brazilian Iron Ore Production, 1999
(millions of tons)

Company	Processed	Pellets	Total	Market share
CVRD	77.3	22.5	99.8	51.7
MBR	25.5	0	25.5	13.2
Ferteco	12.4	4.0	16.4	8.5
Samitri	16.3	0	16.3	8.5
Sanmarco	3.1	10.4	13.5	7.0
CSN	10.4	0	10.4	5.4
Italminas	5.0	0	5.0	2.6
Other	6.1	0	6.1	3.1
Total	156.1	36.9	193.0[a]	100.0

Source: BNDES (2000) from Sinferbase and DNPM.
[a] Total from BNDES.

content), although their export volumes have been converging over the last decade (Figure 8.6).

Despite the economic crises of the second half of the 1990s, the internal and external demand for Brazilian ore has remained strong. Domestic sales suffered relatively more, whereas exports increased from less than 37 million tons in 1994 to almost 40 million tons in 2000 (BNDES, 2000).

Domestic iron consumption is mainly concentrated in the steel sector and totaled 36.9 million tons in 1999. Iron ore consumption is expected to increase based on a forecast of 3 percent average annual growth in Brazilian steel production in the 1999–2010 period (BNDES, 2000). Brazil's demand for iron ore is concentrated in fines and lump ore because the country's steel industry is highly concentrated in blast furnace production. The use of pellets is still limited because of pellets' higher price. Accordingly, the growth in the domestic supply of iron ore is expected to continue to be focused on fines and lump ore, with growth in the supply of pellets concentrated in export sales.

As regards the destination of Brazilian iron ore exports in 1999, major export markets are Japan (18 percent), Germany (14 percent), China (11 percent), South Korea (9 percent), Belgium (5 percent), and the United States (4 percent). Among these, exports have been increasing

Figure 8.6. Volume and Unit Value of Iron Ore Exports for the Two Major World Exporters

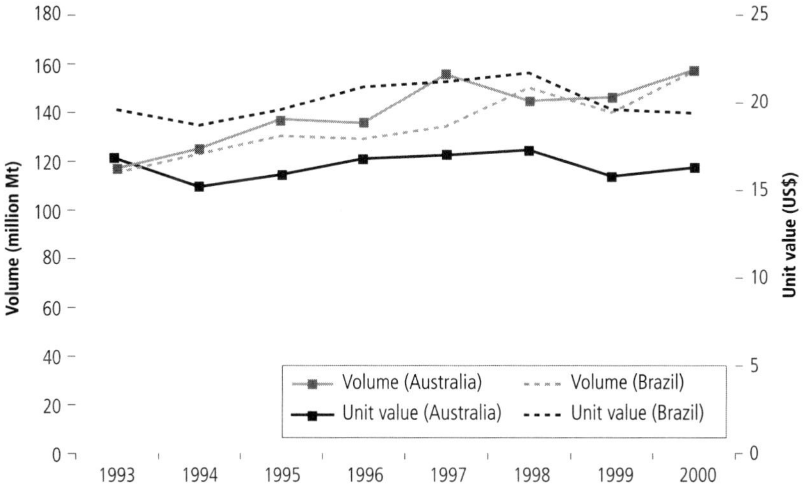

Source: Elaborated from UN Comtrade.

only to China, and they have been decreasing to Japan and South Korea (BNDES, 2000).

The future competitiveness of the steel sector in Brazil depends on several economic and noneconomic factors at the international level. The closing of steel mills in the United States and Europe as a result of obsolescence and environmental problems is likely to open new market opportunities for emerging economies. Moreover, technological progress in the steel industry is likely to lead to a restructuring of the industry worldwide, with greater utilization of slabs acquired in the open market by integrated mills with insufficient furnace capacity. This signals an opportunity for competitive iron ore producers, such as those in Brazil, to consider the integration of slab production, given the ability to produce low-cost slabs. The ability to ensure a high degree of competitiveness in the future will depend on the vertical integration of iron ore producers into the slab production process (BNDES, 2000).

A Case of Downgrading: The Wooden Furniture Industry in Mexico

The wooden furniture industry—traditionally a low-tech, resource- and labor-intensive industry—is often considered to be an industry in which developing countries should enjoy a comparative advantage. But the furniture industry is also important for industrialized countries: many high-income economies still maintain an above-average performance (Maskell, 1998). Indeed, only three out of the ten major world exporters of all wooden furniture in 2000 were developing economies (China ranked fourth, Malaysia sixth, Indonesia ninth).[13]

Even considering that emerging and developing economies are not among major importers of wooden furniture, the ranking of the largest net exporters of furniture includes only a few developing countries within the top 15 (Malaysia ranks fourth, Indonesia sixth, China seventh, and Mexico ninth). On the other hand, Italy has traditionally been and still remains by far the largest gross and net exporter, with increasing net exports during the 1990s.

In this section we analyze the position of Mexico in the global market for wooden furniture. We assess to what extent the country can compete with other major world exporters in different segments of the same market.

The analysis of market shares and export unit values for the wooden furniture sector in Mexico shows that the country has modest market shares in all of the products considered and is further decreasing its share in three out of four product markets (Table 8.4). This suggests a lack (or loss) of international competitiveness in the sector. Mexico has experienced downgrading in office furniture: a slightly increasing market share combined with a sharp decrease in export unit value relative to competitors. The country is progressively withdrawing from the other segments of the market, with falling shares and falling export unit values.

---

[13] Mexico ranked only 15th, with less than 2.5 percent of world export value.

Table 8.4. Export Performance of Mexican Wooden Furniture Relative to Major World Competitors, 1990–2000

	Export earnings[a]	Competitiveness	Unit value
(a) Office furniture—external market conditions:[a] 16%			
Mexico	**50%**	**0.35%→1.61%**	**−22.89%**
China	19%	n.a.→47.22%	116.84%
Malaysia	53%	0.85%→29.39%	−35.64%
Thailand	39%	0.51%→7.61%	−34.85%
Denmark	9%	14.89%→1.20%	−6.17%
Italy	0%	3.12%→0.91%	47.68%
Germany	3%	49.14%→0.75%	35.36%
(b) Kitchen furniture—external market conditions:[a] 11%			
Mexico	**39%**	**0.20%→0.08%**	**−29.80%**
Thailand	16%	3.36%→57.88%	−50.17%
China	29%	n.a.→13.01%	72.89%
Malaysia	30%	0→22.23%	102.81%
Germany	1%	67.87%→0.24%	37.64%
Italy	8%	0.77%→0.17%	19.33%
Denmark	3%	12.06%→0.03%	90.72%
(c) Bedroom furniture—external market conditions:[a] 15%			
Mexico	**40%**	**0.97%→0.68%**	**3.31%**
Thailand	23%	0.59%→63.38%	−32.34%
China	19%	n.a.→24.35%	50.98%
Malaysia	33%	0→3.80%	197.12%
Denmark	9%	21.29%→0.64%	19.20%
Germany	−2%	55.41%→0.56%	47.69%
Italy	0%	3.83%→0.54%	47.41%

Source: Elaborated from UN Comtrade.
[a] Compound annual growth rate.

Thus, the wooden furniture sector in Mexico stands out as the only case of downgrading in the present chapter. These results are consistent with the empirical literature on comparative advantages of developing countries at the aggregate level, which shows that Central and Latin American countries have hardly any comparative advantage in labor-intensive manufacturing, in contrast with Asia. This trend also emerges quite clearly from our data. Three Asian countries rank at the top of world wooden furniture exporters (China, Thailand, and Malaysia). Among these countries, different trends emerge. China is the world's leading exporter of office furniture and of wooden furniture other than kitchen and bedroom furniture and is the second-largest exporter of kitchen and bedroom furniture. In all of the products considered, China has also experienced a significant increase in export unit values, which could signal a shift to higher-quality products. An opposite trend emerges for Thailand, which ranked first among major world exporters of kitchen and bedroom wooden furniture, and third for office furniture, in 2000. Thailand registered an impressive increase in market share combined with a sharp fall in export unit value, which suggests a growing specialization in commodified segments of the market with the risk of immiserizing growth. In comparison, Malaysia shows strong competitiveness in wooden furniture (except office furniture), with increasing market shares and export unit values.

As for the other exporters, some interesting trends emerge. Although the lack of comparable data limits the possibility of assessing South Africa's position in the wooden furniture market, it seems that the country is experiencing upgrading, at least in some products. Among developed countries, three rank among major world exporters: Italy, Denmark, and Germany. All of them registered decreasing market shares and increasing export unit values (with the exception only of office furniture from Denmark). This suggests that industrially advanced countries are shifting to higher-quality segments of the market, that is, they can sell at higher export unit values, although on much lower market shares.

Conclusions

In this chapter we investigated the position of some Latin American countries in international markets for selected primary and manufactured products. Our aim was to detect any upgrading paths in those markets during the 1990s. We found evidence of some high-performing primary sectors—table fish in Chile, fruit in Brazil—and an increasingly competitive primary sector—dairy products in Nicaragua. We also found evidence of a competitive resource-based manufacturing sector—the iron ore sector in Brazil. To summarize: the market for salmon in Chile now ranks among the highest performing in the world, having surpassed that in the countries that had traditionally been the world leaders (northern European countries and Canada). Moreover, Chile has also improved its position in processing activities that allow the capture of higher export margins. The fresh fruit industry in Brazil is gaining competitiveness in international markets, although this sector is traditionally characterized by a vast majority of production for domestic consumption. Brazil is investing in higher-quality products, especially apples, to improve competitiveness in European markets.The dairy industry in Nicaragua is still mostly oriented to the domestic market but is becoming more and more competitive in international markets (at least at the regional level). The iron ore industry—the only capital-intensive industry considered in this study—is a sector in which Brazil has traditionally been competitive and in which public investment in the last decades has improved the position of the country in international markets. The wooden furniture industry in Mexico is the only case of downgrading included in this study.

Although our results cannot be generalized to other countries or sectors in Latin America, we believe that they can at least contribute to a long-lasting discussion of the potential for export-oriented industrialization in Latin America. The debate originated with the belief that East Asia's success in exporting manufactures was the result of export push policies, replicable by other developing countries. Some empirical research, however, suggests that many developing countries—including those in Latin America—do not have a comparative advantage in manufacturing because of their low ratio of human resources to natural resources (Wood and Berge, 1994, 1997). Further research has suggested that primary processing could provide an alternative route to export-oriented industrialization to countries with low skill-to-land ratios and that countries with moderate levels of skill per worker, such as much of Latin America, could pursue a strategy of resource-based industrialization that is consistent with their pattern of comparative advantages (Owens and Wood, 1997). Indeed, Latin

America is nowadays the region with the highest percentage of processed primary exports out of total exports.

The evidence presented in this chapter is consistent with previous research on international comparisons of export competitiveness. All the sectors (except one) considered experienced a process of upgrading during the 1990s, with rising market shares on international markets, and increasing export unit values. We suggest that this outcome can be interpreted as a case of loss of international competitiveness due to emerging Asian economies with much higher comparative and competitive advantage in labor-intensive manufacturing than Latin American countries.

References

Banco Nacional de Desenvolvimento Econômico e Social (BNDES). 2000. Iron Ore in Brazil: Restructuring with Growth. Sectoral Study, BNDES, Rio de Janeiro. http://www.bndes.gov.br/english/studies/is88.pdf.

Bhagwati, J. 1958. Immiserizing Growth: A Geometrical Note. *Review of Economic Studies* 25:201–205.

Cook, R. 1998. International Trends in the Fresh Fruit and Vegetable Sector. *Acta Horticulturae* 495:143–156.

Dolan, C., J. Humphrey, and C. Harris-Pascal. 1999. *Horticultural Commodity Chains: The Impact of the UK Market on the African Fresh Vegetable Industry.* Working Paper no. 96, Institute of Development Studies, University of Sussex, Brighton.

Flam, H., and E. Helpman. 1987. Vertical Product Differentiation and North-South Trade. *American Economic Review* 77(5):810–822.

Fontagné, L., and M. Freudenberg. 1997. *Intra-industry Trade Methodological Issues Reconsidered.* Working Paper No. 1997-01, Centre d'Études Prospectives et d'Informations Internationales (CEPII), Paris.

Fontagné, L., M. Freudenberg, and N. Péridy. 1998. *Intra-industry Trade and the Single Market: Quality Matters.* Discussion Paper No. 1959, Centre for Economic Policy Research (CEPR), London.

Food and Agriculture Organisation (FAO). 1997. *Review of the State of World Aquaculture.* FAO Fisheries Circular No. 886, Fisheries Department, FAO, United Nations, Rome. http://www.fao.org/docrep/003/w7499e/w7499e00.htm.

Gereffi, G. 1999a. A Commodity Chains Framework for Analysing Global Industries. Department of Sociology, Duke University, Durham, N.C. Unpublished.

———. 1999b. International Trade and Industrial Upgrading in the Apparel Commodity Chain. *Journal of International Economics* 48(1):37–70.

Gibbon, P. 2001. Upgrading Primary Production: A Global Commodity Chain Approach. *World Development* 29(2):345–363.

Kaplinsky, R., and M. Morris. 2001. *A Handbook for Value Chain Research.* Prepared for the International Development Research Centre (IDRC), Ottawa, Ontario, Canada. http://sds.ukzn.ac.za/files/handbook_valuechainresearch.pdf.

Kaplinsky, R., and J. Readman. 2000. Globalisation and Upgrading: What Can (and Cannot) Be Learnt from International Trade Statistics in the Wood Furniture Sector? Centre for Research in Innovation Management, University of Brighton, Brighton, U.K., and Institute of Development Studies, University of Sussex, Brighton, U.K. Unpublished. www.centrim.bus.brighton.ac.uk/go/global/.

Maskell, P. 1998. Low-Tech Competitive Advantages and the Role of Proximity: The Danish Wooden Furniture Industry. *European Urban and Regional Studies* 5(2):99–118.

Owens, T., and A. Wood. 1997. Export-Oriented Industrialization through Primary Processing? *World Development* 25(9):1453–1470.

Parisot, M. D. 2001. South America: A Booming Market (interview with Fructidor). http://www.fructidor.com/letter/sept2001/page2.htm.

Schott, P. K. 2001. *Do Rich and Poor Countries Specialize in a Different Mix of Goods? Evidence from Product-Level US Trade Data.* Working Paper No. 8492, National Bureau of Economic Research, Cambridge, Mass.

Schurman, R. 1996. Snails, Southern Hake and Sustainability: Neoliberalism and Natural Resource Exports in Chile. *World Development* 24(11):1695–1710.

Wood, A., and K. Berge. 1994. *Exporting Manufactures: Trade Policy or Human Resources?* Working Paper No. 4, Institute of Development Studies, University of Sussex, Brighton, U.K.

———. 1997. Exporting Manufactures: Human Resources, Natural Resources and Trade Policy. *Journal of Development Studies* 34(1): 35–59.

World Bank. 1999. *Global Commodity Markets* 7(1).

CHAPTER 9

Upgrading in Global Value Chains: Lessons from Latin American Clusters

Carlo Pietrobelli, Roberta Rabellotti, and Elisa Giuliani

In this chapter we present the main empirical findings of our study based on our sectoral taxonomy. We investigate the hypothesis that enterprise upgrading is simultaneously affected by firm-specific efforts and actions and by the environment in which firms operate. The environment is crucially shaped by three characteristics: (1) the collective efficiency of the cluster in which SMEs operate, (2) the pattern of governance of the value chain in which SMEs participate, and (3) the peculiar features that characterize learning and upgrading patterns in specific sectors. Therefore, for each sectoral group we present the impact of the degree of collective efficiency and of the pattern of value chain governance on upgrading. We present them in sequence. In addition, some evidence of the origins of the various clusters is also presented as it may provide useful insights for the discussion and interpretation of the evidence. In each of the sections below, we address in turn each type of sector identified in our taxonomy: traditional manufacturing, natural-resource-based sectors, complex products industries, and specialized suppliers.

On the Origins of Clustering

In traditional manufacturing, the existence of clusters of geographically agglomerated and sectorally specialized enterprises is well documented in the literature (Nadvi and Schmitz, 1994). One of the necessary conditions—albeit not a sufficient one—for clustering to generate the development of collective efficiency is *time*. The Italian literature has drawn attention to the long historical roots of most industrial districts. In some of the Latin American cases analyzed, the industry specialization of the cluster is also historically rooted. This is clearly true for the two Mexican shoe clusters of Guadalajara and León, where ever since the last century there has been a tradition of shoe production in small workshops to satisfy local demand (Rabellotti, 1997).

However, there are also cases of clusters emerging more recently because of the successful growth of a leading firm. This is the case of the Mexican furniture cluster located in Chipilo, Puebla, which originated at the end of the 1980s from the success of an individual firm, Segusino, established in 1987 with less than 20 workers and two subcontractors. However, the village of Chipilo, a little community of 5,000 inhabitants, mainly of Italian origin, was traditionally specialized in cattle breeding and artisan dairy industry with no previous tradition in the furniture sector. The amazing performance of Segusino transformed the local economic structure in less than a decade. Many cattle sheds were rapidly turned into carpenter's shops, and many farmers learned how to produce furniture pieces or parts.

Thus, in the case of Segusino, the boost factor for the sector's initial growth was the opportunity to export to the U.S. market, and one large firm sparked the creation of the cluster. The initial competitive factor for Segusino was the identification of a very specialized market niche: Mexican country-style furniture, later favored by a growing demand in the United States and by the competitive price resulting from the 1994 devaluation of the Mexican peso.

In sum, among the most common initial conditions for the emergence of a cluster specialized in traditional manufacturing are the existence of a historical craft tradition or the establishment of a local leading firm following a business opportunity, together with access to a market.

In natural-resource-based sectors, clusters have originated in very different ways, as we see in the examples of fish in Chile and fruit in Brazil. The start of the Chilean salmon cluster was due to enlightened public–private cooperation and a process of collective learning that was catalyzed by the rise of external demand and an active horizontal policy to support exports (Maggi, Chapter 4 in this book). The first experiments to explore the potential of Chile's southern region (Tenth Region) for open-sea farm-ranching—unknown in this part of the world at that time—were attempted in the 1960s and generated significant progress in specialized technical knowledge but did not lead to major success. In 1981, Fundación Chile bought the plants of Domsea Farms (a Chilean subsidiary of Union Carbide) and founded Salmones Antártica, which turned out to be the first firm (in 1988) to produce more than 1,000 tons of salmon (Pietrobelli, 1998) and set a model to emulate. Other initiatives were carried out in the Llanquihue Lake, supported by Corfo, the Japanese company Nishiro, and the fishing company Mytilus (now Mares Australes). Later, the Asociación de Productores de Salmón y Trucha de Chile (APSTC, today SalmónChile) facilitated the coordination of exporters targeting quality-demanding markets. Thus, *the interaction of public and private initiatives in a new and risky business was critical to setting successful models and providing the essential public goods* in the Chilean salmon cluster.

The transformation of the local economy of Petrolina-Juazeiro, Brazil, into a dynamic mango and grape cluster is rather the result of centralized government planning (Gomes, Chapter 3 in this volume). In 1948, the federal government created the San Francisco River Valley Development Agency (CODEVASF), a parastatal targeting the promotion of navigation, irrigation, and agricultural and industrial development in the San Francisco River Valley. In the 1960s and 1970s in Petrolina-Juazeiro, CODEVASF expropriated land to implement public irrigation projects, enlisted different-sized growers and agricultural processing firms in each project, provided incentives for agricultural industries to establish themselves in the region, and supported the creation of a grower association (VALEXPORT) that was crucial for the formation of export channels. This led to a structure of production consisting of both large and small growers, through land provision, technical assistance, and cheap credit.

The story of the inception of the apple cluster in Santa Catarina, Brazil, is somewhat different, as the cluster is the result of *the initiative of pioneer entrepreneurs together with public support and extension policies*. In Santa Catarina State, apple production is spread across two main growing regions centered in the cities of Fraiburgo and São Joaquim, now known as the "Brazilian apple capital." Commercial apple production in Santa Catarina dates back to the 1960s when private entrepreneurs began experimenting with different apple varieties. German and French immigrants led the efforts in Fraiburgo, while Japanese immigrants led those in São Joaquim. These pioneers were instrumental in experimenting with different apple varieties and in establishing a market for domestically produced apples at a time when Brazil imported 90 percent of its apples.[1] Following the example of the pioneers, many other growers came, and today a great variety of firms and growers prevail. However, initially public policies, and later institution building efforts, also played an important role in generating this cluster. Essentially support came through the early federal fiscal incentives and the agricultural credit, extension, training, and research provided by the Agricultural Credit and Extension Agency, ACARESC (subsequently transformed into the Santa Catarina State Agricultural Research Agency, EPAGRI).

In contrast, melon production in Mossoró, Rio Grande do Norte, Brazil, did not begin because of public sector support. In fact, the cluster was generated by *the early initiative of two innovative and risk-prone entrepreneurs who foresaw a window of opportunity*. These pioneering

[1] In addition, the pioneers in each case established the very different structures of production which still dominate today, with large firms in Fraiburgo and small growers in São Joaquim. This is consistent with the prevailing natural environment, with the rolling hills in Fraiburgo favoring large landholdings, and the rocky, mountainous terrain in São Joaquim favoring smaller holdings (Gomes, Chapter 3 in this volume).

firms were first-movers in every respect (Gomes, Chapter 3 in this volume). The first firm ventured into melon production in the late 1980s in Mossoró, sensing a potential for this crop in a region traditionally specialized in the production of cotton, corn, and beans, by hiring a grower experienced with melon production from São Paulo. By the mid-1990s, this firm was the single largest melon grower in Brazil. Its success inspired another entrepreneur from São Paulo to establish what turned out to be the second-largest firm in the sector. They were both helped by the provision of abundant and highly subsidized venture and investment capital in the mid-1970s. Their venture into melon production was crucial to boosting the emergence and growth of a cluster. They proved that Rio Grande do Norte has a favorable environment for melon production, identified suitable melon varieties, established domestic and export marketing channels, and trained hundreds of field workers and agronomists who subsequently spread their expertise throughout the cluster. Many small growers followed suit, and they represent nearly 40 percent of production today.

The clusters specialized in complex products industry sectors tend to emerge as a result of the operations of transnational companies through *maquila* operations in industries such as cars and consumer electronics. This generates various tiers of suppliers that are, in some cases, clustered local enterprises.

The software clusters analyzed all rely on the existence of a critical mass of local demand, a local favorable environment, and a good endowment of educated labor. In addition, some of the clusters have also benefited from an intense spin-off of skilled personnel from local plants of high-tech transnational companies. In Mexico there is a presence of IBM and Hewlett-Packard, among others, in Guadalajara, and of Xerox and Texas Instruments in Aguascalientes (Ruiz Durán, Chapter 7 in this volume). Similarly, in the Brazilian software cluster of Blumenau, many of the existing software firms are spin-offs of a large center for data processing, created in 1969 to satisfy the needs of local textile firms, which then became the largest Brazilian enterprise in this field (Bercovich and Swanke, 2003).

Collective Efficiency and Sectors

Using the concept of collective efficiency, first introduced by Hubert Schmitz (1995), we define the competitive advantages that may be enjoyed by firms located in clusters, advantages derived from local external economies and joint action. Our empirical evidence suggests that the degree of collective efficiency attained in the clusters analyzed varies across the four sectoral groups (Table 9.1). More specifically, collective efficiency reaches higher levels in natural-resource-based and special services clusters. In contrast, clusters in complex products industries record lower levels of collective efficiency, largely because of the very few joint actions undertaken. All clusters share the advantages of a local labor market, which is a byproduct of geographical clustering. Inputs are also locally sourced, except in complex products industries, in which the logic of global sourcing prevails. Below, we examine the differences in *collective efficiency* across sectors by looking in turn at *external economies* and *joint actions*.

External Economies

In the traditional manufacturing sector, clusters show an intermediate degree of collective efficiency, with the two footwear clusters of Sinos Valley and León clearly ahead of the others. In a very few clusters, among them

Table 9.1. Collective Efficiency across Sectors: Index of Collective Efficiency
(average)

	External economies (EE)	Joint actions (JA)	Collective Efficiency Index
Traditional manufacturing	7.60	5.23	6.31
Natural-resource-based	8.91	7.36	8.20
Complex products	7.61	4.80	6.19
Specialized suppliers	9.10	7.80	8.70

Source: Authors' database.
Note: Collective Efficiency Index = 0.5*EE + 0.5*JA.

Chipilo and Torreón in Mexico (Zepeda, Chapter 5 in this volume; Bair and Gereffi, 2001), the degree of collective efficiency is low.

A first significant finding is that in general, external economies are more common than joint actions, as the theory would lead us to expect. This argument was introduced in Nadvi and Schmitz (1999) and is confirmed for a large number of cases in this study. Joint actions are rare because they require specific investments, and firms get involved in cooperation only if they have to face external challenges, such as new competitors, an innovation to adopt, or a new market to enter. However, clustering in traditional manufacturing sectors facilitates externalites such as pools of skilled workers, diffusion of information, and access to markets.

The most widely diffused form of external economy in traditional manufacturing clusters is a pool of labor with specialized skills. Such pools of industry-specific skills are present in many clusters in Latin America, and this represents a very important competitive advantage because the manual experience of the workforce significantly influences the quality of products.

Moreover, clustering facilitates the *diffusion of specialized expertise and information* in traditional manufacturing, another important externality. Information diffusion takes place through informal channels facilitated by the cluster's social cohesion. In Chipilo, Mexico, circulation of information is facilitated by strong family ties within the small local community, which is characterized by common Italian heritage. A similar point is made by Bazan and Schmitz (1997) in their analysis of the role of social capital in the growth process in the Sinos Valley footwear cluster, stressing the importance of a strong local community spirit based on their common German heritage. This also applies to the furniture cluster of São Bento do Sul.

Finally, the grouping of producers in geographic proximity facilitates *market access*. The initial export success of the Sinos Valley footwear cluster was made possible when U.S. shoe importers looking for new shoe suppliers in low-wage countries identified an established cluster in the Sinos Valley, which included a mass of shoe producers and some specialized local input suppliers (Schmitz, 1995). Southern Italian clusters also tend to be located near urban centers, to exploit the larger markets.

Minimal external economies, as in Chipilo, may be explained by a combination of factors: the very recent origin of the cluster and the prevailing organizational pattern, which in the case of Chipilo is dominated by vertical relationships between Segusino, the leading firm, and its network of subcontractors (Zepeda, Chapter 5 in this volume). The predominance of these strong vertical relationships interferes with the development of external economies and, especially, of horizontal joint actions. Moreover, the lack of a strong industrial tradition before the inception of the cluster, which was generated by the explicit, intentional action of the leading firm, further hindered the development of joint actions and collective efficiency. The export boom of Segusino induced many local farmers to turn themselves rapidly into carpenters, but this is a process requiring time and training. In Chipilo, skilled workers are still a rarity, and the scarcity of skilled labor is still a major limitation.

In natural-resource-based clusters, as in the traditional manufacturing sector, there are more sources of external economies than joint actions; these external economies may arise as a spontaneous, often unintentional, effect of agglomeration.

Sectoral and geographical concentration of productive activities tends to create a pool of specialized skills that benefits both workers and firms. Perhaps in some relatively less developed areas, labor skills are not very advanced, but skills tend to match technologies, so this does not appear to negatively affect production efficiency. This is the case in the dairy cluster in Nicaragua (Artola and Parrilli, Chapter 2 in this volume). Furthermore, in a dynamic cluster the endowments of skilled labor tend to rise over time, as a result of individual firms' training activities, or joint actions in training, or the intervention of the public sector. The Chilean salmon cluster is a good example of powerful efforts to create relevant specialized programs in local universities and to promote training at the firm level (Maggi, Chapter 4 in this volume). Most of the available literature stresses the idea that clustering enhances the easy, informal, and rapid flow of information and knowledge among local producers, traders, and institutions. The crucial asset of knowledge is shared and created though a process of "collective learning" in the cluster, with substantial "spillovers in the air" (Maskell, 2001).[2]

However, this model is called into question by the empirical evidence of knowledge flows in the Colchagua Valley wine cluster in Chile. In this case, knowledge does not flow freely in the air by virtue of geographical proximity, but rather flows within cliques of actors and firms that have similar absorptive capacity and belong to the same epistemic community (Giuliani, 2003). The mysteries of trade are not in the air, but rather residing in people (professionals) who embody both tacit and codified knowledge. The most valuable knowledge flows and produces important changes within these cliques. Firms' capacity to transfer and absorb knowledge is not evenly spread, but is rather the result of specific skills and capabilities with which only a few firms are endowed.

Drawing on Allen's (1977) terminology, Giuliani (2003) identifies three different types of firms in Colchagua, as regards their position in the flow of knowledge. Technological gatekeepers are those actors that have a high level of knowledge interconnectedness with other local firms and also with extracluster sources of knowledge. They are often locally owned firms, channeling new knowledge into the cluster and diffusing it locally. External stars are highly interconnected with external sources of knowledge but have hardly any cognitive interaction with other local firms, and isolated firms are scarcely interconnected either locally or externally.

In Colchagua, the strongest link of firms with networks of knowledge is represented by the so-called flying winemakers, consultant oenologists who advise firms and keep them informed of the latest technological developments. They are often (56 percent) foreign experts who visit the wineries at least four times a year and serve more than one local firm, thus enhancing the diffusion of knowledge within the cluster. National experts

---

[2] In Marshall's "industrial atmosphere," "the mysteries of the trade become no mysteries, but are as it were in the air, and children learn many of them, unconsciously" (Marshall, 1920:225).

also exist and constitute what has been called an "epistemic community," which represents a local highway for learning and technical improvements (Giuliani, 2003). Endowed with a common technical knowledge base, they easily connect national and foreign professionals and facilitate the alignment of intra- and extracluster knowledge flows. Foreign advisors also play a similar important role in Brazilian wine clusters (Vargas, 2001a).

In other cases, however, information flows informally across the agents, often eased by extension initiatives of international development cooperation (see Artola and Parrilli, Chapter 2 in this volume, on dairy clusters in Nicaragua). In other cases, a host of public and private education programs and research institutions helps substantially (e.g., the role of local universities in the Chilean salmon cluster; Maggi, Chapter 4 in this volume).

The level of external economies appears especially low in complex products industry clusters, such as the electronics and automotive industries. This probably reflects their history and intrinsic logic of operation. In most cases they were created following the initiative of a large transnational company (a leader or an assembler) searching for local providers, often indirectly through the working of the first-tier suppliers, following the leader. To some extent, the metalworking cluster in Espírito Santo, Brazil, represents an exception, with local SMEs that are beginning to supply local anchor firms with local inputs and services (Villaschi, Cassiolato, and Lastres, Chapter 6 in this volume). Access to information, as well as market access, is eased by clustering to a varying extent, reflecting the dominant role of the quasi-hierarchical value chain leaders.

In software clusters, the local labor market is characterized by a concentration of highly skilled people moving from one firm to another, which represents an important external economy of learning and knowledge exchanges within the clusters. Proximity of firms is an important factor facilitating information exchange through the movement of skilled people across firms, and public policies often aim at fostering joint location. The common social and cultural background of many entrepreneurs, who often share past work experience at large transnational companies such as IBM and HP or come from the same local university, also helps. The study on Blumenau (Bercovich and Swanke, 2003) also underscores the positive impact on local software firms of a nationally recognized image of the cluster. The recognition of Blumenau as a high-tech pole initially came from the growth of a center for data processing that was created to cater to local needs but then rapidly extended its market to the rest of the country. Moreover, some local firms have also contributed to this image by obtaining national awards.

Joint Actions

In the traditional manufacturing sector, the footwear cluster of Chipilo is characterized by intense *vertical cooperation* between Segusino and its subcontractors because in the beginning the leading firm made the explicit choice to adopt an organizational model based on a strong division of labor. Segusino organized its network of subcontractors, each specializing in specific products (e.g., chairs, tables), with Segusino assisting many of the workshops technically and financially, training the workforce, and continually checking the quality of products. At the same time, the best subcontracting firms were able to participate in the process of quality improvement and sometimes also contributed to the introduction of new designs (Zepeda, Chapter 5 in this volume).

In some of the clusters analyzed, an increase in cooperation between producers and suppliers has been the local *response to an external challenge.* This was the case in the footwear clusters of Sinos Valley, Guadalajara, and León, and in the furniture cluster of São Bento do Sul. For instance, in Guadalajara since the opening of the domestic market and the increase in imports of shoes and shoe components, the manufacturer–supplier relationship has undergone a profound process of change. Suppliers, who were also hit by liberalization, reacted to the crisis by increasing their attention to the quality, variety, and fashion content of their products. For the first time, after many years of copying from European and North American magazines, suppliers have begun regular visits to international trade fairs.

Locally available information has increased and its circulation within the cluster improved since liberalization. In addition, relationships between footwear producers and suppliers have been improving and becoming more collaborative, including joint product development, quality improvement, and improved delivery times (Rabellotti, 1999).

In the Sinos Valley an increase in collaboration between suppliers and shoe producers in reaction to the "Chinese shock" pushed local firms to raise the quality of products and to reduce the time between order and delivery (Schmitz, 1995). In this cluster, *horizontal cooperation through institutions* also played an important role. Initially, the early organization of a trade fair and a program to bring foreign buyers to the Sinos Valley were significant. Later, as the cluster grew and firms' interests diverged, institutions proliferated in a period characterized by the lack of a common purpose at the cluster level (Schmitz, 1995).

However, cases of failure of joint action are also frequent. The predominance of strong vertical relationships interferes with the development of joint actions, other than cooperation between the leading firm and its subcontractors. The attempt to create a technological center to assist the furniture industry in Chipilo and to promote an association among local producers was not successful. This is perhaps because both initiatives were endorsed by Segusino and therefore viewed with suspicion by the rest of the cluster. Local producers not belonging to Segusino's network saw these as initiatives of the leading firm alone, aimed solely at protecting its own private interests (Zepeda, Chapter 5 in this volume). Very similar results are also reported in Torreón's blue jeans cluster, in which the only significant external economy is the creation of a specialized local labor market. Joint action at horizontal level is almost nonexistent, characterized by a generalized distrust among firms and the absence of an institutional environment that would facilitate cluster growth (Bair and Gereffi, 2001).

Joint actions in natural-resource-based sectors are illustrated by evidence from the three clusters of fresh fruit production in Brazil (Gomes, Chapter 3 in this volume). All three clusters enjoy similar levels of external economies. Given the long history (more than 20 years) of production for each of them, each has a labor pool qualified to work the crop, purchase nearly all inputs locally, and share easy access to information on markets and technology. These advantages are spread through both formal (associations, cooperatives, input suppliers-growers) and informal (social) networks. However, the three clusters differ remarkably in terms of joint actions and of the institutions that growers and the public sector have created to aid in the process of upgrading. Further differences among the clusters are related to the role and the governance model of the value chains in which they operate.

At one extreme in terms of joint actions, mango and grape production in Petrolina-Juazeiro is the result of concerted planning by a federal parastatal. At the other extreme, melon production in Rio Grande do Norte is mostly the result of private entrepreneurship and only minimal public support. Somewhere in between is apple production in Santa Catarina, where the public sector was very active with research and extension but did not have as broad a range of interventions as in Petrolina-Juazeiro. Moreover, interventions were mostly in the hands of state-level, not federal-level, government in Santa Catarina.

What can explain such strikingly different levels of joint action in the three clusters? A possible explanation lies in the structure of production: empirical evidence suggests that less concentrated structures of production are associated with a greater level of joint action among growers. In Rio Grande do Norte, two lead firms have historically accounted for over 70 percent of total production, while production is less concentrated in Petrolina-Juazeiro and Santa Catarina, where 5 to 10 firms account for 35 and 50 percent of production, respectively. Thus, scale economies in production and rising sector concentration would not help exploit the advantages of collaboration and joint action.

In Santa Catarina, firms and small growers also interact through vertical coordination, ranging from the outsourcing of production, through long-term contracts, to on-the-spot negotiations at harvest time. In Petrolina-Juazeiro (mangoes and grapes), in some cases the exporting firm visits suppliers weekly, provides technical assistance, does soil analysis for fertilizer schedules, suggests the harvest calendar, harvests and transports mangoes to the pack house, and advances credit to purchase inputs.

Forward and backward linkages in the melon cluster of Rio Grande do Norte are radically different. The two lead firms never managed to collaborate on anything beyond the few activities of the melon growers association, PROFRUTAS, which was itself created only in response to demands from the U.S. Department of Agriculture, but remained a weak and disarticulated association, with limited reach and limited voice. Thus, the highly concentrated Rio Grande do Norte cluster stands out for its comparatively low level of joint action.

The fruit clusters in Brazil provide a stark contrast to the experience of the salmon cluster in southern Chile (Maggi, Chapter 4 in this volume). In salmon farming, policy requirements have changed and evolved with the development of the local system, and public policies, together with private initiatives, have generated several remarkable joint actions. In the evolution of this cluster, three different phases may be identified, each of which presents different opportunities for joint action.

In a first, initial learning phase (1978–1985), the central challenge was to learn to produce a new product under new conditions, which required a great deal of precompetitive investments in R&D and pioneer risky initiatives, with both private and public entities investing in the new venture. This would later provide a demonstration effect to convince new investors to engage in the business. This initial learning phase consisted chiefly of the actions of public actors such as Fundación Chile and IFOP (Instituto de Fomento Pesquero) and international development cooperation agencies. Their policies reflect the conditions of this phase and are directed to the creation of essential public goods, such as basic physical and research infrastructure, knowledge and technology for breeding salmon in this environment, and successful models to imitate.

In a second, maturing phase (1986–1995), the imperative to gain competitiveness was to standardize production quality and increase production quantity. This required better infrastructure and better local providers of cages, nets, and food; the local agglomeration of providers of such goods and services gained importance. Moreover, efforts to upgrade functionally emerged, through promotion and marketing of Chilean salmon abroad. Policies differed in this period from those in the previous phase: subsidies are offered by public agencies such as Corfo and ProChile to create technological capacities. For example, INTESAL (Instituto Tecnológico del Salmón) was created as a public/private (70/30 percent) initiative to strengthen local technical skills and improve technology transfer; Salmo-Food, a public/private (20/80 percent) venture involving 13 local salmon producers, was founded to enter the strategic segment of food production, which was until then dominated by foreign producers; Salmocorp brought together 13 national producers—30 percent of total production—to sell abroad; and ProChile, in collaboration with Chilean producers, promoted salmon in the United States to develop new markets in collaboration with Canadian producers.

In a third, globalization phase (since 1996), the aim has been to raise productivity through technology transfer (foreign missions) and biotechnology (genetic improvements and remedies for fish illnesses). Moreover, several efforts have been made to improve the regulatory aspects of the sector. Thus, for example, public policies introduced environmental controls, and a collective agreement on clean production was reached among the cluster firms, the Salmon Producers' Association, and state regulatory (Conama) and support (Corfo) agencies. New environmental regulations (RAMA) were also introduced. Interestingly, the technical mechanism for allocating resources shifted from direct subsidies, which were utilized in the early stages of the cluster, toward public funding assigned through competitive tenders. This was possible only with the acquired evolution and maturity of the cluster.

In summary, the experience of this cluster has been characterized by remarkable joint actions involving a variety of private firms and public institutions throughout all three phases (Maggi, Chapter 4 in this volume, Table 4.6). These cooperative actions were first mainly directed to promoting access to export markets and later, in the globalization phase, to addressing "second-order" priorities, typical of a mature cluster, such as science and technology and environmental and regulatory issues.

Useful lessons may also be drawn from failures to carry out joint actions in natural-resource-based clusters. Thus, for example, the Rio Grande do Norte melon cluster experienced a puzzling disconnect between growers and public sector research, such as the local federal agricultural school (ESAM) and the EMBRAPA center in the neighboring state of Ceará. However, this caused less damage than it might have because of characteristics of the market for melons and melons' production cycle. Upgrading with melons is much easier than with other fruits. The two traditionally dominant very large growers in Rio Grande do Norte could do much of the upgrading themselves without feeling the need to pressure the government for public support for the entire cluster (Gomes, Chapter 3 in this volume).

In the dairy cluster of Nicaragua (Artola and Parrilli, Chapter 2 in this volume), horizontal, bilateral, and multilateral relations have improved in the past few years, as a result of the creation of several cooperatives for processing cheese (CANISLAC, Alianza Amerrisque) and their important lobbying and service activities. The creation of many cooperatives has been favored by international cooperation, which had to expend much effort to reverse the widespread negative attitude toward the concept of the cooperative, a negative attitude that was entrenched in the population after the Sandinista period. A successful example of such a cooperative is Cantores, with 37 cheese manufacturers in Boaco, which is planning to set up its own pasteurizing plant with UNIDO and CIDA advice.

Another, different example of joint action in the Nicaraguan dairy cluster is the creation of the milk producers' chamber CANISLAC in 2000, following the advice of UNIDO and PRODEGA (a Finnish cooperation project that has operated in the sector for several years). CANISLAC plays a primarily lobbying role, working on issues such as international trade negotiations following the closing of the Salvadoran market to Nicaragua's milk, and the Nicaraguan government plan (Vaso de Leche Escolar) to subsidize the provision of a daily glass of milk to all schoolchildren in the country. The large companies in the country, such as Parmalat and Nestlé-Prolacsa, also participate in CANISLAC, demonstrating its strength and weakness simultaneously, given the diversity of the interests CANISLAC represents.

Another example of joint action is the creation of the Brazilian Institute of Wine (IBRAVIN) in the 1990s in the wine cluster of Serra Gaúcha, Rio Grande do Sul, Brazil. IBRAVIN was originally founded with the purpose of managing and executing a series of projects approved through the so-called Fund for Support to the Wine Sector (Fundovitis), which utilized resources coming from the state government's tax waiver. Initially, IBRAVIN tried to integrate the efforts of the main sector associations in order to upgrade the whole wine production chain. This process involved development projects in several areas, including market information, improved viticulture practices, cooperation between growers and wineries, improvements in wine and grape quality, creation of a viticulture directory in the region, and a new proposal of legislation for the sector (Vargas, 2001a).

In natural-resource-based clusters, collective actions are especially important for promoting science and technology research and development, as is revealed in several field studies. In the Brazilian wine cluster, for example, the National Center for Research on Grape and Wine (CNPUV) of EMBRAPA and the JK Agro-Technical Federal School, both in the city of Bento Gonçalves, constitute the main research and human resource development centers of this cluster. CNPUV is a national reference center for wine research. Created in 1975, its main purpose is the development of product and process technologies related to the wine agro-industrial complex. Most R&D activities related to viticulture systems in the cluster are performed by this center. The JK Agro-Technical Federal School was created in 1959 and is the only educational institution in Brazil that offers training as a technician in oenology as an intermediate degree. Since 1995, the school has also been offering a graduate degree program in technology in viticulture and oenology and collaborates with ENFA (National School of Agronomic Formation) in Toulouse, France, and with the Federal University of Rio Grande do Sul (UFRGS). In another example, the Brazilian Apple Growers Association in the Santa Catarina apple cluster has a special focus on research and development for the apple sector. The association adopted its technology program in 1992, establishing a phyto-sanitary alert station (in collaboration with the Ministry of Agriculture and the Santa Catarina State Secretary of Agriculture) and implementating a hail control system to reduce the impact of hailstorms on the region's apple orchards (Gomes, Chapter 3 in this volume).

In complex products industry sector clusters, joint actions are generally limited, with the exceptions of the aeronautics cluster around Embraer in São João do Campo, Brazil, and the metalworking cluster in Espírito Santo, Brazil. In Espírito Santo, forward vertical linkages with the large anchor firms have notably improved. Moreover, the local Center for the Development of the Capixaba Metalworking Industry (CDMEC) has been dynamically fostering networking ("articulating") within the cluster and fostering relationships between the large anchor firms and small local providers of parts and services. CDMEC was created in 1988 with the strong leadership of the Development Bank of the State of Espírito Santo (BANDES), all the anchor companies, and a few local SMEs. It also benefited from the personality of the individual directors who have managed it over time. In the aeronautics cluster in São João do Campo, Brazil, developed around Embraer, a fair degree of interfirm cooperation among subcontractors is observed, along with frequent spin-offs and upgrading of second- and third-tier subcontractors. In the automobile cluster of Nova Serrana, the chain leader (Fiat) has succeeded in developing a network of local suppliers, but at the same time these suppliers do not cooperate in the exchange of knowledge (Lemos et al., 2000). It is therefore more common that local suppliers link vertically with the leader firm (i.e., Fiat) rather than horizontally with other suppliers. This reduces the possibilities for joint actions at the cluster level.

Firms cooperate vertically (backward and forward) in the few cases in which the "buyer" (e.g., IBM in the electronics cluster in Jalisco) promotes local acquisition of services and goods. More typically, vertical cooperation with the buyer is rare (e.g., Intel in Costa Rica imported 85 percent of its inputs in 1999; Vargas and Lindegaard, 2002).

In the specialized services sector, the number and variety of joint actions through collective institutions is surprisingly higher in software clusters. Intense joint action is explained by diffused specific policies at the local level, high human capital intensity, strong personal relationships (sometimes developed in universities) linking small entrepreneurs, and deep relationships with institutions of research and higher education. In all these clusters horizontal cooperation among firms is common, consisting mainly of agreements to offer customers full systems satisfying all their needs. In some cases, these agreements may also imply technological cooperation to match the different software programs. However, institutions substantially help to create horizontal joint actions. In the Mexican clusters of the D.F., Guadalajara, and Aguascalientes, there are very active business associations, promoting various initiatives as training courses, joint promotion and collective catalogs of products and of the human resources locally available. In Aguascalientes, the business association has been created within the framework of a state cluster program aimed at the development of *agrupamientos industriales* in various sectors (e.g., automobile, furniture, clothing).[3]

A strategic issue is a certification program aimed at collectively obtaining the Capability Maturity Model (CMM) certificate. The issue of CMM certification is also among the main future collective projects of the business associations in the D.F. and in Guadalajara (Ruiz Durán, Chapter 7 in this volume).

Another very interesting collective initiative has been recently promoted in Blumenau, Brazil, where the local business association joined with the city government to launch Programando o Futuro, a project aimed at increasing the local availability of a skilled labor force. The program consists of organizing training courses, financed jointly by the local firms and the municipality, to prepare middle-level technicians. The local sustenance of

[3] In each cluster, the program promotes the establishment of an association involving local enterprises, the state government, and other relevant local institutions. In the case of the software cluster of Aguascalientes, the association includes 34 enterprises, the Economic Secretary of State, three local universities, and the national institute of statistics (INEGI), located in Aguascalientes.

the cluster is confirmed by the establishment of Blusoft, an incubator of new software businesses, created in 1992 by an agreement between the city government, the local university, and the business association. Blusoft is a very successful incubator and plays an important role in promoting the image of the software "made in Blumenau." Blusoft also helps firms access various sources of financing, and organizes training courses and visits of foreign experts to the cluster, as well as foreign trips of local entrepreneurs to get to know other successful software clusters (Bercovich and Swanke, 2003). Finally, in all the software clusters analyzed, there is a very strong relationship between firms (through their business associations) and local universities, including collaboration for reorganizing curricula and two-way exchanges of people between universities and firms.

Chain Governance and Sectors

In light of other work on global value chains, one would expect the quasi hierarchy to be the dominating pattern of governance in the traditional manufacturing sector (Gereffi, 1999). However, according to our sample, the reality is characterized by a greater variety of forms of organization and governance of value chains, with remarkable differences across sectors. Evidence shows that in some cases different value chains coexist in the same cluster, with firms participating in local as well as global value chains, especially in traditional manufacturing and natural-resource-based sectors (Table 9.2).

Although inclusion in global value chains generally provides an open window on the global market, foreign buyers do not always provide support for local upgrading (Humphrey and Schmitz, 2002a). However, in traditional manufacturing sector industries, buyers usually provide upgrading support. This is because products are generally not customized: in these industries information on products and processes cannot be easily codified in technical norms, and the quality of products depends on the specialized skills of local producers (or alternatively, even if processes could be codified, local firms lack the capability to decode and use such codes and translate them

Table 9.2. Value Chains' Pattern of Governance

	Market	Network	Quasi-hierarchy	Hierarchy
Traditional manufacturing sector				
Textiles				
Medellín (Colombia)	0	0	1	0
Itaji, Santa Catarina (Brazil)	3	0	0	0
Apparel				
Bucaramanga (Colombia)	2	0	0	0
Gamarra (Peru)	1	0	0	0
Torreón (Mexico)	0	0	2	0
Shoes				
Sinos Valley (Brazil)	3	0	2	0
León (Mexico)	1	1	2	0
Guadalajara (Mexico)	1	1	2	0
Campina Grande (Brazil)	N/A	N/A	N/A	N/A
Furniture				
Serra Gaúcha (Brazil)	1	0	0	0
Uba, Minas Gerais (Brazil)	1	0	0	0
Espírito Santo (Brazil)	1	1	0	0
São Bento do Sul (Brazil)	0	1	2	1
Segusino/Chipilo (Mexico)	3	0	1	0
Tiles				
Santa Catarina (Brazil)	2	0	0	0
Natural-resource-based sector				
Tobacco				
Rio Pardo, Rio Grande do Sul (Brazil)	0	0	2	0
Wine				
Colchagua (Chile)	3	0	2	0
Serra Gaúcha, Rio Grande do Sul (Brazil)	3	0	0	0
Sugar				
Valle del Cauca (Colombia)	3	0	0	0
Marble				
Espírito Santo (Brazil)	1	0	2	0
Copper				
Cuajone-Toquepala (Peru)	2	0	2	0
Salmon				
Region Austral (Chile)	0	2	2	0
Milk-dairy				
Boaco, Chontales (Nicaragua)	1	1	2	2
Mangoes and grapes				
Petrolina-Juazeiro (Brazil)	1	0	3	0
Melons				
Rio Grande do Norte (Brazil)	1	0	3	0

(continued on next page)

Table 9.2. Value Chains' Pattern of Governance (continued)

	Market	Network	Quasi-hierarchy	Hierarchy
Apples				
Santa Catarina (Brazil)	1	0	3	0
Complex products sector				
Aircraft				
SJC Aeronautics, São Paulo (Brazil)	0	0	2	0
Automotive				
Nova Serrana (Brazil)	0	0	2	0
Caxias do Sul, Rio Grande do Sul (Brazil)	0	2	2	0
Juárez (Delphi) (Mexico)	2	0	2	0
Metalworking				
Espírito Santo (Brazil)	0	0	1	0
Electronics				
Jalisco (Mexico)	0	0	2	0
Audiovisual equipment				
Baja California (Mexico)	0	0	0	2
ICT				
San José (Costa Rica)	2	0	0	0
Campinas, São Paulo (Brazil)	2	2	2	0
Specialized suppliers sector				
Software				
Joinville (Brazil)	1	1	0	0
Distrito Federal (Mexico)	1	1	0	0
Guadalajara (Mexico)	1	1	0	0
Aguascalientes (Mexico)	1	0	0	0
Monterrey (Mexico)	1	1	3	0

Note: 0 = absent; 1 = domestic chain; 2 = global chain; 3 = domestic and global chain.

into idiosyncratic routines). Because they rely on the competencies of their local suppliers, global buyers are obliged to assist producers in improving products and processes, the buyers' support being particularly crucial in the first stages of new producers' integration into a global value chain. In fact, in traditional manufacturing industries, global buyers look constantly for lower-cost production sites, which implies that when buyers integrate new producers into a global value chain, they must assist the producers in meeting requirements that frequently do not apply to the producers' domestic market. Thus, we may expect that in these cases, quasi-hierarchical governance is needed both because new suppliers lack knowledge of international markets, so buyers must be involved in products' design, and because close monitoring and control is required to ensure that products meet international standards (Humphrey and Schmitz, 2002a).

An interesting example of a cluster operating simultaneously in different value chains is the Sinos Valley footwear cluster, in which, in addition to the chain dominated by U.S. and European buyers, there are other minor chains oriented to the Brazilian and the Latin American market (Bazan and Navas-Alemán, 2004). These different chains are characterized by different patterns of governance. The U.S. value chain is a typical quasi-hierarchical chain, dominated by U.S. buyers, while firms selling in the domestic market and exporting to Latin America operate under market conditions. In the quasi-hierarchical chain, U.S. buyers impose their conditions concerning product design, marketing, and branding on Brazilian producers. The buyers are the undisputed leaders in the chain, exerting control over intermediaries, local producers, and often input suppliers as well. According to Bazan and Navas-Alemán (2004), this asymmetrical relationship with local producers can be explained by several factors, the most important being the marked concentration of exports in a small number of export agents in the U.S. market. Moreover, the numerous sourcing options (e.g., China, Spain, and Portugal) open to the buyers, in the unlikely scenario that local producers did not accept their terms, made the buyers stronger.

The organization of the domestic value chain is completely different from the quasi-hierarchical global chains. The relationships between producers and buyers in domestic chains are market-based:

> This is reflected by a number of different indicators such as the low degree of buyer concentration and sales concentration to main clients, the strategic option of selling directly to retailers by using the producer's own sales representatives and, more importantly, the main strategic activities (design, branding and marketing) are carried out by producers instead of buyers. Sales representatives are hired by producers and this sets

> them apart from exporting agents (who are hired by buyers) in the quasi-hierarchical chains. Therefore, the main differences are that sales representatives are accountable to the producers, buyers (local wholesalers and retailers) do not control any of the strategic activities mentioned above and these conditions, combined with the atomized local footwear demand make market-based relations the main trend in the chain (Bazan and Navas-Alemán, 2004:116).

Similarly, the two Mexican footwear clusters of Guadalajara and León operate simultaneously in different chains: in quasi-hierarchical chains dominated by U.S. buyers and in the domestic market, sometimes under market conditions and also in a few cases in network chains. While in the quasi-hierarchical value chains, U.S. buyers control design and product development, in network-governed chains there is cooperation among firms of more or less equal power, which share their competencies within the chain. This is an increasingly common pattern in these clusters, in which one of the effects of trade liberalization has been an increase in cooperation between domestic buyers and producers (Rabellotti, 1999).

The literature on global value chains generally agrees that the quasi-hierarchical form of governance tends to prevail in natural-resource-based sectors, with international buyers playing a leading role. However, our evidence reveals that a great variety of forms of organization and governance actually occur. In the Nicaraguan dairy case (Artola and Parrilli, Chapter 2 in this volume), firms in the cluster participate in three different types of productive chains: (1) a chain led by a transnational company, (2) chains headed by Salvadoran medium-sized processing plants and traders, and (3) a chain led by some local small cooperatives. A clear pattern of hierarchical governance is evident in the productive chain led by the transnational company and in the chains led by the Salvadoran agents, while a form of network-like governance prevails in the value chain led by local cooperatives. The cooperatives value chain is contributing most to raising dairy exports from Nicaragua and substantially upgrading the dairy industry's processes and functions.

Brazilian fresh fruit value chains (Gomes, Chapter 3 in this volume), show a clear tendency toward the dominance of quasi-hierarchical forms of governance associated with the restructuring of food retail, in which retailers are increasingly shifting away from middlemen and wholesalers to alternative, more direct forms of procurement. In practice, however, there remains a surprisingly wide range of possible relationships between buyers and suppliers, including arm's length and, in a few cases, hierarchy (e.g., Del Monte in Rio Grande do Norte, Alpine in Petrolina-Juazeiro, and the French-dominated Agrícola in Santa Catarina).

Hierarchical governance styles of global value chains involving transnational companies in natural-resource-based sectors may have different roles in product upgrading. In the tobacco cluster of the Rio Pardo Valley in Brazil, a few large conglomerates dominate (British American Tobacco, Philip Morris, Dimon) and are all present locally. They buy tobacco leaves from local SMEs and essentially convey to the SMEs standards and specifications that the international market requires, without providing business or technical support. The governance of these relationships is eminently hierarchical, in which large transnational companies set the requirements and signal the standards demanded by the market and retain the core capabilities that in this sector are related to basic research and marketing. Local actors provide a negligible contribution to the process of technological innovation in the cluster (Vargas, 2001b).

Subsidiaries of transnational companies also entered the wine cluster of Serra Gaúcha, Brazil, but they maintain a less hierarchical relationship with local grape producers and small wineries. Small family-owned wineries are today at the very center of the wine cluster upgrading process (Vargas, 2001a).

In complex products industry sector clusters, there is a prevalence of quasi hierarchy in global value chains led by transnational companies and their first-tier suppliers, while in the specialized suppliers' software clusters, relationships with clients are mainly of a market/network type, and the main market is local. In some cases, the relationship between software producers and their clients could be seen as a network-type value chain, because it involves a great deal of feedback and information exchanges between the software firms and the users, which provides important upgrading opportunities. There are only a very few cases in Mexico of local enterprises integrated in quasi-hierarchical global value chains. The most well known case is Softtek, a lead provider of software development, implementation, maintenance, and support services in Latin America, with 2,000 employees and offices in Argentina, Brazil, Colombia, Mexico, Peru, Spain, and Venezuela.

Upgrading, Collective Efficiency, and Global Buyers across Sectoral Groups

The empirical evidence presented so far suggests that different sectoral groups tend to show different degrees of collective efficiency and a range of governance environments. In this section, we explore whether it is possible to associate a level of collective efficiency and a particular form of chain governance with upgrading across different sectoral groups. Our analyses show that upgrading is achieved in different sectors in considerably different ways.

Collective efficiency does not seem to be equally strongly related to upgrading in all sectors (Table 9.3). While collective efficiency is positively associated with upgrading in traditional manufacturing, natural-resource-based, and specialized suppliers (software) clusters, the relationship is not significant in complex products industries. As far as governance is concerned, the impact of global leader firms on cluster upgrading is very mixed. Global leader firms tend to have a positive effect on product and process upgrading in traditional manufacturing and natural-resource-based clusters, while they have only a moderate impact on the same types of upgrading in complex products industry clusters. Most interestingly, global buyers show a weak or, in some cases, negative relationship with functional upgrading in all three of these sectoral

Table 9.3. Patterns of Learning and Upgrading across Sectors

	Traditional manufacturing	Natural-resource-based	Complex products	Specialized services
Pattern of learning according to Pavitt taxonomy	Supplier-driven	Supplier-driven, science-based	Scale-intensive specialized suppliers	Specialized suppliers
Relation between collective efficiency and				
Product upgrading	Positive	Positive	Neutral[b]	Positive
Process upgrading	Neutral[a]	Positive	Neutral[b]	Positive
Functional upgrading	Neutral	Positive	Neutral[b]	Positive
Impact of global buyers'/leaders' operations on				
Product upgrading	Positive	Positive[c] (but passive)	Neutral[d] (indirectly positive)	None[c]
Process upgrading	Positive	Positive[c] (but passive)	Neutral[d] (indirectly positive)	None[c]
Functional upgrading	Often negative	Neutral/negative	Neutral/ negative	None[c]
Other critical sources of knowledge	Suppliers, local institutions, national buyers alternative to the global leaders	Suppliers, university and research labs, technology extension services, producers' associations, and cooperatives	Consultants, local agencies (network brokers)	Users, universities and higher-education institutions

[a] Process innovations in this sector are usually driven by technology suppliers, and in none of the sample clusters is there local production of technology.
[b] Often little collective efficiency is detected.
[c] Global leaders set the target and provide market outlets but do not normally engage in supporting initiatives.
[d] Only indirect impact through the incentive to enter global value chains and fulfill the standards required. Not attained through the direct support of buyers.
[e] "None" refers to the case in which the global buyer is not present.

groups.[4] In the sections that follow, we provide a detailed analysis of the findings for each type of sector.

Upgrading in the Traditional Manufacturing Sector

An important result of our research is that there appears to be a *positive relationship between product upgrading and the degree of collective efficiency* in traditional manufacturing industries (Table 9.4). This positive relationship can be explained by several factors. First, circulation of information, knowledge, and labor force facilitates the process upgrading of clustered firms. Second, product upgrading is facilitated by vertical joint action with local suppliers and with buyers. Third, multilateral horizontal cooperation plays an important role in product upgrading through various actions, such as participation in international trade fairs, collection of information about international fashion trends, and easier connections with international buyers.

The positive relation between collective efficiency and product upgrading is illustrated by two Mexican footwear clusters and that in the Sinos Valley. Rabellotti (1999) shows how efforts to improve the quality and fashion content of components undertaken by some manufacturers together with their suppliers have percolated all over the Guadalajara cluster. Moreover, she stresses the importance of a program undertaken in León aimed at promoting the standardization of components for product upgrading at the cluster level. Schmitz (1995) underscores the importance of various cluster programs in the Sinos Valley aimed at supporting the participation of local producers in international trade fairs and at bringing international buyers into the cluster, all at an early stage of development.

In contrast, there seems to be a clear link between collective efficiency and process upgrading on the basis of available empirical evidence. This link

[4] Specialized services are not mentioned because none of the cases analyzed form part of a quasi-hierarchical value chain.

Table 9.4. Upgrading in Traditional Manufacturing Clusters

	Degree of collective efficiency	Product upgrading	Process upgrading	Functional upgrading	Intersectoral upgrading	Sum of upgrading
Textile						
Medellín (Colombia)	Medium	2	2	1	1	6
Itaji, Santa Catarina (Brazil)	Medium	3	3	1	0	7
Apparel						
Bucaramanga (Colombia)	Medium	1.5	1.5	N/A	0	3
Gamarra (Peru)	Medium	1	1	0	0	2
Torreón (Mexico)	Low	1	3	1	0	5
Shoes						
Sinos Valley (Brazil)	High	3	3	1.5	0	7.5
León (Mexico)	High	2	2	1	0	5
Guadalajara (Mexico)	Medium	2	2	1	0	5
Campina Grande (Brazil)	Medium	1.5	1.5	0	0	3
Furniture						
Serra Gaúcha (Brazil)	Medium	2.5	2.5	0	0	5
Uba, Minas Gerais (Brazil)	Low	1	1.5	0	0	2.5
Espírito Santo (Brazil)	Medium	1.5	1.5	1	0	4
São Bento do Sul (Brazil)	Medium	1	2	1	0	4
Chipilo (Mexico)	Low	2	2	1	0	5
Tiles						
Santa Catarina (Brazil)	Medium	3	3	1	0	7
Total		28	31.5	10.5	1	
Average		1.86	2.10	0.70	0.06	4.73

Source: Authors' database.
Note: 3 = high; 2 = medium; 1 = low; 0 = absent; N/A = not available.

can be explained by a combination of factors. In traditional manufacturing industries, technology suppliers drive process innovations, and in none of the clusters analyzed is there a local production of technology. Therefore, most Latin American clusters lack the virtuous and close relationship between technology producers and technology users that is so important in explaining process upgrading in Italian industrial districts.

Furthermore, in some of the cases analyzed, *process and product upgrading has been facilitated by international large buyers*. This result confirms Gereffi's (1999) view that producers entering a quasi-hierarchical chain have good prospects for upgrading their processes and products. Along the same lines, Humphrey and Schmitz (2002a) agree that "local producers learn a great deal from global buyers about how to improve their production processes, attain consistency and high quality, and increase their speed of response to customer orders."

That buyers often provide support for upgrading can be related to characteristics of the products, which are not standardized. In these industries, information on products and processes cannot be easily codified in technical norms, and the quality of products depends on the specialized skills of local producers (or alternatively, even though the processes could be codified, local firms lack the capability to decode and to use the codes to transform the processes into idiosyncratic routines). Relying on the competencies of their local suppliers, global buyers are obliged to assist the suppliers in improving products and processes, their support being particularly crucial in the first stages of new producers' integration into global value chains. This upgrading effect is well documented in the Sinos Valley, where according to Bazan and Navas-Alemán (2004), a rapid process and product upgrading has been facilitated by inclusion in the U.S. value chain. A similar effect was also detected in León, Mexico, where, since the 1994 devaluation of the peso, U.S. buyers have begun to play a very significant role in upgrading. Again, U.S. buyers have contributed in an important way to process and product upgrading in the blue jeans cluster of Torreón, in Coahuila, Mexico (Bair and Gereffi, 2001). In all these cases, integration in global value chains has supported rapid enhancement of product and process capabilities.

Large buyers have a different effect on *functional upgrading*. Although inclusion in global value chains facilitates product and process upgrading, firms become tied into relationships that often prevent functional upgrading and leave the firms dependent on a small number of powerful customers (Bazan and Navas-Alemán, 2004; Humphrey and Schmitz, 2002b; Rabellotti, 2004). In the Sinos Valley, local suppliers were discouraged from functional upgrading by their main U.S. buyers, who did not want to share their core competencies in design, marketing, and sales. Since the acquisition of capabilities to engage in the higher-value-added activities requires great investments, Brazilians have been feeding into the footwear value chain mostly as producers, and their buyers have been more than happy to keep the status quo for as long as is possible (Bazan and Navas-Alemán, 2004).

If functional upgrading is prevented by buyers' power in quasi-hierarchical chains, it more readily occurs in market-based value chains. In these chains producers experience neither support for, nor blockages to, upgrading (Humphrey and Schmitz, 2002b). In the Sinos Valley, functional upgrading in design, branding, and marketing has been achieved by those firms selling to buyers in the domestic and regional markets in Latin America. Bazan and Navas-Alemán (2004) explain that in those markets buyers are smaller and buy ready-designed shoes, often sold under the producers' brand. A similar process of functional upgrading can also be detected among the Mexican footwear producers selling in the domestic market and in some cases also in the rest of Latin America (Rabellotti, 1999). In the textile sector, the Brazilian cluster of the Valle de Itaji in the state of Santa Catarina has experienced a similar process of functional upgrading (Campos, Ferraz Cário, and Nicolau, 2000).

Finally, we observe a positive (albeit weak) relationship between functional upgrading and collective efficiency (Table 9.4). Complementing this information with the available qualitative evidence, we can conclude that the association is due to external economies, such as the circulation of information and skilled labor, and joint action initiatives, such as participation in international trade fairs, collection of information about fashion trends, training programs for designers, and collective promotion of local brands.

To conclude, in order to functionally upgrade, firms must invest in design, branding, and marketing, and because the funds involved are often large, SMEs need to take advantage of the ongoing collective initiatives in a cluster to improve their access to information, expertise, and knowledge about markets. In other words, the degree of collective efficiency positively affects the SMEs' chances of functional upgrading.

Upgrading in the Natural-Resource-Based Sector

In natural-resource-based clusters, process and product upgrading are strongly tied to advances in science and technology in related industries, such as plants and seeds, machinery and tools, chemicals and pharmaceuticals. New methods, inputs, and machinery are introduced through interactions between suppliers and research labs, which carry out the majority of the research activity. Especially given the high uncertainty and low appropriability conditions of knowledge in the natural-resource-based sector, public research centers and universities play an important role in upgrading (Pray and Umali-Deininger, 1998).

SMEs have successfully upgraded in clusters characterized by public–private initiatives aimed at supplying research and technology extension services. For example, in the mango and grape cluster of Petrolina-Juazeiro in Brazil, the local San Francisco River Valley Development Agency (CODEVASF) promoted a sequence of crops that facilitated the learning process of small growers.[5] Similarly, in the wine cluster of Serra Gaúcha

[5] Most of the local small growers had never previously worked with irrigated agriculture. Thus, they first produced a combination of annual crops, including beans, corn, and melons, followed by widespread adoption of industrial tomatoes, and subsequently higher-value fruit crops, including

(Vargas, 2001a), CNPUV and the JK Agro-Technical Federal School, both located in the city of Bento Gonçalves, constitute the main research and human resource development centers of the cluster.

In southern Chile in the early 1980s, development of the salmon cluster was fostered by the Chile Foundation, which ventured into salmon farming, an industry which had until then been unknown in the region, proving that this activity could be profitable. Several private firms and transnational companies then followed this example, initially set up by a public actor (Pietrobelli, 1998). Later, joint actions led by the private sector and supported by public policies (e.g., a trade market, joint promotion abroad) paved the way to further strengthening and evolution of the cluster. In the late 1990s, R&D funds were allocated through competitive tenders (Maggi, Chapter 4 in this volume). Hence, public–private horizontal joint action positively affects product and process upgrading, which is achieved through several channels, including a local institutional network, public support of local joint actions, research centers, universities, and international cooperation. Cases demonstrating successful public–private joint action include the salmon cluster in Chile (Maggi, Chapter 4 in this volume), the Petrolina-Juazeiro mango cluster, and the apple cluster in Santa Catarina, Brazil (Gomes, Chapter 3 in this volume). These results suggest a positive relation between collective efficiency and product and process upgrading, although positive effects on functional upgrading are very rare (see Table 9.5).

In natural-resource-based clusters operating within buyer-driven chains, foreign buyers facilitate the link with the international market by signaling the need for and modes of necessary upgrading. Nevertheless, requirements of the international market are often codified by standards (e.g., HACCP). Buyers relay information on the standards that must be met but do not normally support the SMEs' upgrading process; rather,

---

mangoes and grapes. The transition from phase to phase involved a combination of conventional and more innovative support policies to help growers in each (consecutively more difficult) phase (Gomes, Chapter 3 in this volume).

Table 9.5. Upgrading in Natural-Resource-Based Clusters

Main product	Location	Degree of collective efficiency	Product upgrading	Process upgrading	Functional upgrading	Intersectoral upgrading	Sum of upgrading
Tobacco	Rio Pardo, Rio Grande do Sul (Brazil)	Medium	3	3	0	0	6
Wine	Colchagua (Chile)	Medium	3	3	0	0	6
Wine	Serra Gaúcha, Rio Grande do Sul (Brazil)	Medium	3	3	0	0	6
Sugar	Valle del Cauca (Colombia)	High	3	3	2	1	9
Marble	Espírito Santo (Brazil)	Medium	2	2	0	0	4
Copper	Cuajone-Toquepala (Peru)	Low	2	2	0	1	5
Salmon	Region Austral (Chile)	High	3	3	2	2	10
Milk-dairy	Boaco, Chontales (Nicaragua)	Medium	2	2	2	0	6
Mangoes and grapes	Petrolina-Juazeiro (Brazil)	High	3	3	0	0	6
Melons	Rio Grande do Norte (Brazil)	Medium	2	1	0	0	3
Apples	Santa Catarina (Brazil)	High	3	3	0	0	6
Total			29	28	6	4	
Average			2.64	2.55	0.55	0.60	6.09

Source: Authors' database.
Note: 3 = high; 2 = medium; 1 = low; 0 = absent.

buyers select SMEs that are able to comply with these standards. Such an example is that of the fresh fruit cluster in Petrolina-Juazeiro, Brazil (Gomes, Chapter 3 in this volume).

In the Nicaraguan milk and dairy products cluster, upgrading dynamics have taken very different forms. The hierarchical value chain led by a transnational company has fostered upgrading of products and processes but hindered functional upgrading (Artola and Parrilli, Chapter 2 in this volume). However, the value chain led by the semi-industrial cooperative has enhanced functional upgrading as well as improvements in products and processes. An interesting and promising issue that has emerged from this study is that value chains of types other than the quasi-hierarchical ones dominated by buyers or transnational companies may facilitate a smoother and more continuous process of learning, thereby creating the conditions for firms to functionally upgrade over time. Global buyers are not necessarily the optimal solution for upgrading; national chains also offer alternative, promising, and often more sustainable opportunities.

Upgrading in the Complex Products Sector

In complex products sector industries, levels of process (and to a lesser extent, product) upgrading are remarkable, but functional upgrading has been achieved only in a few cases (Table 9.6). In one case of functional upgrading, the Delphi automotive cluster in Juárez, Mexico, has experienced functional upgrading at a local level because of the development of the design and engineering center of Delphi (Carrillo and Lara, 2004). Local second- and third-tier suppliers have started producing higher-value-added products and services, mainly in electronics and informatics (Dutrénit, Vera-Cruz, and Gil, 2002). A similar example is the São João do Campos cluster in São Paulo, Brazil (Bernardes and Pinho, 2002).

In all other cases, the predominant pattern seems to be only product and process upgrading, with very limited support from the lead firms. In the sport shoes cluster in Nova Serrana, Brazil, local subsidiaries are

Table 9.6. Upgrading in Complex Products Clusters

Main product	Location	Degree of collective efficiency	Product upgrading	Process upgrading	Functional upgrading	Intersectoral upgrading	Sum of upgrading
Aircraft	SJC, São Paulo (Brazil)	Medium	2	2	2	0	6
Automotive	Nova Serrana (Brazil)	Medium	3	3	1	0	7
Automotive	Caxias do Sul, Rio Grande do Sul (Brazil)	Medium	1.5	2.5	0	0	4
Automotive	Juárez (Delphi) (Mexico)	Medium	3	3	2	0	8
Metalworking	Espírito Santo (Brazil)	Medium	2	3	0	0	5
Electronics	Jalisco (Mexico)	Low	2.5	2.5	0	0	5
Audiovisual equipment	Baja California (Mexico)	Low	2.5	2.5	1.5	0	6.5
Intel ICT	San José (Costa Rica)	Low	3	3	1	0	7
High-tech	Campinas, São Paulo (Brazil)	Medium	2.5	2.5	1	0	6
Total			22	24	8.5	0	
Average			2.44	2.70	0.94	0.0	6.06

Source: Authors' database.
Note: 3 = high; 2 = medium; 1 = low; 0 = absent.

not involved in new design development; what is done locally is rather to adapt designs to local conditions (*tropicalização*) (Santos, Crocco, and Lemos, 2002; Lemos et al., 2000). In the case of the television industry in Baja California, Mexico, upgrading affects predominantly foreign first-tier suppliers (Carrillo and Hualde, 2000). In Costa Rica (under Intel), there has been a very limited upgrading of locally owned firms into more-value-added activities: "With the reorganization of the plant after 1999, the process attracts some other suppliers and promotes local interaction with the software industry . . . major services are in low-tech low-value-added activities, except for some recent software contracts" (Vargas and Lindegaard, 2002:9–10).

Similarly, Quadros (2002) reports that in the GM and Volkswagen automotive cluster in São Paulo, Brazil, local suppliers improved the quality standards of production and achieved ISO 9000 certification, but leading firms in the Brazilian automotive chain have expended little effort to assist suppliers in the adoption of quality standards. Instead, firms received technical support mainly from consultancies and accredited certification institutions. Similar evidence is also observed in other cases (e.g., in the automotive sector in Argentina and Mexico; Albornoz, Milesi, and Yoguel, 2002; Dutrénit, Vera-Cruz, and Gil, 2002).

Interactions between leader firms and local suppliers have fostered product and process upgrading in some reported cases (e.g., Santos, Crocco, and Lemos, 2002; Bernardes and Pinho, 2002). However, according to our evidence, this effect is limited to very few cases, because market liberalization has produced a displacement of most local first-tier suppliers in favor of global outsourcing strategies by multinational assemblers. This further suggests that participation in a value chain offers no *direct* advantages to upgrading in these industries. Rather, it is the interest of local small firms in operating as suppliers that induces them to try to keep up with technological advances. In other words, most evidence suggests that *upgrading is left to the market*, leaving firms to upgrade through market mechanisms in order to improve their capabilities, by contracting consultants or exploiting other sources of knowledge available in the market. Most of the upgrading effort is not led by or conducted jointly with the buyer, who merely acts as an external stimulus to and spectator of the process.

Another interesting result of the current study is that collective efficiency does not appear to be related to upgrading in any way in most complex products sector clusters. In his study of industrial policies in the plastics and automobile industries in the Regional Chamber of ABC in São Paulo, Quadros (2002) concludes that technical collaboration with customers to achieve certification is limited and rarely systematic and that assistance has rather come from private consultants. Certification has not improved collaboration within the value chain, as the design of light components is carried out entirely by customers who provide the suppliers with detailed designs.

The strategic alternative for upgrading in very specific niches that are created by the presence of a local large firm is illustrated by the metalworking cluster in the state of Espírito Santo, Brazil (Villaschi, Cassiolato, and Lastres, Chapter 6 in this volume). This is an atypical SME cluster in that large commodity exporters (of steel, iron ore pellets, paper pulp) act as *anchors* of the local system, and the cluster SMEs manufacture parts, components, and machinery that service industrial maintenance and assembly lines.[6] So, strictly speaking, these firms should not be considered as part of a complex products cluster, but they still provide a useful example of how small local firms may collaborate with large (transnational) firms that act according to their own global strategy. Although the large firms do not follow the rationale of modular systems to manufacture complex products, the extent of tacit uncodified knowledge they employ is limited, and the ensuing need for continuous interactions with local suppliers is reduced, as is their interest in local providers' learning and upgrading. Therefore, this case offers valuable suggestions for the more general study of SMEs' upgrading in complex products clusters and value chains.

---

[6] These large firms have acted as carriers of industrial development based on an import-substituting strategy since the 1940s, when state-owned enterprises were set up to exploit the abundant local natural resources (iron mines, forests, and wood).

Although local SMEs sell in the domestic market, they are indirectly part of global commodity chains. These firms have experienced a remarkable upgrading, illustrated by the recent rise of local purchases by the large anchor firms (from 1 percent in the 1980s, to 10 percent in 1990, to 35 percent in 2002). In addition, local cluster firms are proving increasingly able to compete with firms from larger and more industrialized states (e.g., São Paulo and Minas Gerais) in servicing anchor firms out of Espírito Santo. Several factors interact to explain this successful process of upgrading. One important factor is the combination of customers committed to exporting commodities in highly competitive international markets and local SMEs' willingness to improve their industrial capabilities and become suppliers of the anchor companies. Another factor is the pragmatic collaboration that has gradually built between some of the anchor firms and a group of local SMEs. This has taken time to develop and has not been equally successful with all anchor companies. Collaboration has been helped by the personal trust generated by the local small entrepreneurs' being mostly spin-offs of the large companies. Small firms started by selling only to one large firm and later diversified their portfolio. A third factor promoting upgrading is the active and dynamic role of a local institution, CDMEC, which has been acting as an effective "network broker" of the cluster, or as it is locally defined, a true *articulador.*

The role played by the local government and support institutions cannot be underestimated. Local finance and support institutions, such as BANDES, provided varying support but contributed usefully in at least two major ways. First, they provided financial support during the early years of CDMEC, funding studies that initiated consciousness of the local small metalworking sector, of the role and value of interfirm cooperation, and of the firms' potential as local providers to the large commodity producers. Local support was also crucial for using all formal and informal political tools to induce large firms to source their intermediate inputs and services locally. For example, the State Environment Ministry had among its tools the ability to grant investment authorization in exchange for the preservation of the local environment and for better conditions for the local manpower: this implicitly meant more local sourcing.

Inducing large transnational companies and assemblers to opt for a cooperative attitude with the local productive system is always a very complex task. However, the Espírito Santo metalworking case shows that some effective options are available and should be pursued actively by local government authorities. Therefore, provided that some conditions are fulfilled (e.g., institutions articulating relationships between SMEs and large firms, local government negotiating to enhance collaboration, willingness of the local SMEs to upgrade through relationship with large firms), local SMEs may seek a niche in which to grow and upgrade by servicing large firms active in complex productive systems.

Upgrading in the Specialized Suppliers Sector (Software Clusters)

In specialized suppliers sector, our empirical analysis focuses on *software* clusters in Brazil and Mexico. In all the software clusters studied, levels of product and process upgrading are generally high. Regarding *product upgrading*, Ruiz Durán (Chapter 7 in this volume) presents five different types of products with increasing value added: data processing, outsourcing (offshore and near shore), ad hoc software development, development of software packages, and development of registered packages. Some of the oldest enterprises in the Mexican software clusters analyzed began their activity supplying data processing services, and most of them have since upgraded to ad hoc software packages, often adapting existing packages to the specific needs of their customers. In these cases, most of the product upgrading consists of incremental improvements, which are favored by the existence of network relationships with users.

Another form of product upgrading, also increasingly common in Blumenau, Brazil, is the supply of complete systems, instead of specific subsystems for bookkeeping, human resource management, and so on. With SMEs beginning to adopt enterprise resource planning (ERP) solutions, the market for full and integrated systems has expanded, opening the opportunity to be competitive in these systems to small software firms (Bercovich and Swanke, 2003). Finally, in all the clusters analyzed, a few firms have been able to evolve from producing ad hoc solutions to developing standardized systems, which are developed and sold to a large number of customers. For example, a small enterprise in Aguascalientes has developed software for ophthalmologists, translating existing packages into Spanish and adapting them to Mexican doctors' needs. This software is now exported to other Latin American countries.

According to available empirical evidence, in all of these clusters the degree of collective efficiency is positively related to product upgrading. Most of the entrepreneurs interviewed in Mexico and Brazil consider the exchange of information and the flow of skilled people within the clusters to be very important determinants of product upgrading. Moreover, the various collective initiatives undertaken in most of these clusters also contribute to enhancing firms' knowledge, access to information and skills. In the Mexican clusters *process upgrading* is very strongly related to obtaining the CMM certification. In addition, the linkages between software firms and local universities also importantly enhance process upgrading.

Finally, *functional upgrading* appears to be more common in the special services sector than in others. In all of these software clusters, firms make efforts to improve their marketing activity through collective initiatives. Examples include joint participation in trade fairs in Blumenau and the creation of a cluster catalog in Aguascalientes, with some joint marketing initiatives by the local business association.

Concluding Remarks: Clusters, Value Chains, and Sector-Specific Upgrading Patterns

Clustering and participating in a (global) value chain are increasingly considered by development scholars and policymakers as possible strategies to enhance enterprise competitiveness in international markets. In this chapter we show, and support with novel empirical evidence on Latin America, that collective efficiency affects enterprise upgrading, but the impact is different, and follows different routes, in different industrial sectors. On the whole, collective efficiency appears to reach higher levels in clusters in natural-resource-based and specialized suppliers (software) sectors. As expected, clusters in the complex products industry sector record lower levels of collective efficiency, largely because of the low degree of joint action. All clusters share the advantages of a local labor market, sometimes as a byproduct of geographical clustering. Inputs are also locally sourced, except in complex products sector industries, in which the logic of global sourcing prevails.

Moreover, passive external economies are more common than the various forms of joint action in all four of the sectors considered. This confirms our theoretical hypothesis that joint actions require specific investments and that firms get involved in cooperation only if they must face some external challenges, such as new competitors, adopting an innovation, or entering a new market.

In some cases, a low degree of collective efficiency may seriously hinder upgrading. The studies in this book and in the literature yield some important general lessons. First, a cluster takes time to develop; passive external economies may be present, but cooperative attitudes and joint actions take much longer to develop. The Chilean salmon cluster has taken nearly a decade to develop; the metalworking cluster in Espírito Santo put effort into promoting joint actions for almost a decade before getting successful results.

Second, the predominance of strong vertical relationships interferes with the development of external economies and hinders joint actions. This occurred in Chipilo, dominated by vertical relationships between the leading firm, Segusino, and its network of subcontractors. Very similar results are also reported in Torreón's blue jeans cluster. In the Nicaraguan dairy industry, foreign aid projects helped develop a cooperative attitude that later enhanced joint actions and the upgrading efforts of small breeders and producers.

However, collective efficiency is not the only thing that matters; the mode of governance of the value chain in which firms participate also affects the scope and extent of local firms' upgrading and how upgrading is pursued. More specifically, in quasi-hierarchical value chains, the pressure to comply with the standards imposed by the chains' leaders often enhances product and process upgrading but almost always inhibits functional upgrading. This result is common to all four sectors, but the way of pursuing product and process upgrading differs by sector. In traditional manufacturing sector industries, buyers directly facilitate product and process upgrading, because the characteristics of the manufactured products are not customized in these industries. Knowledge of products and processes cannot easily be codified in technical norms and is largely tacit, so the quality of products depends on the specialized skills of local producers. Therefore, foreign buyers and value chain leaders have an incentive to help local providers upgrade products and processes, because of the high risks of noncompliance and high cost of late deliveries or products of insufficient quality. Thus constant monitoring and supervision of local producers is an imperative for the buyers and value chain leaders. In contrast, in natural-resource-based and complex products sector clusters, upgrading is left to the SMEs themselves. Global value chains dominated by large buyers or producers from the developed world facilitate the link with the international market by signaling the need for upgrading (and modes of upgrading necessary), but they do not normally foster and support the SMEs' upgrading process.

Functional upgrading is rarely achieved in the clusters analyzed, and this is also the result of the strategic governance of the value chain leaders. In traditional manufacturing, natural-resource-based, and complex products sector clusters, local suppliers are discouraged from functional upgrading by their main buyers, who do not want to share their core competencies in design, marketing, and sales with local suppliers.

In most cases, global value chains are characterized by quasi-hierarchical governance structures. The leaders of these chains control the production phases with the highest value added (generally design, marketing, and branding), and producers from developing countries often rely on a few buyers. However, different types of chains often coexist in the same cluster. Many of the clusters do not participate exclusively in quasi-hierarchical chains but simultaneously in chains in which market conditions dominate. The chains with market condition structures offer the best opportunities for functional upgrading, as is seen in the Nicaraguan dairy cluster and the Brazilian shoe cluster in the Sinos Valley.

Moreover, chain governance is a dynamic process. Given that power is relational, the exercise of power by one party depends on the powerlessness of other parties in the chain. Therefore, existing producers or their spin-offs may acquire new capabilities or explore new markets, and this changes the power relationships. Secondly, establishing and maintaining quasi-hierarchical governance is costly for the leader firm and leads to inflexibility because of transaction-specific investments. In sum, the governance of value chains may change and evolve in ways that are more favorable to developing countries' SMEs (Humphrey and Schmitz, 2002a).

In conclusion, firm-level strategies for pursuing upgrading differ substantially across the four industrial sectors. Clustering and collective efficiency play a key role in some sectors (traditional manufacturing and natural-resource-based) but not in others (complex products) where the global logic of foreign buyers prevails and SMEs need to learn to cope with more competent (and often larger) players. Future empirical research will need to build rigorous quantitative methods to address some of the issues raised in this book.

References

Albornoz, F., D. Milesi, and G. Yoguel. 2002. New Economy in Old Sectors: Some Issues Coming from Two Production Networks in Argentina. Paper presented at the DRUID Summer Conference, "Industrial Dynamics of the New and Old Economy: Who Embraces Whom?" Copenhagen, June 6–8. www.druid.dk.

Allen, T. J. 1977. *Managing the Flow of Technology: Technology Transfer and the Dissemination of Technological Information within the R&D Organization.* Cambridge, Mass.: MIT Press.

Bair, J., and G. Gereffi. 2001. Local Clusters in Global Chains: The Causes and Consequences of Export Dynamism in Torreón's Blue Jeans Industry. *World Development* 29(11):1885–1903.

Bazan, L., and L. Navas-Alemán. 2004. The Underground Revolution in the Sinos Valley: A Comparison of Upgrading in Global and National Value Chains. In *Local Enterprises in the Global Economy: Issues of Governance and Upgrading,* ed. Hubert Schmitz. Cheltenham, U.K.: Elgar.

Bazan, L., and H. Schmitz. 1997. *Social Capital and Export Growth: An Industrial Community in Southern Brazil.* Discussion Paper No. 361, Institute of Development Studies, University of Sussex, Brighton, U.K.

Bercovich, N., and C. Swanke. 2003. *Cooperação e competitividade na indústria de software de Blumenau.* Working Paper No. 138, Serie Desarrollo Productivo, ECLAC/United Nations, Santiago de Chile.

Bernardes, R., and M. Pinho. 2002. *Aglomeração e aprendizado na rede de fornecedores locais da Embraer.* Nota Técnica, Instituto de Economia, Universidade Federal do Rio de Janeiro. www.ie.ufrj.br/redesist.

Campos, R., S. Ferraz Cário, and J. A. Nicolau. 2000. *Arranjo produtivo têxtil-vestuário do Vale do Itajaís/SC.* Nota Técnica No. 20, Instituto de Economia, Universidade Federal do Rio de Janeiro.

Carrillo, J., and A. Hualde. 2000. Existe un cluster en la maquiladora electrónica en Tijuana. In *¿Aglomeraciones locales o clusters globales? evolución empresarial e institucional en el Norte de México,* ed. J.

Carrillo, 99–139. Tijuana: Fundación Ebert and El Colegio de la Frontera Norte, Universidad Autónoma de Ciudad Juárez.

Carrillo, J., and A. Lara. 2004. Maquiladoras de cuarta generación y coordinación centralizada. *Estudios Sociológicos* 22(66).

Dutrénit, G., A. O. Vera-Cruz, and J. L. Gil. 2002. *Desafíos y oportunidades de las Pymes para su integración a la red de proveedores: el caso de la maquila automotriz en Ciudad Juárez.* Nota Técnica, Instituto de Economia, Universidade Federal do Rio de Janeiro. www.ie.ufrj.br/redesist.

Gereffi, G. 1999. International Trade and Industrial Upgrading in the Apparel Commodity Chain. *Journal of International Economics* 48:37–70.

Giuliani, E. 2003. Knowledge in the Air and Its Uneven Distribution: A Story of a Chilean Wine Cluster. Paper presented at the DRUID Winter Conference, Aalborg, Denmark, January 16–18. www.druid.dk.

Humphrey, J., and H. Schmitz. 2002a. How Does Insertion in Global Value Chains Affect Upgrading Industrial Clusters? *Regional Studies* 36(9):1017–1027.

———. 2002b. *Developing Country Firms in the World Economy: Governance and Upgrading in Global Value Chains.* Report No. 61, Institute für Entwicklung und Frieden der Gerhard-Mercator-Universität, University of Duisburg, Duisburg, Germany. http://www.ids.ac.uk/ids/global/vwpap.html.

Lemos, M. B., C. B. Diniz, F. Teixeira dos Santos, M. A. Crocco, and O. Camargo. 2000. *O arranjo produtivo da Rede Fiat de Fornecedores.* Nota Técnica No. 17, Instituto de Economia, Universidade Federal do Rio de Janeiro. www.ie.ufrj.br/redesist.

Maskell, P. 2001. Towards a Knowledge-Based Theory of the Geographical Cluster. *Industrial and Corporate Change* 10(4):921–943.

Marshall, A. 1920. *Principles of Economics.* 8th ed. London: Macmillan (1st ed. 1890).

Nadvi, K., and H. Schmitz. 1994. *Industrial Clusters in Less Developed Countries: Review of Experiences and Research Agenda.* Discussion

Paper No. 339, Institute of Development Studies, University of Sussex, Brighton, U.K.

———, eds. 1999. Industrial Clusters in Developing Countries [Special Issue]. *World Development* 27(9).

Pietrobelli, C. 1998. *Industry, Competitiveness and Technological Capabilities in Chile: A New Tiger from Latin America?* Basingstoke, U.K.: Macmillan.

Pray, C. E., and D. Umali-Deininger. 1998. The Private Sector in Agricultural Research Systems: Will It Fill the Gap? *World Development* 26(6):1127–1148.

Quadros, R. 2002. *Global Quality Standards, Chain Governance and the Technological Upgrading of Brazilian Auto Components Producers.* Working Paper No. 156, Institute of Development Studies, University of Sussex, Brighton, U.K.

Rabellotti, R. 1997. *External Economies and Cooperation in Industrial Districts: A Comparison of Italy and Mexico.* Basingstoke, U.K.: Macmillan.

———. 1999. Recovery of a Mexican Cluster: Devaluation Bonanza or Collective Efficiency? *World Development* 27(9):1571–1585.

———. 2004. The Effect of Globalisation on Industrial Districts in Italy: The Case of Brenta. In *Local Enterprises in the Global Economy: Issues of Governance and Upgrading,* ed. Hubert Schmitz, 140–173. Cheltenham, U.K.: Elgar.

Santos, F., M. Crocco, and M. B. Lemos. 2002. *As MPMEs em Espaços industriais periféricos: os casos de Nova Serrana e da Rede de Fornecedores da Fiat.* Nota Técnica, Instituto de Economia, Universidade Federal do Rio de Janeiro. www.ie.ufrj.br/redesist.

Schmitz, H. 1995. Collective Efficiency: Growth Path for Small-Scale Industry. *Journal of Development Studies* 31(4):529–566.

———, ed. 2004. *Local Enterprises in the Global Economy: Issues of Governance and Upgrading.* Cheltenham, U.K.: Elgar.

Vargas, M. A. 2001a. Local Systems of Innovation in Developing Countries: A Study of Technological Learning in Local Productive Arrangements in Brazil. Paper presented at the DRUID Winter Conference, Aalborg, Denmark, January 16–18. www.druid.dk.

———. 2001b. *Forms of Governance, Learning Mechanisms and Upgrading Strategies in the Tobacco Cluster in Rio Pardo Valley-Brazil.* Working Paper No. 125, Institute of Development Studies, University of Sussex, Brighton, U.K.

Vargas, L., and K. Lindegaard. 2002. New Economies and Innovation for Developing Countries. The Case of Intel in Costa Rica. Paper presented at the DRUID Summer Conference, "Industrial Dynamics of the New and Old Economy: Who Embraces Whom?" Copenhagen, June 6–8. www.druid.dk.

Chapter 10

Supporting Enterprise Upgrading in Clusters and Value Chains in Latin America

Carlo Pietrobelli and Roberta Rabellotti

What can we learn for public policies from the rich and varied empirical evidence presented in this book? What implications may be drawn for their design and implementation? Notions like clusters and (global) value chains have gained so much popularity these days that they often shape and encompass the whole industrial and SME policy approach in developing (and developed) countries. However, we believe that these concepts are often used too vaguely, and as such they do not represent effective tools for designing and implementing policies to improve SMEs' competitiveness and enhance their upgrading prospects, notably in developing countries.

In this final chapter we pull together the main insights that may be useful for policy purposes and put them in a historical perspective. After discussing policies for cluster development, we explore the policy options for cluster and value chain development to support upgrading in specific industrial sectors. Identifying four distinct groups of industrial sectors (Pietrobelli and Rabellotti, Chapter 1 in this volume) has proven to be a useful tool for analyzing the challenges that confront different industries and for identifying policy solutions that address these challenges effectively.

Policy Approaches Prevailing in the 1990s

Prevailing wisdom in the 1990s was that effective business support policies should be based on the principles of neutrality, horizontality, and demand orientation (Dini, 2003). Neutrality implied the ex ante definition of universal rules to separate support institutions from potential pressures from private or public lobbies. Horizontality referred to the application of policies and rules to all businesses independent of their size, location, or industrial sector. Finally, support initiatives should respond to an explicit demand from the enterprise sector that, in turn, was required to provide cofinancing.

Consensus on this approach was reached internationally through repeated meetings of the Committee of Donor Agencies for Small Enterprise Development, representing most international donors active in this field. This committee's guiding principles, based on a private-sector-led, market economy framework, are (1) a fundamental belief in the principles of a market economy, in which the state has a role in providing an enabling environment, in correcting market failures, and in the provision of public goods; (2) the assumption that the majority of business services are private goods, and hence market rules apply; and (3) the expectation that with appropriate product design, delivery, and payment mechanisms, business support services can always be provided on a commercial basis (Committee of Donor Agencies, 1997, 2001).

Within this general framework, most countries have been recently enacting SME support policies with much emphasis on clusters and value chains, sometimes without a clear understanding of what these concepts mean and imply. However, macroeconomic constraints in Latin America have often created *a remarkable gap between statements of principle and the design of SME support policies and their actual implementation*, which is hardly of the size and outreach foreseen. In stark contrast with what is occurring in more industrialized countries, the private sector is still insufficiently involved in the design and management of policy initiatives and policy evaluations (Pietrobelli and Rabellotti, 2002, on Italy). Evaluations, although increasingly necessary to get access to public funds, are often weak and lack independence.

However, the major shortcoming of the present policy approach in most Latin American countries appears to be the *lack of a comprehensive and consistent vision of local SME development and upgrading*. Thus, policy packages tend to address either the issue of technical training, or that of local cluster development, or that of the development of value chain providers. Yet, as has been shown repeatedly in this book, SMEs simultaneously face the challenge of upgrading through the advantages offered by geographical clustering and collective efficiency *and* through the opportunities and pressures offered by participation in global value chains and collaboration with foreign buyers. Any attempt to enhance local SMEs' upgrading should therefore take such a comprehensive approach.

A preliminary question needs to be addressed here, related to the definition of what we really mean by "cluster development policies." Thus, in order to design and then manage a policy to support a cluster, the two main dimensions that characterize a cluster must be explicitly taken into account. These are the *territorial factor* (i.e., social and cultural identity as well as geographical concentration and specialization) and the *linkage factor* (i.e., the richness of vertical and horizontal linkages occurring within a cluster) (Dini, 2003).

Thus, in principle, cluster development policies correspond to the *intersection* between these two policy areas (Figure 10.1). A proper cluster development policy aimed at fostering collective efficiency should explicitly consider both the development of local competitive factors and the promotion of networks and linkages. Policies aimed at enhancing collective

Figure 10.1. Cluster Development Policies

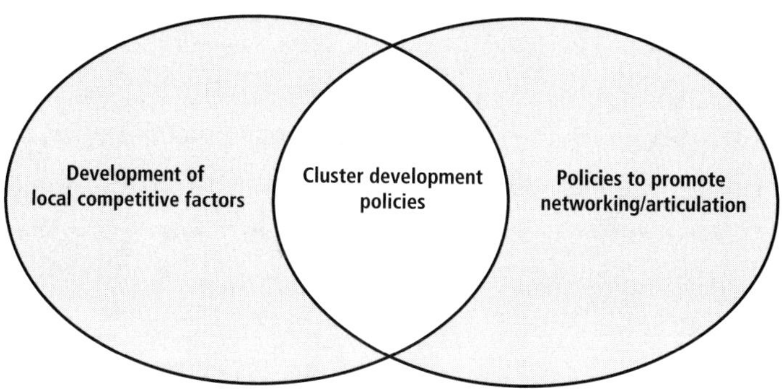

efficiency will target both the development of local competitive factors (including tangible factors such as infrastructure and intangible factors such as local expertise) and the promotion of linkages among economic actors in the cluster (e.g., programs to upgrade subcontractors, establishment of consortia or business associations) (Dini, 2003).

As shown in this book, external economies are much more frequent than joint actions in most Latin American clusters. This is due to the complex and lengthy process of building up trust and developing social capital locally. *Human capital* and *time* are the two essential resources for such policies. This point has been clearly stressed also by the Organisation for Economic Co-operation and Development (OECD) (Boekholt and Thuriaux, 1999).

Despite a coherent theoretical vision, in practice, cluster development policies may differ remarkably. Recent evidence on cluster support policies implemented in European countries reveals that each country adopts different policy instruments, although the policies may share a number of key objectives and characteristics (Observatory of European SMEs, 2002). Not all these goals and actions are appropriate in the Latin American context, but the distillation of the European experience may offer useful guidelines for developing Latin American cluster policies. Some of the key findings in regard to European cluster policies are the following:

- Cluster policies are considered a means to promote economic development and structural changes, often by enhancing (regional) innovation capacity.
- Policies are based on improved business cooperation and networking, which may require the stimulation of social processes.
- Policies emphasize the linking of firms to the (regional) technological infrastructure of education and R&D institutions and, in particular, try to bring new technology to regional networks of SMEs. In the end, policies imply enhancing "regional innovation systems."

- Public or semipublic organizations have a role as mediators in encouraging interfirm networks and joint projects. Especially in the early stage of cluster development, a third party often needs to take care of the flow of information, of the building of mutual trust among cluster members, and of supporting the organization of business networks. Policies underline the need to improve innovation capability and knowledge management in firms. Underlying these policies is a focus on the need to stimulate the creation of specialized factors and, in particular, specialized knowledge.

Given that Latin American countries are often constrained by limited financial resources, which must be used as efficiently as possible, two general principles may be added: selectivity and decentralization with local financial autonomy. As regards selectivity, clusters to be supported should be selected on the basis of their strategic potential for future growth. In addition, interventions should address a few essential priorities, as also stressed for OECD countries (Boekholt and Thuriaux, 1999). To make selectivity—itself a very hard task—easier, good tools for mapping and analyzing clusters need to be developed, investing adequate financial resources in the exploratory and diagnostic phase *before interventions*. In fact, the information available is often insufficient and collected for different purposes. Well-directed and purposeful analyses of local circumstances should always precede all policy design and implementation. Several techniques are available and could be usefully employed.[1] As regards decentralization, local, competent, and financially autonomous organizations should be promoted and strengthened to address the specific problems of SMEs.

A Menu of Actions for Cluster Development

In this section we present a menu of actions aimed at supporting the upgrading of SMEs located in clusters and integrated into value chains.

---

[1] See, for example, the methodology used for the present book, and also that of PACA (Participatory Appraisal of Competitive Advantage) (http://www.paca-online.de).

It is worth remembering that these proposals are based not on abstract theorizing, but on the detailed scrutiny of our original case studies and on international comparisons and best practices available from the specialized literature and thoroughly analyzed in this book.

The menu of actions is presented in Table 10.1 and explained in detail thereafter. The actions proposed are organized according to three complementary goals: enhancing the development of external economies, promoting linkages, and strengthening local positions within a value chain. The approach suggested here is not normative and does *not* aim to suggest *general* principles to apply in *all* circumstances. In contrast, it advocates a *context-specific approach to policy design and implementation.* Which action (or combination of actions) should be chosen for a specific cluster depends on the cluster's characteristics, its actual degree of collective efficiency, its sector of specialization, and the characteristics of the value chains in which it operates—most importantly, the value chains' mode of governance. In addition, the chosen actions should also depend on the stage of the cluster's life cycle, given that policies need to evolve over time to reflect cluster evolution.

Table 10.1. A Menu of Actions to Support Cluster Development

Facilitate the development of external economies
- Build specialized labor force skill centers

Promote linkages among firms
- Create and enhance trust among firms
- Promote the establishment of collective projects
- Create and strengthen business associations
- Strengthen local supply of financial and nonfinancial services
- Facilitate the external connections of the cluster
- Promote innovation

Strengthen the local position within value chains
- Attract the chain leaders into the clusters
- Sustain the upgrading of suppliers
- Facilitate interaction within value chains
- Promote access to new markets and value chains
- Assist SMEs in meeting international standards

Source: Based on authors' field studies.

Facilitate the Development of External Economies

Build a Specialized Labor Force

General basic education and human resource development policies are of course necessary conditions for local development and for the improvement of local factor endowments. However, they cannot be considered proper cluster development policies.

For our present aims, more specific, cluster-oriented interventions must be designed and implemented. The Chilean and Mexican clusters offer good evidence of the positive effects of investments in human capital, aimed at satisfying the specific local requirements in terms of skills (Maggi, Chapter 4, and Ruiz Durán, Chapter 7 in this volume). An example would be the design of curricula taught in technical schools and local universities by introducing reality and context into the education and aligning programs with real workplace needs. Even the most basic programs, such as vocational English, can be taught more effectively if the vocabulary is related to that used in the cluster (Rosenfeld, 2002). Moreover, direct involvement of students within local firms for a short period of their school curriculum is usually a very effective means of encouraging students to follow career paths in the cluster.

The notion of a *cluster skill center* associated with an existing institution may help in this regard. This need not be a physical but rather a *virtual center* that might organize teams from various colleges to work on particular problems, conduct R&D, or develop curricula and diffuse these results throughout the cluster (Rosenfeld, 2002). A cluster skill center should aim at surveying industry labor needs, developing new curricula, updating skill standards, benchmarking practices in other places, and collecting information about the cluster labor market. Moreover, cluster skill centers can serve as gateways, for example, to help firms bombarded with more information than they can digest and help them determine which training programs offer the most relevant staff experience and technologies and the best track record and are most familiar with the industry. The private sector should be actively involved in the operation of such skill centers.

Promote Linkages among Firms

Create and Enhance Trust among Firms and Promote the Establishment of Collective Projects

In Latin America and elsewhere, an increasing number of projects are aimed at *stimulating the development of linkages among firms.* In Chile, one of the oldest and best-known projects, which has been effectively promoting collective projects among firms for more than a decade, is PROFO (Programa de Fomento Asociativo) (Dini, 2004). UNIDO has also implemented various projects with a similar aim in developing countries as varied as Honduras, Nicaragua, and India (Ceglie and Dini, 2000; Rabellotti, 1998). In South Africa, a project to develop "learning networks" in the auto components industry has been remarkably successful. An automobile components benchmarking club was created to compare SMEs to both their domestic and their international competitors. After a period of months the participating firms were helping each other improve, meeting at members' plants, and sharing expertise through best-in-class workshops. The result has been a dramatic improvement in production and management efficiency (Kaplinsky, 2001). This shows that *collective action helps improve collective efficiency.*

Typically, these projects provide incentives and technical assistance to compensate firms for some of the costs of participating in activities with uncertain returns and very high transaction costs. However, the idea of offering financial incentives for firms' participation can be strongly questioned because some firms may be induced to participate in the project to access funds, without a real intent of cooperation. Therefore, incentives must be temporary, decreasing with time and also involving the financial participation of the receiving firms. Moreover, the use of funds is often restricted and usually excludes the purchase of machines or raw materials or the payment of wages. However, financial incentives are not sufficient by themselves to induce joint actions and build trust. Specialized technical assistance is extremely valuable for this goal and should be provided by people trained as network "brokers," able to promote trust, to increase firms' awareness about the importance of cooperation, and to help firms elaborate and implement collective projects (UNDP, 2000). These brokers may be individuals or institutions with strong technical skills, highly independent of local lobbies and vested interests, and enjoying sound credibility with local actors.

Another crucial condition for the success of cluster development programs is the so-called *ownership of local actors*, who must participate actively and be engaged in the initiative in order to guide and develop any policy intervention successfully (Dini, 2003). This has been observed in several of the successful joint actions in our field studies (e.g., the metalworking and fresh fruit clusters in Brazil [Chapter 3] and the salmon cluster in Chile [Chapter 4]). In this respect, the participatory process of enhancement of the local context involving a coalition of local public and private actors to identify and then implement collective entrepreneurial and infrastructural projects is an interesting experience to analyze (Meyer Stamer, 2004).

A final remark concerns the *long-term perspective that this type of project needs to take*. In a recent survey of different projects implemented in Latin America, Dini (2004) notes that at least 12 months are needed to create a real change in entrepreneurs' attitude toward cooperation, and at least two years to impact firms' internal capacity. Although exact measurements for cluster development projects are not available, it is extremely likely that the time required may be even longer: the evolution of the Chilean salmon cluster (Chapter 4) took over a decade, and the UNIDO program in the Boaco and Chontales, Nicaragua, dairy cluster has been in place for five years (Chapter 2).

Create and Strengthen Business Associations at the Cluster Level

Business associations are the collective voice of the cluster, providing it with a collective identity. They can play an important role in articulating demands of the private sector as well as in providing services to member firms. Generally, business associations tend to be weak in most Latin American countries. Therefore, the first step is to examine the existing trade, labor, professional, and civic associations with respect to membership requirements, mission and services supplied. If appropriate associations do not exist, interested companies may be assisted in forming one. Furthermore, it is important to verify how associations represent different types of firms and particularly how they represent the interests of SMEs as opposed to those of large firms.

If the cluster is already served by specialized and local business associations, they can assume additional responsibilities. Useful services might include advice to local institutions and governments on the design of appropriate policies and strategies; development of networks of firms; direct provision of some services, like information about new markets; collective participation in international trade fairs; and facilitation of external connections of the cluster by participating in international networks of business associations.

Strengthen the Local Supply of Financial and Nonfinancial Services

Various instruments may be used to enhance SMEs' access to financial services and, indirectly, spur collaboration. Thus, funds may be tied to financing projects involving multiple firms; for instance, awarding grants to groups of firms for training associate companies. The experience of the recently created "cluster banks" in Brazil should be carefully observed and monitored (Vargas, Britto, and Cassiolato, 2001).

In addition to financial services, *"real" business development services are especially needed.* These services are geared to promote and facilitate structural changes at the enterprise level and may be provided through various means. In advanced countries, these services may be more easily acquired on the market and may be effective without public subsidies. Public subsidies may be necessary only in an initial stage but not later (e.g., this was true for quality management and certification in Italy; Pietrobelli and Rabellotti, 2002). Careful location-specific analysis of each case should guide policymakers.

The creation of a local business development services center may be an instrument to support the development of a supply of services whenever current services are inadequate. The center's capability to provide services demanded by firms depends on its embeddedness in the local business environment. An alternative to the direct provision of services is to support existing institutions in the development of the missing services. In this case, business development service centers would act more as "network facilitators" than as service providers. Nevertheless, this desirable model requires the prior existence of institutions, such as universities, research centers, laboratories, and training centers, in order to set up the network. This may not be so obvious everywhere, especially in the least developed countries. This is often a feasible alternative in more industrially advanced Latin American countries that are already endowed with numerous institutions with diverse missions and objectives but may lack a unitary and integrated vision or duplicate their functions without enhancing their effectiveness. In poorer countries, where industry is still incipient, a business development services center is often bound to operate on its own, in the absence of other agents and institutions supporting local industrial development. This requires a different strategy. Within such a context, a business development services center should first improve its management and technical skills and the quality of the services it provides. This would in turn improve the center's reputation and raise enterprises' demand for its services. Once it has established its presence in the local economy, the center should also aim to create linkages with the existing firms and institutions and to convince firms of the mutual advantage of close collaboration.

Business development services centers also have a role in *stimulating firms' demand for new services.* This requires anticipating tacit, unexpressed needs and convincing firms of their relevance for future competitiveness. This is especially true in less developed regions, where firms have not developed a full understanding of their own needs and lag behind in adopting a strategic and forward-looking business attitude. Some of these needs may become, in a relatively short time, perceived by enterprises under the pressure of competitive markets, such as in the case of laboratory testing and quality certification services. But in the case of other services, such as innovative services, R&D projects, and development of new technological solutions, such services may need to be subsidized for a long time given their public good content.

Finally, the activities of business development services centers should be constantly monitored, and their effectiveness, efficiency, and impact regularly evaluated. Although the *evaluation* of a center's activities is a difficult task, it is nevertheless necessary. It is worth making efforts to quantify benefits, costs, and impacts, although indicators should be used very carefully. Moreover, evaluation should be repeated on a regular basis to facilitate effective learning and improvements in methods and practices. Self-sustainability should not necessarily be an objective, but given that budget constraint is probably a common problem, collection of even some crude measures of efficacy and value for money spent may be an important asset for policymakers (Pietrobelli and Rabellotti, 2002).

Facilitate External Connections of the Cluster

External connections are crucial for innovating and for entering new markets. Several instruments can be adopted, such as study tours of entrepreneurs, creation of connections between local institutions and business associations and their foreign equivalents, and invitations of external consultants to the cluster. This is especially relevant for industries in which technologies constantly evolve and local external economies in the form of information exchanges may not suffice to ensure the necessary levels of innovation and technology development.

In the case of an Italian industrial district studied by Rabellotti (2004), a very effective way of creating external connections consisted of an informal program of exchange between the children of the local entrepreneurs and the children of their German buyers. In this way, the producers could acquire some direct knowledge about their final market and also improve their German language skills, while the buyers could learn some production skills and some Italian. Furthermore, both the Italian producers and their German buyers also emphasized the positive impact of this experience on their mutual trust.

In the Italian and Taiwanese clusters studied by Guerrieri, Iammarino, and Pietrobelli (2001), the ability to link up with foreign firms and value chains marked a substantial difference in performance across clusters active in industries as different as garments and computer electronics. Such linkage activities have been fostered through several policy interventions and *domestic linkages developed in parallel with international linkages.* Examples of specific programs include informal peer group networks for technological knowledge and brand name recognition; hierarchical center-satellite systems, often subsidized and directed by government policies; linkages with large domestic firms, often in the form of cross-sectoral business groups; and business groups centered around a holding company.

In the Chilean wine cluster of Colchagua, international experts played the strategic role of "flying winemakers" (i.e., consultant oenologists) who advised firms and kept them informed of the latest evolutions of technology and who fostered the external linkages of the cluster. Because knowledge in this cluster did not "flow freely in the air" by virtue of geographical proximity, it rather required professionals to embody both tacit and codified knowledge and to diffuse their knowledge locally (Giuliani, 2003).

Promote Innovation

Several instruments may be adopted to support research and technology transfer inside and among SMEs and between SMEs and research institutes and universities and generally to promote innovation. In a cluster promoting collective efficiency, access to grants and subsidies may be tied to the establishment of linkages and agreements of cooperation between two or more firms or institutions. Foreign experts and consultants may often facilitate access to innovation and foster its adoption and adaptation to local circumstances.

In addition, technology centers and incubators are one of the most popular instruments of economic and technology support at the cluster level. The basic concept of these centers is to create a favorable environment for start-ups, especially innovative and technology-oriented firms, by reducing fixed costs and sharing services, combined with providing technical assistance and easy interactions with research institutes and universities. These technology centers and incubators appear to be especially relevant for new, emerging industries, such as software clusters (Ruiz Durán, Chapter 7 in this volume).

In a cluster, local universities and other advanced institutions can be encouraged to concentrate part of their research on topics relevant for the local economy. In the Chilean salmon cluster, this is being achieved through competitive tenders for joint research projects proposed by universities and cluster firms and financed by the government (Maggi, Chapter 4 in this volume). Furthermore, review criteria adopted for evaluating the performance of local universities could add further relevance to the regional economy and to the commercial potential of research relevant for the cluster (Rosenfeld, 2002).

Strengthen the Local Position within Value Chains

In designing and implementing policies and programs, the enhancement of collective efficiency must be accompanied by explicit attention to the value chains in which local SMEs are integrated and specifically to the value chains' mode of governance. Several factors greatly affect the intensity of the linkages among firms belonging to the same value chain, the opportunities offered by the chain for SME upgrading, and the ability of SMEs to exploit opportunities. These factors include the pattern of governance of the value chain, the existence of alternative value chains in which firms can operate, and the sector of specialization. For instance, in traditional manufacturing industries, product specifications cannot be easily codified in technical norms and require a substantial amount of tacit knowledge. As buyers rely on the competencies of their suppliers, they are obliged to assist the suppliers' upgrading.

Attract the Chain Leaders into the Clusters

A preliminary type of support is oriented to attracting the chain leaders into the clusters and supporting their process of choice with the provision of relevant information. National or local programs of fiscal incentives and subsidies are often adopted to attract these firms. In some cases, when the balance of power allows it, these incentives are tied to the commitment of the leading firms to assisting local suppliers in process and product upgrading. For instance in Chile, Corfo has implemented a program to sustain a process of suppliers' upgrading, the cost of which is shared among the local supplier, its buyer, and Corfo itself (Dini, 2003).[2]

Sustain the Upgrading of Suppliers

Support is especially necessary for strengthening skills and abilities in the backward production stages along the chain. In Mexico, a program to sustain the upgrading of suppliers has recently been implemented by National Financiera and the United Nations Development Programme (UNDP) (2000). One of the first results of the program has been the elaboration of an interactive method for training consultants specialized in facilitating suppliers' upgrading. The program provides financial services, such as credit and guarantee, and also nonfinancial services, such as technical assistance and training. Based on this experience, both suppliers and customers appear to enjoy substantial benefits. The main benefits obtained by the customer firms are quality improvement of inputs, reduction of delivery time, more competitive price, and increased flexibility to adapt to changes in demand. On the supplier side, the most common benefits are increase in sales and profits, more stable demand, productivity increase and cost reduction, improved access to technology, and adoption of a more quality-oriented approach.

From what has been said so far, it can be concluded that the success of the initiatives aimed at supporting SMEs' upgrading within quasi-hierarchical value chains depends on the interest of the leaders of the chains in getting involved and directly sustaining the process. But why should a leader be interested in supporting the upgrading process of its providers?

---

[2] For similar evidence on Singapore's attracting FDI and tying it to a clear commitment to train local human capital, see Manzocchi and Pietrobelli (2001).

A leader's interest may depend on how important the inputs produced in the cluster are, how easily local provider firms could be replaced by other providers located elsewhere (i.e., the opportunity cost of local firms' lack of upgrading), and the weight of the main chain within the total market of the cluster (i.e., the providers' dependence on a single value chain as a market outlet). In addition, the general impact of a program to sustain SMEs' upgrading in value chains depends on the intensity of the relationships existing within the cluster (i.e., on the cluster's degree of collective efficiency). When vertical relationships between suppliers and leading firms predominate, and when suppliers are not fully embedded and integrated in the local cluster, there are limited spillovers toward the rest of the cluster. In contrast, when firms in the cluster are highly integrated within the local system, the results of their upgrading strategies percolate to other firms, generating a process of diffuse upgrading at cluster level which may open the opportunity to successfully enter new alternative markets and extend the upgrading process to other SMEs.

For this reason, even when leading firms actively collaborate in the upgrading process of their providers, it is always useful for providers to develop an alternative strategy, seeking at the cluster level access to new markets and assistance in exporting. The objective for local producers is to reduce their risk of being locked into just one global value chain, being strongly dependent on the leader's strategy, clearly outside the cluster's control.

Facilitate Interaction within Value Chains

The role of *consultants as intermediaries between suppliers and their customers* is particularly useful when the economic structure is extremely polarized. Intermediaries facilitate interaction among parties, reducing the transaction costs and enhancing the development of trust. A role of this kind is played by CDMEC in the metalworking cluster of Espírito Santo, Brazil (Villaschi, Cassiolato, and Lastres, Chapter 6 in this book). In addition, consultants and other intermediary institutions also contribute, with their technical assistance, support to the process of modernization of local suppliers. However, the success of this upgrading process is also strongly dependent on the buyers' commitment to guaranteeing a stable and substantial demand.

Business associations may also have an impact on the development of the relationships between SMEs and chain leaders (UNCTAD, 2000). Business associations can contribute in several ways, including providing assistance in preselection: they have an important role in facilitating and enhancing the formation of the linkages between potential local firms as suppliers to leading firms in the chain by preparing updated records of enterprises' profiles and supplying clear and relevant information on the existing and potential capabilities of enterprises interested in entering the chain. Business associations can also foster partnerships between potential customers and local suppliers through improved contacts between them and by organizing fairs and other trading events and increasing awareness of the benefits from improved relationships, and they can provide the institutional assistance required for SMEs' upgrading. Furthermore, business associations can play a very crucial role in the search for new alternative markets in which local firms may be able to overcome the obstacles to functional upgrading that are common in most quasi-hierarchical chains.

Promote Access to New Markets and Value Chains

Individual small firms often lack the resources and knowledge to effectively enter new markets. Marketing, especially exporting, is usually one of the most widely accepted horizontal forms of cooperation. Therefore, an important set of interventions is related to the promotion of firms' linkages with markets, including provision of information, particularly on overseas markets, and promotion of products in these markets, particularly through participation in trade fairs. Joint stands at key international trade fairs are an example of a way to pool resources and act together. Participating in these trade fairs is not just about selling; it is also about learning through direct contact with potential customers (Humphrey, 2002).

A more ambitious objective of a cluster—which may be the goal of a support program—is to try to promote and market itself to investors and customers, creating a brand that identifies the cluster with quality, establishes customer loyalty, and becomes a prime destination of buyers. This may be especially valuable for getting access to multiple value chains and for exploiting the opportunities for learning and for more advanced forms of upgrading (i.e., functional, in addition to product and process, upgrading), otherwise impossible when locked in by participation in a single hierarchically governed value chain. This appears to have helped SMEs upgrading in the Sinos Valley shoemaking cluster in southern Brazil, as well as in the Nicaraguan dairy cluster (Chapter 2).

Assist SMEs in Meeting International Standards

Globalization of value chains has been sustained by the parallel drive toward the standardization of practices and procedures. Firms' interactions along the value chain require conformity with agreed-upon standard business practices in contracting, accounting, environmental management, labor standards, health regulations, and the communication of product design and engineering information (Nadvi and Waltring, 2004; UNIDO, 2002). Access to international markets is conditional upon fulfillment of these standards, and noncompliance frequently offers the opportunity for value chain leaders and foreign buyers to reject products. To this end, technical assistance may be very effective, especially if it is administered at the cluster level and through collective institutions and joint actions, involving small firms together with buyers and chain leaders.

The implementation of an adequate *regulatory framework* may be the right instrument for urging local producers to respect environmental and sanitary controls and health and labor standards. This is often a need that is not perceived in the earliest stages of a cluster's life cycle. However, as soon as the cluster approaches the international market, and eventually starts to enjoy success and threatens the consolidated market shares of existing exporters, protectionist measures may start to bite. The Chilean salmon cluster experience offers an example of this evolution. Although salmon exporters initially gained market shares relatively easily with minimum formalized standard requirements, as their market shares began to grow, they started facing rising barriers, often of a nontariff nature (Maggi, Chapter 4 in this volume).

A Sectoral Approach to Policy Design and Implementation

Given the remarkable sectoral differences emerging from the empirical evidence presented in this book, in spite of some overlap, policy priorities are different in several respects for each of the four sectors. In this section we review the sectors in sequence, identifying policy priorities for each sector (Table 10.2).

Table 10.2. A Sectoral Approach to Policy Design

Traditional manufacturing sector clusters

- Ensure consistency between micro support policies and programs and the overall macroeconomic framework
- Promote linkages among firms
- Promote access to new, additional value chains

Natural-resource-based sector clusters

- Promote public-private collaboration in research and disseminate research to SMEs
- Improve skills and abilities of producers in the backward stages of the value chain (e.g., agriculture, breeding)
- Facilitate the entry of SMEs into markets and value chains
- Promote the adoption of quality and sanitary standards and environmental regulations and enforce quality inspections and controls
- Promote access to foreign markets and overcome nontariff barriers
- Improve the access and availability of good basic infrastructures

Complex products sector clusters

- Promote/support the active and dynamic role of actors working as "network brokers" (*articuladores*) of the cluster, and notably of the relationships between the large anchor firms and the local small suppliers
- Set up an incentive framework aimed at inducing large firms to source their intermediate inputs and services locally and to support their suppliers' upgrading strategies

Specialized suppliers sector (software) clusters

- Invest in highly skilled professionals
- Intensify industry-research collaboration

Source: Based on authors' field studies.

Traditional Manufacturing Sector Clusters

A preliminary condition that should be ensured by all possible means and that is relevant in all clusters, but especially in traditional manufacturing sector clusters, is the need to *maintain macro conditions under control.* Recent examples from Mexico and Argentina illustrate this point. Research has shown that in traditional manufacturing clusters, *external economies and, above all, joint actions remarkably help upgrading*, as does the participation of the cluster—or some of its firms—in a global value chain. The development of collective efficiency in the cluster (promoting vertical and horizontal joint actions, increasing firms' sensitivity to cooperation) may be sustained with several actions described above.

Finally, *support to promote access to larger (and foreign) markets* is especially relevant in the traditional manufacturing sector. A cluster policy should constantly monitor new developments in technologies and international markets and help provide local producers with market outlets other than their current value chain and with stronger powers of negotiation with their current value chain. Actions that foster clusters' search for markets alternative to their main value chains include support for marketing and branding of the cluster (e.g., the "Made in Brazil" project in the Sinos Valley shoe cluster, or Salmoexport in the Chilean salmon cluster), support for the creation of export networks, and support for collective participation in international trade fairs. Strengthening local producers is especially necessary when the value chain is quasi-hierarchically governed, as most chains in traditional manufacturing sectors are. A value chain with this governance structure allows only for product and process upgrading, but by keeping a strong hold over its core areas of competence, very often inhibits the functional upgrading of its providers.

Natural-Resource-Based Clusters

In natural-resource-based sector clusters, an essential area of intervention is *access to scientific knowledge*, clearly a necessary condition for participating in global value chains. If research is concentrated in the leaders of the chain, SMEs do not easily gain access to the information (e.g., the melon clusters in Rio Grande do Norte, Brazil; Gomes, Chapter 3 in this volume). The role played by local public research institutions aimed at carrying out research, disseminating findings, and assisting SMEs in adapting and internalizing research advances in their production process is therefore very important.

However, development of efficient and effective local public research institutions is often difficult for various reasons. Often, there is no collaboration between SMEs and whatever local institutions and large enterprises carry out substantial research. In addition, large firms may also control the connections with the market from which the stimulus to innovation usually derives. And finally, as in the Rio Grande do Norte melon cluster (Chapter 3), large firms may also extend their power of control over local institutions, participating in the definition of their research strategy.

Therefore, policy programs should *help disseminate research to SMEs*, as in the programs developed by EMBRAPA/SEBRAE with seedless grape varieties in Petrolina-Juazeiro and the development of integrated production practices in Petrolina-Juazeiro and Santa Catarina (Chapter 3). This effort could be undertaken in collaboration with a public sector agricultural research agency active in each case, whenever such an agency exists, as in Brazil with EPAGRI in Santa Catarina and EMBRAPA in Petrolina-Juazeiro.

To this end, public–private collaboration in research should be promoted. Given the paucity of research on the effectiveness of different mechanisms to promote public–private collaboration in research in Latin America, investigations in this area are especially needed. Efforts to engage SMEs in collaborations with research institutions should be pursued, in order to help guide institutional research priorities in directions that are useful to SMEs as well as (and not exclusively) to large firms and traders.

In these natural-resource-based sectors, SMEs often face higher entry costs in several productive activities and in value chains. Programs and projects that explicitly benefit production by SMEs along with larger growers should be promoted. This effort could be undertaken with public sector agricultural agencies whenever they exist (Gomes, Chapter 3 in this volume). Useful actions would include allocation of land in public projects to SMEs and larger growers, availability of working and investment capital by development banks, access to appropriate storage facilities at ports, and support for participation in national and international trade fairs where SMEs could display their products and make contacts with potential buyers.

Moreover, in the natural-resource-based sector, support is also especially necessary to strengthen skills and abilities in the backward production stages along the chain. Thus, for example, the dairy cluster in Nicaragua needs to help cow breeders and small milk producers improve their technical and managerial expertise, and their expertise in areas and with techniques that could be usefully applied but that are little known (e.g., cows' productivity, cheese manufacturing). The main value chain led by Parmalat contributed to introducing and diffusing a culture of quality in the sector and imposed higher standards than in the past (Artola and Parrilli, Chapter 2 in this volume). However, in this chain Parmalat did not directly help small producers fulfill such requirements, which was a hard task for all producers, and especially for those not involved in producers' cooperatives.

Quality, sanitary, and environmental standards and patenting are playing a growing role in natural-resource-based sectors. To this end, technical assistance may do a lot, especially if administered at the cluster level and through collective institutions and joint actions, involving small growers together with buyers and chain leaders. Policy support actions should be designed and developed with local cluster agencies or business associations. Policy support actions may include awareness-raising campaigns directed at small producers about the importance of environmental and hygienic standards, technical assistance to help local SMEs fulfill the requirements imposed by international standards, technical assistance to strengthen local regulatory institutions and institutions setting environmental and sanitary standards for local producers, and the conditioning of access to loans and grants on the effective implementation and maintenance of quality and sanitary standards.

In addition to the rising requirements that international standards create, other forms of nontariff barriers to international trade are widespread in natural-resource-based sectors. While larger firms usually have the competencies and means to overcome these barriers, SMEs are especially threatened by them. Several examples may be cited. A cooperative of small enterprises in Pará, in the Brazilian Amazon, tried to export to Europe traditional sweets made with *cupuaçú* (a very tasty Amazon fruit) and learned that a Japanese trading company had already registered the Indian name *cupuaçú* in the European Patent Office, together with the traditional process of extracting the pulp and making the sweet. Now, with the support of the Brazilian government, these firms are suing the Japanese firm, but the process will take some time, and harm has already been done. There are several similar cases, including the attempt to increase exports of *cachaça*, the Brazilian sugar cane spirit, to the United States, by a cluster of SMEs in Minas Gerais.[3] These cases show that access to external markets, when attempted by SMEs independently, can be very difficult, revealing the need for *programs to support SMEs' access to international markets.*

Finally, *availability of and access to good basic infrastructure* (e.g., roads, water, energy) is a key competitive factor for the natural-resource-based sector. Competitiveness policies at the local level should cater to these needs.

Complex Products Sector Clusters

According to the evidence presented thus far, *the complex products sector offers the fewest opportunities for SMEs' upgrading*, as it is governed by the

[3] José Cassiolato, personal communication, March 7, 2003.

global logic of large transnational companies and by quasi-hierarchical value chains. However, to exploit the limited chances for upgrading, some policies may still be useful.

A "network broker" may be the appropriate institution to help the local cluster improve its collective efficiency and, notably, build bridges and negotiate with large value chain leaders. Who should play the broker's role? There is no hard and fast rule. For a while the broker could be someone from an existing organization (e.g., local firms; cooperatives; institutes; universities; or agencies in charge of promotion, development, or financing) or an individual agent (e.g., a leading entrepreneur, researcher, consultant, or policymaker). As the constraints and opportunities become clearer to the cluster, the broker must be someone who will be available for a considerable period of time. The case of CDMEC in Espírito Santo, Brazil, suggests that the broker can at times be someone from a development agency run by the government. At other times it may be crucial that the broker be someone chosen from among the SMEs' peers, and on still other occasions the best choice might be someone with deeper understanding of what is taking place in the frontier of the industry who might therefore be better prepared to foresee opportunities and challenges for the local cluster. In the Espírito Santo metalworking cluster, the person who became the main cluster broker had technical credibility within the cluster (his previous work was with an engineering consultant firm) and the political ability to build bridges between SMEs and their anchor customers (Villaschi, Cassiolato, and Lastres, Chapter 6 in this volume).

Financial backing at this stage is also essential. In the Espírito Santo cluster, the local development bank (BANDES) played an important role when in 1995 it helped CDMEC to finance a study about the potential of SMEs to supply the anchor companies during their expansion projects.

Moreover, the direct involvement of anchor firms is crucial to promoting local SMEs' upgrading. In the Espírito Santo metalworking cluster, the anchor (leader) Aracruz Celulose was essential in opening doors abroad and allowing SMEs to visit some of the paper pulp industry's leading international companies. This enabled SMEs to present themselves as potential local partners for these top firms, and as they interacted with the those firms, they learned from technologically better-equipped customers. Nevertheless, if there is no obvious reward for anchors to collaborate and promote suppliers' upgrading, *some external pressure must be sought.* Pressure could come from a financial institution in the form of a clause which requires improvement in their local suppliers/customers when anchor companies are being financed. Or pressure could come from the local government if a special license (e.g., an environmental license) were required for the operation of the anchor companies (Villaschi, Cassiolato, and Lastres, Chapter 6 in this volume).

The evidence above suggests that *local governments may play an indispensable role in attracting large chain leaders in the cluster and moreover convincing them to foster local SMEs' upgrading efforts.* Traditionally, local-content and trade-balancing requirements were among the instruments used to induce transnational companies to cooperate with local small providers. However, requirements have often produced disillusioning results, revealing that *forcing transnational companies* usually leads to multiple inefficiencies and undermines the competitiveness of the cluster as a whole (Altenburg and Meyer-Stamer, 1999). Rather, the advantages accruing to chain leaders should be emphasized, in an effort to engage them in cooperative and mutually beneficial initiatives. Nowadays, large multinationals are increasingly looking for ways to demonstrate their social responsibility and therefore they may be pleased to understand the positive impact of their efforts in sustaining SMEs upgrading on national and local economies housing these SMEs. This implication may represent an increasing important appeal to for-profit corporations.

Related policy programs should, whenever possible—that is, whenever a tradition of collaboration is already in place and has produced mutual benefits—assist second- and third-tier suppliers in accumulating the financial and managerial expertise needed to internationalize when they have the opportunity to follow sourcing (i.e., supplying services and parts to the same anchor firm in its different locations).

Specialized Suppliers Sector (Software)

Analyses of the Brazilian (Bercovich and Swanke, 2003) and Mexican software clusters (Ruiz Durán, Chapter 7 in this volume) reveal that endowments and constant investments in educational institutions provide high returns, as large multinational corporations and national companies often have an unmet demand for the qualified and specialized human capital created by these institutions. To this end, *integration with universities and higher education institutions should be sought in order to orient the curricula in directions useful for the industry*. Moreover, policy programs may grant incentives for highly qualified migrants (e.g., groups of Mexicans producing software in Boston) to come back and work for the cluster's firms. Similar efforts have been successful in other software clusters elsewhere in the world, such as in Bangalore, India. Furthermore, the recent Mexican experience (Ruiz Durán, Chapter 7 in this volume) suggests that cluster-based Technopoles and incubators may provide useful *infrastructure support to start-ups* in this sector. Also in this sector, international certification is a process that is increasingly gaining strategic importance and could be usefully supported by international agencies and development banks.

Conclusions

What are the lessons we may draw for policy design and implementation from the rich original analysis and evidence presented in this book? How can we summarize all the insights and implications that we have derived? The general lesson is that policy priorities are different according to sectoral specificities. In traditional manufacturing clusters there is a need for interventions aimed at sustaining the development of collective efficiency and at favoring the access to new additional chains. In natural-resource-based clusters, governments should actively seek to raise local quality, sanitary, and environmental standards through regulation, at the same time assisting SMEs in fulfilling the requirements increasingly imposed in the international markets. Besides, in these clusters the promotion of public–private collaboration in research and efforts in disseminating findings to SMEs are key policy priorities. The identification of the right incentives to get large corporations involved in their local suppliers' upgrading is the decisive policy objective in complex products sector clusters. Finally, in the software clusters it appears that governmental efforts to invest in educational institutions and specialized human capital provide high returns.

Beyond sectoral policy priorities, there are some further considerations that should be borne in mind when designing and carrying out policies to foster SMEs' upgrading in clusters and value chains.

First of all, policies must be *context-specific*. They need to take into account the local specificities of the cluster and its collective efficiency, along with the mode of governance of the prevailing value chain(s) and the detailed sectoral specialization of the local area. *No general recipes are valid and may be applied everywhere*, in disregard of local history, idiosyncrasies, and peculiarities.

Secondly, *policies need to evolve over time* and take into consideration the evolution of clusters and value chains. Interfirm linkages vary, as do firms' bargaining power and potential for upgrading. What may be useful today may not work tomorrow. In this regard, analysis of the phases of development of the Chilean salmon cluster offers a remarkable example (Maggi, Chapter 4 in this volume).

Thirdly, policies are very *intensive in coordination and in human capital*. Several agents, firms, and institutions are involved and constantly interact in ways that could not have been predicted at the outset and that call for constant supervision and coordination. This, in turn, requires specialized and dynamic human capital.

Fourthly, favorable *macroeconomic conditions are important* for all types of clusters and are essential in the traditional manufacturing sector. Unfavorable macro conditions may rapidly convert success into failure. *Local potential competitive advantages*, sometimes rooted in external economies and joint actions, *cannot overcome unfavorable macroeconomic conditions*, such as exchange rate management discriminating against exports.

Finally, we need to remember that *cluster policies are not a panacea for all economic development problems.* In recent times, local and national policymakers have often labeled as "cluster policies" generic initiatives to support SMEs, sectors, or regions, creating confusion, false expectations, and a great deal of disillusionment and reluctance among firms to spend time and effort on such projects. The emphasis on cluster policies has overlooked the need of firm-level efforts to upgrade and, using a different terminology, to acquire and deepen firms' technological capabilities (Morrison, Pietrobelli, and Rabellotti, 2006).

Moreover, costs and benefits from clustering should also be taken into consideration and evaluated. The costs of collective action are usually neglected and hardly evaluated, but they may be almost insuperable for most potential clusters. In other cases, returns from clustering may be lower than expected, as when every firm invests in the same direction and in the end nobody is differentiated from anyone else. There is a strong need for investing in the *measurement of cost-adjusted returns of cluster policies.*

This volume presents very rich empirical evidence and represents a first and consistent effort in the direction of building more rigorous theory and quantitative testing.

References

Altenburg, T., and J. Meyer-Stamer. 1999. How to Promote Clusters: Policy Experiences from Latin America. *World Development* 27(9):1693–1713.

Bercovich, N., and C. Swanke. 2003. *Cooperação e competitividade na indústria de software de Blumenau.* Working Paper No. 138, Serie Desarrollo Productivo, ECLAC/United Nations, Santiago, Chile.

Boekholt, P., and B. Thuriaux. 1999. Public Policies to Facilitate Clusters: Background, Rationale and Policy Practices in International Perspective. In *Boosting Innovation: The Cluster Approach,* ed. Organisation for Economic Co-operation and Development. Paris: OECD.

Ceglie, G., and M. Dini. 2000. *SME Clusters and Network Development in Developing Countries: The Experience of UNIDO.* Technical Working Paper, Private Sector Development Branch, United Nations Industrial Development Organization (UNIDO), Vienna.

Committee of Donor Agencies for Small Enterprise Development. 1997. Business Development Services for SMEs: Preliminary Guideline for Donor-Funded Interventions. Committee of Donor Agencies for Small Enterprise Development, International Labour Organization, Geneva. www.ilo.org/public/english/employment/ent/sed/bds/donor/guide.htm.

———. 2001. Business Development Services for Small Enterprises: Guiding Principles for Donor Intervention. Committee of Donor Agencies for Small Enterprise Development, International Labour Organization, Geneva. Unpublished.

Dini, M. 2003. Consideraciones sobre políticas para el desarrollo de cluster. AGORA 2000 for the Inter-American Development Bank, Rome, April. Unpublished.

———. 2004. Programas de fomento de la articulación productiva: experiencias en América Latina en los noventas. In *Pequeñas empresas y eficiencia colectiva,* ed. M. Dini and G. Stumpo. Santiago, Chile: ECLAC.

Giuliani, E. 2003. Knowledge in the Air and Its Uneven Distribution: A Story of a Chilean Wine Cluster. Paper presented at the DRUID Winter Conference, Aalborg, Denmark, January 16–18. www.druid.dk.

Giuliani, E., C. Pietrobelli, and R. Rabellotti. 2005. Upgrading in Global Value Chains: Lessons from Latin American Clusters. *World Development* 33(4):549–573.

Guerrieri, P., S. Iammarino, and C. Pietrobelli. 2001. *The Global Challenge to Industrial Districts: SMEs in Italy and Taiwan*. Cheltenham, U.K.: Elgar.

Guerrieri, P., and C. Pietrobelli. 2004. Industrial Districts' Evolution and Technological Regimes: Italy and Taiwan. *Technovation* 24:899–914.

Humphrey, J. 2002. *Opportunities for SMEs in Developing Countries to Upgrade in a Global Economy*. Small Enterprise Development (SEED) Working Paper No. 43, International Labour Organization, Geneva.

Kaplinsky, R. 2000. Globalisation and Unequalisation: What Can Be Learned from Value Chain Analysis? *Journal of Development Studies* 37(2):117–146.

———. 2001. Learning Networks in the South African Auto Components Industry. *Innovation News* (Pretoria, South Africa).

Kaplinsky, R., and J. Readman. 2001. *How Can SME Producers Serve Global Markets and Sustain Income Growth?* Working Paper, University of Brighton, Brighton, U.K., and University of Sussex, Brighton, U.K. Unpublished. http://www.ids.ac.uk/ids/global/pdfs/rkjr2.pdf.

Manzocchi, S., and C. Pietrobelli. 2001. La globalización de los mercados financieros y sus implicaciones para los países en vías de desarrollo. ¿Es la inversión directa extranjera una panacea para las economías en vías de desarrollo? In *El problema de la deuda externa*, ed. P. García Ruiz. Pamplona, Spain: Ediciones Universidad de Navarra S.A. (EUNSA).

Meyer Stamer, J. 2004. The Theory and Practice of Policy, Polity and Politics around Local Economic Development. In *The Theory and Practice of Local Development Opportunities for Cooperation between Mediterranean Regions*, ed. Nicola Bellini, Elisa Giuliani, Carlo Pietrobelli and Roberta Rabellotti. Firenze, Italy: Regione Toscana.

Morrison, A., C. Pietrobelli, and R. Rabellotti. 2006. Global Value Chains and Technological Capabilities: A Framework to Study Industrial Innovation in Developing Countries. CREI, University of Rome 3. Unpublished.

Nadvi, K., and F. Waltring. 2004. Making Sense of Global Standards. In *Local Enterprises in the Global Economy: Issues of Governance and Upgrading*, ed. Hubert Schmitz. Cheltenham, U.K.: Elgar.

Observatory of European SMEs. 2002. *Regional Clusters in Europe*. No. 3/2002, DG Enterprise, European Commission, Brussels.

Pietrobelli, C., and R. Rabellotti. 2002. *Business Development Service Centres in Italy: An Empirical Analysis of Three Notable Regional Experiences—Emilia Romagna, Lombardia and Veneto*. Working Paper No. 130, Serie Desarrollo Productivo, ECLAC, United Nations, Santiago, Chile. http://www.eclac.org/cgi-bin/getProd.asp?xml=/publicaciones/xml/4/11094/P11094.xml&xsl=/ddpe/tpl-i/p9f.xsl&base=/tpl/top-bottom.xslt.

———. 2004. *Upgrading in Clusters and Value Chains in Latin America: The Role of Policies*. Sustainable Development Department Best Practices Series, MSM (Micro, Small, and Medium Enterprises) 124, Inter-American Development Bank, Washington, D.C. http://www.iadb.org/sds/mic/publication/publication_159_3586_e.htm.

Rabellotti, R. 1997. *External Economies and Cooperation in Industrial Districts: A Comparison of Italy and Mexico*. Basingstoke, U.K.: Macmillan.

———. 1998. Helping Small Firms to Network—The Experience of UNIDO. *Small Enterprise Development* 9(1):25–34.

———. 2004. How Globalisation Affects Italian Industrial Districts: The Case of Brenta. In *Local Enterprises in the Global Economy: Issues of Governance and Upgrading*, ed. Hubert Schmitz. Cheltenham, U.K.: Elgar.

Rosenfeld, S. 2002. Creating Smart Systems: A Guide to Cluster Strategies in Less Favoured Regions. Regional Technology Strategies, Carrboro, North Carolina. Unpublished.

Schmitz, H., ed. 2004. *Local Enterprises in the Global Economy: Issues of Governance and Upgrading*. Cheltenham, U.K.: Elgar.
United Nations Conference on Trade and Development (UNCTAD). 2000. *Enhancing the Competitiveness of SMEs through Linkages*. Geneva: UNCTAD.
United Nations Development Programme (UNDP). 2000. Introducción a la integración productiva. UNDP, Mexico City. Unpublished.
United Nations Industrial Development Organization (UNIDO). 2002. *World Industrial Development Report*, 2002–03. Vienna: UNIDO.
Vargas, M. A., J. Britto, and J. E. Cassiolato. 2001. *Instrumentos financeiros para arranjos e sistemas de MPME*. Nota Técnica No. 1.11, Universidade Federal do Rio de Janeiro.

Contributors

Alessia Amighini, United Nations Conference on Trade and Development (UNCTAD), Geneva, Switzerland

Ner Artola, Institute Nitlapan, Central American University (UCA), Nicaragua

José Eduardo Cassiolato, Federal University of Rio de Janeiro, Brazil

Elisa Giuliani, University of Pisa, Italy, and Science Policy Research Unit (SPRU), University of Sussex, United Kingdom

Raquel Gomes, Oxfam America and Massachusetts Institute of Technology (MIT), United States

Helena Lastres, Federal University of Rio de Janeiro, Brazil

Claudio Maggi Campos, Chile Foundation, Chile

Mario Davide Parrilli, Birmingham Business School, University of Birmingham, United Kingdom

Carlo Pietrobelli, Center for Research on the Economics of Institutions (CREI), University of Rome 3, Italy

Roberta Rabellotti, University of Piemonte Orientale, Italy

Clemente Ruiz Durán, Universidad Nacional de México, Mexico

Arlindo Villaschi Filho, Inter-American Development Bank and Federal University of Espírito Santo, Brazil

Eduardo Zepeda Miramontes, Universidad Autonoma de México, Mexico, and United Nations Development Programme (UNDP)